S0-CBM-706

COST CONTROL FOR THE HOSPITALITY INDUSTRY

COST CONTROL FOR THE HOSPITALITY INDUSTRY

Second Edition

Michael M. Coltman

JOHN WILEY & SONS, INC.

New York • Chichester • Weinheim • Brisbane • Singapore • Toronto

A NOTE TO THE READER
This book has been electronically reproduced from
digital information stored at John Wiley & Sons, Inc.
We are pleased that the use of this new technology
will enable us to keep works of enduring scholarly
value in print as long as there is a reasonable demand
for them. The content of this book is identical to
previous printings.

Cover design by Caliber Design Planning, Inc.
Cover photo by SPG International
Example of computerized guest room key, exhibit 14.1, page 357, used courtesy
of Forum Hotel, London, England

This book is printed on acid-free paper. ⊖

Copyright © 1989 by John Wiley & Sons, Inc. All rights reserved

Published simultaneously in Canada

No part of this publication may be reproduced, stored in a retrieval system or transmitted
in any form or by any means, electronic, mechanical, photocopying, recording, scanning
or otherwise, except as permitted under Sections 107 or 108 of the 1976 United States
Copyright Act, without either the prior written permission of the Publisher, or
authorization through payment of the appropriate per-copy fee to the Copyright
Clearance Center, 222 Rosewood Drive, Danvers, MA 01923, (978) 750-8400, fax
(978) 750-4470. Requests to the Publisher for permission should be addressed to the
Permissions Department, John Wiley & Sons, Inc., 111 River Street, Hoboken, NJ 07030,
(201) 748-6011, fax (201) 748-6008.

This publication is designed to provide accurate and authoritative information in regard to
the subject matter covered. It is sold with the understanding that the publisher is not
engaged in rendering professional services. If professional advice or other expert
assistance is required, the services of a competent professional person should be sought.

Library of Congress Cataloging-in-Publication Data:

Coltman, Michael M., 1930-
    Cost control for the hospitality industry / Michael M. Coltman.—2nd ed.
       p.   cm.
    Includes index.
    ISBN 0-471-28859-4
    1. Hotels, taverns, etc.—Cost control.   2. Restaurants, lunch
rooms, etc.—Cost control.   3. Foodservice—Cost control.
I. Title.
 TX911.3.C65C63   1989
647'.94'0681—dc19   88-34340

Printed in the United States of America

16   15   14   13   12   11   10   9   8

CONTENTS

PREFACE

This book is concerned with cost control. No enterprise, regardless of size, can do without some forms of cost control. This has become more obvious in recent years. Traditional profit margins have been eroded, while costs of all types have increased, and the raising of prices to combat this has begun to meet with customer resistance. The only alternative for owners and operators is to implement more effective cost control systems to limit expenditures, or at least hold them at levels that produce reasonable net incomes. A cost control system is simply an accounting-oriented information system. However, the cost control system differs from the accounting system. The accounting system only records costs. The control system tells management how, when, and where a cost was created, what the amount of the cost is, and how much it differs from its budgeted, anticipated, or standard cost. The cost control system allows management to see what is happening to costs, particularly on a trend basis, so that rational decisions can be made and necessary actions implemented to correct undesirable situations.

As small enterprises grow, cost control becomes even more important, but, because of the myriad of other day-to-day operating decisions that need to be made, cost control may be pushed aside. For example, in the purchasing aspects of cost control, it is so easy to rely more and more on suppliers as the number of products purchased increases. In other words, the supplier rather than the operator begins making the decision about which product the establishment should be provided with. Larger establishments, and particularly chain operations, can solve this problem by staffing separate purchasing departments with skilled employees who have a wide product knowledge, are aware of what is available on the market, and are familiar with the price that should be paid for products that suit the organization's needs.

It should be emphasized that a control system is not intended as an employee policing device. Rather, it is a set of objectives, policies, and procedures made known to all involved employees so that they can perform their jobs effectively without needless restrictions. The result should be that the organization meets its objectives. For example, an objective might be to have a given number of room-cleaning personnel (a labor cost) on duty each day for any given level of guest room occupancy. To meet this objective a system must be established so that the housekeeper can be advised ahead of time how many rooms each night are anticipated will be occupied. In this way the housekeeper can schedule the appropriate personnel for the following day. After each day the control system should quickly be able to provide information, such as the forecast and actual number of rooms occupied, and the forecast and actual number of room-cleaning personnel hours used. Analysis of this information can then be made, and corrective action taken where necessary to improve the effectiveness of personnel scheduling for the future.

Obviously, the larger the enterprise the more procedures should be implemented so that information is provided for each area or department of the operation. However, even in a large operation, the control system should not become so complex that the information provided is neither timely nor relevant. Nor should it provide too much information. A person responsible for decision-making can easily be provided with so much information that the time needed to sort, assimilate, and analyze it costs more than the benefits the information provides. Information must be selective.

Information also must be communicated to those who need the information in order to carry out their work effectively. For example, if a daily food cost is calculated by the food and beverage control office, then that cost information should be provided to the food and beverage manager and to the chef, since they are primarily responsible for ensuring that the operation achieves its food cost objective.

One advantage of a good cost control system is that it allows performance to be standardized (for example, the number of rooms to be cleaned in a standard shift), and quality to be controlled (for example, written recipes to ensure quality consistency). A good cost control system also helps ensure that assets such as food and beverage and other inventories are protected from wastage, misuse, or theft. Finally, a good cost control system makes it easier to plan for the future. For example, the documentation of past costs for various revenue levels simplifies the budgeting process. These are only some of the advantages of good cost control. Other advantages for specific departments or areas will be indicated throughout the book.

Even though the need for good cost control systems cannot be overemphasized, a word or two of caution is necessary. A good cost control system, however good it is, cannot substitute for other necessary methods of management. Management supervision is still required not only to ensure that the control system is effective, but also to do what a control and information system cannot do to achieve management's overall goals. Further, a control system cannot cure problems. It can only indicate that problems exist. It is still management's responsibility to make decisions and implement necessary corrective action.

The first chapter in this book introduces the reader to the concept of cost and the terminology of various types of cost. It illustrates how knowing the type of cost that one is dealing with in any specific situation can help one make the right decision.

Budgeting is covered in chapter 2. Although budgeting in general is discussed, the chapter concentrates on the preparation of departmental income and expense statements or budgets, since those budgets are primarily concerned with the ongoing, day-to-day operations and cost incurrence.

Chapter 3 covers the important aspects of establishing a purchasing system. Costs are initially incurred as the result of the purchasing decision. This chapter also covers the ordering, receiving, and inventory-control process.

The next three chapters discuss food cost control. Chapter 4 covers food purchasing, receiving, and inventory control. Chapter 5 concentrates on the food cost percent calculation, menu item costs, and the selling prices needed to achieve a food cost objective. Chapter 6 discusses ways to evaluate food cost results. It demonstrates different approaches, and concludes with a discussion of gross-profit analysis.

Chapters 7 and 8 cover alcoholic beverage cost control. Chapter 7 discusses purchasing, receiving, and storeroom control. Chapter 8 concentrates on the bar area, where most losses are likely to occur. Various methods that can be implemented to reduce or eliminate these losses are illustrated.

Labor cost control is covered in the next two chapters. Chapter 9 introduces the many difficulties encountered in trying to keep this major cost in line. Chapter 10 covers the techniques used to establish labor productivity standards to control labor cost and subsequently measure labor cost results.

Chapter 11 demonstrates a system for control of direct operating costs other than food, beverages, and labor. Control of undistributed costs (those not the responsibility of the operating departments) through a system of zero-based budgeting is included in this chapter, as is the technique of variance analysis.

Control of the purchase cost of long-term investments such as furniture and equipment is the topic of chapter 12. The control techniques illustrated include the average rate of return, the payback period, net present value, and internal rate of return.

The concluding chapter continues the discussion of long-term or fixed investments and demonstrates various methods for calculation of long-term asset depreciation. The chapter illustrates a technique for determining whether fixed assets should be purchased or leased. The chapter concludes with current-asset control.

PREFACE TO
SECOND EDITION

Since the first edition of *Cost Control for the Hospitality Industry* appeared, some eight years have gone by. As the result of comments and suggestions from users of the book, both students and teachers, some changes have been made to this second edition. Some of these modifications are minor, others are major. Following is a chapter-by-chapter summary of the changes made.

Chapter 1, Costs and Decision Making, has not been altered.

Chapter 2, Cost Control by Budgeting, has had a new section added on special budgeting situations.

Chapter 3, Purchasing and Inventory Cost Control, has had several new sections added throughout the chapter in such areas as centralized purchasing, considerations about suppliers, types of purchasing, perpetual inventory cards, and purchase rebates and kickbacks.

Chapter 4, Food Purchasing, Receiving, and Inventory Control, has had one major change: expansion of the section on ways in which frauds can occur in the delivery of food items.

Chapter 5, The Food Cost Percent, has had material added concerning employee and promotional meals, the accuracy of the daily food cost, and portion control.

Chapter 6, Evaluating Food Cost Results, remains substantially unchanged.

Chapter 7, Beverage Purchasing, Receiving, and Storeroom Control, has a substantial amount of new material added, considerably expanding the first edition's comments about beverage purchasing. The balance of the chapter is unchanged.

Chapter 8, Beverage Cost Control: The Bar, has had new material introduced concerning the purchase of alcoholic beverage dispensing equipment.

Chapter 9, Labor Cost Control: Employee Policies, is a completely new chapter. The content of this chapter lays the foundation for proper labor cost control—the subject of the next two chapters.

Chapter 10, Measurement of Labor Cost, has a new section that introduces three methods (other than labor cost percent) of looking at labor cost, as well as some new material on the use of part-time employees and overtime.

Chapter 11, Labor Cost Standards, has been left basically unchanged, other than the wording of some sections.

Chapter 12, Control of Other Direct and Indirect Costs, has not been altered.

The last two chapters of the first edition have been eliminated, because they were more centrally concerned with long-run management control than with day-to-day operating cost control. In their place, two entirely new chapters have been added. These are chapter 13, Information Systems and Control, and chapter 14, Computers and Cost Control.

I would like to express my appreciation to the many individuals who provided comment and offered suggestions for the creation of the second edition of *Cost Control for the Hospitality Industry*. I hope that the users of this second edition will find it considerably improved over its predecessor.

COST CONTROL FOR THE HOSPITALITY INDUSTRY

Costs and Decision-Making

1

Objectives

After studying this chapter, the reader should be able to do the following:

- Briefly define, and give examples of, some of the major types of cost such as direct, indirect, relevant, fixed, and variable.
- Prorate indirect costs to revenue areas.
- Use relevant costs to help determine which piece of equipment to buy.
- Use a knowledge about fixed and variable costs for a variety of different business decisions, such as to close or not to close during the off-season.
- Define the term *high operating leverage* and explain its advantages and disadvantages.
- Explain and use each of the three methods (maximum/minimum calculation, multipoint graph, and regression analysis) to separate semifixed or semivariable costs into their fixed and variable elements.

THE MEANING OF COST

A cost is an asset

In the typical hospitality industry operation, as much as ninety cents of each sales dollar is used to pay for costs. It is obvious that cost management must be an extremely important part of the successful management of an establishment.

In accounting terminology, a *cost* is defined as an asset. This asset could be one with a very long life, such as a hotel building, or one with a relatively short life, such as food inventory. Theoretically, as these assets or costs are used up, they become expenses and are so recorded on income statements.

Assets become expenses

For example, if our hotel building were expected to have a twenty-five-year life, then we might expect, with straight-line depreciation, to see one twenty-fifth of its initial cost recorded each year as depreciation expense on the income statement. Similarly, as our food inventory is used up, it is taken out of the storeroom and put into production. At that time, the asset becomes an expense and is so recorded on the income statement. Unfortunately, and this can be confusing for the nonaccountant, it is recorded as an expense using the terminology cost of goods sold or, more commonly, food cost. On the other hand, some items are paid for and are never considered to be assets. They are classified directly as expenses. This includes items such as wages paid, supplies purchased, and energy consumed, among many others. This can still be confusing since, in industry, we do not always refer to these items as expenses.

Cost and expense are often synonymous

We usually say "wage cost," "supplies cost," and "energy cost." Therefore, it is obvious that the words *cost* and *expense* are commonly interchangeable despite the theory. In order to conform to the language of the industry, we shall use the words cost and expense as synonyms and will only differentiate between one or the other where it becomes important to do so.

One of the ways to better manage expenses or costs is to understand that there are many types of cost, and, if one can recognize the type of cost that is being considered, better decisions can be made about it. Some of the most common types of cost are defined here.

TYPES OF COST

Actual cost. The actual cost is what a cost or expense actually was. For example, the payroll records and checks made out to employees will indicate the actual labor cost for that payroll period.

Budgeted cost. A budgeted cost is what a cost is expected to be for a period of time. For example, for an anticipated level of sales for a month, we might budget or forecast what the labor cost should be for that period. Later, that budgeted cost would be compared with the actual labor cost in order to determine the causes of any differences.

Direct cost. Direct cost is a cost that is the responsibility of a particular department or department manager. Most direct costs will go up or down, to a greater or lesser degree, as revenue goes up and down. Because of this, they are considered to be controllable by, and thus the responsibility of, the department to which they are charged. Examples of this type of cost would be food, beverages, wages, operating supplies and services, and linen and laundry.

Direct costs charged to departments

Indirect cost. An indirect cost is commonly referred to as an *undistributed* cost or one that cannot easily be identified with a particular department or area, and thus cannot be charged to any specific department. For example, property operation, maintenance, and energy costs could only be charged to various departments (such as rooms or food and beverage) with difficulty. Even if this difficulty could be overcome, it must still be recognized that indirect costs cannot normally be made the responsibility of an operating-department manager. Indirect costs are also sometimes referred to as *overhead costs.*

Undistributed or overhead costs

Controllable cost. The mistake is often made of calling direct costs controllable costs, and indirect costs noncontrollable ones. It is true that direct costs are generally more easily controllable than indirect costs, but all costs, in the long run, are controllable by someone.

Joint cost. A joint cost is a cost shared by, and thus the responsibility of, two or more departments or areas. The cost of a dining room waiter who serves both food and beverage is an example. His labor is a joint cost, and should be charged to the food department and to the beverage department (in proportion to revenue or by some other appropriate method). Most indirect costs are also joint costs. The problem is to find a rational basis for separating the cost into parts and charging them to each department.

Indirect costs often joint ones

Discretionary cost. A discretionary cost is one that may or may not be incurred at the sole discretion of a particular person, usually the general manager. Nonemergency maintenance would be an example of a discretionary cost. The building exterior could be painted this year, or the painting could be postponed until next year. Either way, revenue should not be affected. The general manager has the choice. He can use his own discretion; thus, it is a discretionary cost.

Relevant cost. A relevant cost is one that makes a difference to a decision. For example, a restaurant is considering replacing its mechanical sales register with an electronic one. The relevant costs would be the cost of the new register (less any trade-in of the old one), the cost of training employees on the new equipment, and any change in maintenance and material-supply costs on the new machine. As long as no changes were necessary in number of serving

Costs that make no difference to decisions

people required, the restaurant's labor cost will make no difference to the decision and so would not be a relevant one.

Sunk cost. A sunk cost is a cost that has already been incurred and about which nothing can be done. It cannot affect any future decisions. If the restaurant used in the preceding example of relevant costs had spent $250 for the time of an employee to study the relative merits of using mechanical or electronic registers, the $250 would be a sunk cost. It cannot make any difference to the decision.

Opportunity cost. An opportunity cost is the cost of not doing something, or the profit lost. An organization can invest its surplus cash in marketable securities at 10 percent, or leave the money in the bank at 6 percent. If it buys marketable securities, its opportunity cost is 6 percent. Another way to look at it is to say that it is making 10 percent on the investment, less the opportunity cost of 6 percent, therefore the net gain is 4 percent.

Costs not fixed in long run

Fixed cost. Fixed costs are those that, over the short run (a year or less), do not change or vary with volume. Examples of fixed cost would be salaries of management people, fire-insurance expense, rent paid on a square-foot basis, and the committed cost of an advertising campaign. Over the long run, of course, all these costs can change. But, in the short run, they would normally change only, if at all, by a specific top-management decision.

Variable cost. A variable cost is one that varies on a linear basis with revenue. Very few costs are strictly linear, but two that are (with only a minor possibility that they do not always fit this strict definition) are the costs of food and beverages. The more food and beverages sold, the more that have to be purchased. If revenue is zero, then the cost should also be zero.

Most costs are semivariable

Semifixed or semivariable cost. Most costs do not fit neatly into the fixed or the variable category. Most have an element of fixed expense and an element of variable, and then not always variable with revenue on a linear basis. Such costs would include items like maintenance, energy, and many of the direct costs. To make useful decisions, it is generally advantageous to break down these semifixed or semivariable costs into their two elements: fixed or variable. Ways of doing this will be discussed later in this chapter.

Standard cost. A standard cost is what the cost should be for a given volume or level of revenue. For example, a standard cost can be developed by costing the recipe for a given menu item. If ten of these menu items are sold, the total standard cost should be ten times the individual recipe cost. Another illustration would be personnel cost for cleaning a hotel room. If a room attendant is paid $5.00 an hour, and it takes one half hour to clean a room, the standard labor cost for cleaning a room would be $2.50. If 100 rooms are occupied overnight, total standard cost would be $250. Standard costs should be developed individually by each establishment, since many factors influencing standard costs differ from one establishment to another. One use for standard costs is in budgeting or forecasting. Other uses would be in pricing decisions, expansion planning, staff scheduling, and internal control. For example, a comparison of actual costs with standard costs can determine if actual costs are in line with what they should be.

COST DECISIONS

It is important, as was mentioned earlier, to recognize the type of cost when making decisions. Without this recognition, it is quite possible that a wrong decision will be made. Let us have a look at some examples of different types of costs involved in decision-making.

Allocating Indirect Costs to Revenue Areas

One of the difficulties in allocating indirect costs to revenue outlets is determining the correct basis for apportioning the cost to each department. If an allocation of indirect costs is made on an incorrect basis, then decisions could turn out to be unprofitable.

Correct basis for cost allocation

    Consider the following example of a restaurant complex with two main revenue areas, a dining room and a snack bar. Revenue and direct costs for each area and indirect costs for the entire operation for a typical month are shown in exhibit 1.1. The average monthly net income for the total operation is $8,000.

EXHIBIT 1.1. Income Statement with Indirect Costs Not Allocated			
	Dining room	Snack bar	Total
Revenue	$ 70,000	$ 30,000	$100,000
Direct costs	50,000	26,000	76,000
Departmental income	$ 20,000	$ 4,000	$ 24,000
Indirect costs			16,000
Net income			$ 8,000

    Management feels that the indirect costs should be charged to each of the two operating departments, and that the $16,000 total indirect cost should be allocated pro rata according to revenue. This would allocate 70 percent to the dining room and 30 percent to the snack bar. Exhibit 1.2 shows the new monthly income statement and indicates that, by dis-

Indirect costs prorated on revenue basis

EXHIBIT 1.2.   Income Statement with Indirect Costs Allocated

	Dining room	Snack bar	Total
Revenue	$ 70,000	$ 30,000	$100,000
Direct costs	50,000	26,000	76,000
Departmental income	$ 20,000	$ 4,000	$ 24,000
Indirect costs	11,200	4,800	16,000
Net income	$ 8,800	($ 800)	$ 8,000

---

tributing indirect costs on a basis of sales, the snack bar appears to be losing $800 a month. Management of the restaurant complex has an oppor-
tunity to lease out the snack bar, as is, for $500 a month. The new operator
will pay for his indirect costs (administration, advertising, and energy
costs). This seems like a good offer. A $500 net income appears better than
an $800 loss. The dining room monthly income statement after a few
months is shown in exhibit 1.3.

EXHIBIT 1.3.   Dining Room Monthly Income Statement

Revenue	$ 70,000
Direct costs	50,000
Departmental income	$ 20,000
Indirect costs	12,900
Income before rent	$ 7,100
Rent income	500
Net income	$ 7,600

**Net income now less
than before**

This indicates that the dining room's net income, including rent income, is only $7,600. In exhibit 1.2, net income was calculated to have been
$8,800 without any rent income. Overall net income is now less than before
($7,600 versus $8,000). Obviously, a mistake was made in allocating indirect costs to the dining room and the snack bar on the basis of revenue and
then making a decision based on this allocation. A more careful assessment
of indirect costs should have been made, and distribution determined on a
more logical basis. If this had been done using the information we now have
about the dining room's indirect costs as shown in exhibit 1.3, the real situation would have been as shown in exhibit 1.4, which indicates that both
revenue areas were making a profit. In fact, exhibit 1.4 shows that renting
out the snack bar, which is making $900-a-month net income, for $500 a
month would not be a profitable proposition. To look at it another way, $500

EXHIBIT 1.4. Income Statement with Indirect Costs Correctly Allocated

	Dining room	Snack bar	Total
Revenue	$ 70,000	$ 30,000	$100,000
Direct costs	50,000	26,000	76,000
Departmental income	$ 20,000	$ 4,000	$ 24,000
Indirect costs	12,900	3,100	16,000
Net income	$ 7,100	$ 900	$ 8,000

is the opportunity cost of not renting out, but, since that cost is less than the $900 we are presently making, we can comfortably ignore it.

Example of opportunity cost

Which Piece of Equipment to Buy?

One of the ongoing situations all managers face is that of choosing between alternatives: which items to offer on a menu, which employee to hire, and how to spend the advertising budget. One area of decision-making where a knowledge of costs is helpful is that of selecting a piece of equipment. The following might be a typical situation.

A motel owner has asked his public accountant to research the front-office guest-accounting equipment available and to recommend the two best pieces of equipment that are on the market. A decision would then be made by the motel owner about which of the two to use. The accountant's fee for this research was $500. The accountant, in his report, produced the information in exhibit 1.5. (Note that the $500 fee is a sunk cost. It has

Example of sunk cost

EXHIBIT 1.5. Equipment Purchase Information

	Equipment A	Equipment B
Initial cost, including installation	$ 10,000	$ 8,000
Economic life	10 years	10 years
Scrap value at end of economic life	0	0
Initial training costs	$ 500	$ 1,000
Annual maintenance	$ 400	$ 300
Annual forms cost	$ 750	$ 850
Annual wage cost	$ 22,500	$ 22,500

to be paid regardless of the decision and, indeed, would have to be paid if a decision were made to buy neither piece of equipment.)

In order to make the decision, the motel owner must sort out the relevant cost information. This is shown for year 1 in exhibit 1.6. Note that the initial cost of the equipment is not relevant, but the annual depreciation is.

EXHIBIT 1.6. Costs Relevant to Equipment Purchase

	Equipment A	Equipment B
Depreciation	$ 1,000	$ 800
Initial training costs	500	1,000
Annual maintenance	400	300
Annual forms cost	750	850
Total year 1 cost	$ 2,650	$ 2,950

Relevant costs over entire life of item

Wage cost is also not relevant since it is the same in both cases. Exhibit 1.6 shows that, in year one, equipment A is cheaper than equipment B by $300. However, this saving is in year one only. Perhaps the motel owner should look ahead to see what the relevant costs are over the full economic life of the equipment. Exhibit 1.7 shows the information concerning these costs for each of the years two to ten. Note that, in exhibit 1.7, the training cost of year one is now a sunk cost; it is no longer relevant.

EXHIBIT 1.7. Annualized Costs Relevant to Equipment Purchase

	Equipment A	Equipment B
Depreciation	$ 1,000	$ 800
Annual maintenance	400	300
Annual forms cost	750	850
Total annual cost	$ 2,150	$ 1,950
Total cost for years 2 to 10	9 × $2,150 = $19,350	9 × $1,950 = $17,550

Assumptions made

To finalize the decision, the motel manager must then add the total cost for years two to ten to the cost for year one. This is illustrated in exhibit 1.8, which shows that, despite year one, the total ten-year cost is lower with equipment B. In this illustration, certain assumptions have been made, such as that one can forecast costs for ten years, and that the

EXHIBIT 1.8. Total Relevant Equipment Purchase Costs

	Equipment A	Equipment B
Year 1 cost (Exhibit 1.6.)	$ 2,650	$ 2,950
Years 2 to 10 cost (Exhibit 1.7.)	19,350	$17,550
Total cost	$22,000	$20,500

costs as originally estimated are accurate. Also, in the final decision, costs may not be the only factor to be considered.

Can We Sell Below Cost?

The apparent answer to the question, "Can we sell below cost?" would be, "Not unless you want to go broke." But, before we can intelligently answer that question, we should first ask, "Which cost?" If the answer is "below total cost but above variable cost," then yes, indeed, we can sell below total cost under certain circumstances. **Variable costs to be covered**

Consider the case of a catering company that rents its premises for $40,000 a year and has other fixed costs (management salaries, insurance, furniture and equipment depreciation) of $33,000 a year. This is a total fixed cost of $73,000:

$$\frac{\$73,000}{365} = \$200 \text{ a day}$$

The catering company can only handle one function a day, and operates at a variable cost (food, wages for preparation and service staff, and supplies) of 60 percent of revenue. It has been approached by an organization **Unusual situation** that wishes to have a banquet for only 100 people at a price of $4.00 per person. Normally, the catering company would not handle a group as small as this, but, on this occasion, it does not see any likelihood of having the hall used by any other organization that day. If it handles the function, its income statement for that day will be:

```
             Function Income Statement

Revenue 100 persons × $4.00        $ 400
Variable cost: 60% × $400          (  240)
Fixed cost                         (  200)
Net loss                           ($   40)
```

The net loss of $40 does not look good, but what is the loss if the function is not accepted? It will be $200, because the fixed costs for that day will still have to be met. By selling below *total* cost of $440 ($240 fixed plus $200 variable), the loss is less than it would otherwise be.

Concept of contribution margin

In the short run, as long as revenue is greater than variable cost, it pays to accept business because the excess of revenue over variable cost will contribute to, or help pay for, the fixed costs. The income statement can be rearranged to illustrate this concept of the contribution margin:

Income Statement	
Revenue	$400
Variable costs	(240)
Contribution margin	$160
Fixed costs	(200)
Net loss	($ 40)

Should We Close During the Off-Season?

Example of seasonal operation

The same reasoning as in the previous case can be applied to a seasonal operation to answer the question of staying open or closing down during the off-season. Consider a motel that has the following income statement:

Annual Income Statement	
Revenue	$130,000
Expenses	(110,000)
Net income	$ 20,000

The owner decided to do an analysis of his revenue and costs by the month, and found that for ten months he was making money and for two months he was losing money. His variable costs were 20 percent of total revenue and total fixed costs were $84,000, or $7,000 a month. Exhibit 1.9 summarizes his findings.

His analysis seems to indicate that he should close to eliminate the $10,000 loss during the two-month "loss" period. But, if he does, the fixed costs for the two months ($14,000) will have to be paid out of the ten-month **Annual net income reduced by closing** net income. The ten-month net income of $30,000 less two months' fixed costs of $14,000 will reduce his annual net income from its present

EXHIBIT 1.9. Income Statement Broken Down by Season

	10 months	2 months	Total
Revenue	$125,000	$ 5,000	$130,000
Variable costs	$ 25,000	$ 1,000	$ 26,000
Fixed costs	70,000	14,000	84,000
Total costs	$ 95,000	$ 15,000	$110,000
Net income (loss)	$ 30,000	($ 10,000)	$ 20,000

$20,000 to $16,000. If he does not want a reduction in annual net income, he should not close.

There might be other factors to consider in such a situation that would reinforce the decision to stay open. For example, there could be considerable additional close-down and start-up costs that would have to be included in the calculation of the cost of closing. Also, would key employees return after an extended vacation? Is there a large enough pool of skilled labor available and willing to work on a seasonal basis only? Would there be recurring training time (and costs) at the start of each new season? These are some of the types of questions that would have to be answered before any final decision to close was made. **Other questions to be asked**

Which Business to Buy?

Just as a business manager has to make choices between alternatives on a day-to-day basis, so, too, does an entrepreneur going into business or expanding an existing business frequently have to choose between alternatives. Let us look at one such situation. **Choosing between alternatives**

A restaurant chain is anxious to expand. It has an opportunity to take over one of two existing restaurants. The two restaurants are close to each other in location, have the same type of clientele and size of operation, and the asking price is the same for each. They are also similar in that each is presently taking in $1,000,000 annual revenue and each has a net income of $100,000 a year. With only this information, it is difficult to make a decision as to which would be the more profitable investment. But an analysis of their costs reveals the information in exhibit 1.10. **Insufficient cost information**

EXHIBIT 1.10. Income Statement Showing Different Cost Structures

	Restaurant A		Restaurant B	
Revenue	$1,000,000	100.0%	$1,000,000	100.0%
Variable costs	$ 500,000	50.0%	$ 300,000	30.0%
Fixed costs	400,000	40.0%	600,000	60.0%
Total costs	$ 900,000	90.0%	$ 900,000	90.0%
Net income	$ 100,000	10.0%	$ 100,000	10.0%

Structure of costs affects results

Although the revenue and net income are the same for each restaurant, the *structure* of their costs is different, and this will affect the decision about which one could be more profitable. The restaurant chain that wishes to take over either A or B is optimistic about the future. It feels that, without any change in fixed costs, it can increase annual revenue by 10 percent. What effect will this have on the net income of A and B? Net income will not increase for each restaurant by the same amount. Restaurant A's variable cost is 50 percent. This means that, out of each dollar of additional revenue, it will have variable expenses of $0.50 and net income of $0.50 (fixed costs do not increase). Restaurant B has variable costs of 30 percent, or $0.30 out of each revenue dollar, leaving net income of $0.70 from each dollar of extra revenue (again, fixed costs do not change).

Assuming a 10 percent increase in revenue and no new fixed costs, the income statements of the two restaurants have been recalculated in exhibit 1.11. Note that Restaurant A's net income has gone up by $50,000

EXHIBIT 1.11. Effect of Increased Revenue on Costs and Net Income

	Restaurant A		Restaurant B	
Revenue	$1,100,000	100.0%	$1,100,000	100.0%
Variable costs	$ 550,000	50.0%	$ 330,000	30.0%
Fixed costs	400,000	36.4%	600,000	54.5%
Total costs	$ 950,000	86.4%	$ 930,000	84.5%
Net income	$ 150,000	13.6%	$ 170,000	15.5%

(to $150,000), but Restaurant B's has gone up by $70,000 (to $170,000). In this situation, Restaurant B would be the better investment.

A company with high fixed costs relative to variable costs is said to have *high operating leverage*. It will do better from a net income point of view in times of rising revenue than will a company with *low operating leverage* (low fixed costs relative to variable costs). A company with low fixed costs, however, will be better off when revenue declines. Exhibit 1.12 illustrates this, under the assumption that our two restaurants are going to have a decline in revenue of 10 percent from the present $1,000,000 level, and given the assumption of no change in fixed costs. Exhibit 1.12 shows that, with declining revenue, Restaurant A's net income will be higher than Restaurant B's.

High and low operating leverage

EXHIBIT 1.12. Effect of Decreased Revenue on Costs and Net Income

	Restaurant A		Restaurant B	
Revenue	$ 900,000	100.0%	$ 900,000	100.0%
Variable costs	$ 450,000	50.0%	$ 270,000	30.0%
Fixed costs	400,000	44.4%	600,000	66.7%
Total costs	$ 850,000	94.4%	$ 870,000	96.7%
Net income	$ 50,000	5.6%	$ 30,000	3.3%

In fact, if sales decline far enough, Restaurant B will be in financial difficulty long before Restaurant A. If the break-even point were calculated (the break-even point is that level of revenue at which there will be neither net income or loss), Restaurant A's revenue could decline to $800,000, while Restaurant B would be in difficulty at $857,000. This is illustrated in exhibit 1.13.

Break-even point differs

EXHIBIT 1.13. Break-even Income Statements

	Restaurant A		Restaurant B	
Revenue	$ 800,000	100.0%	$ 857,000	100.0%
Variable costs	$ 400,000	50.0%	$ 257,000	30.0%
Fixed costs	400,000	50.0%	600,000	70.0%
Total costs	$ 800,000	100.0%	$ 857,000	100.0%
Net income	0	00.0%	0	00.0%

SEPARATING COSTS INTO FIXED OR VARIABLE

Methods for separating semicosts

In a number of the decision-making situations illustrated so far in this chapter, the concept of fixed versus variable costs has been used. To have a breakdown of all costs into either fixed or variable is valuable information for many different kinds of decisions.

Some costs are easy to identify as either definitely fixed or definitely variable. Others, which are semifixed or semivariable, must be broken down into their two separate elements. A number of different methods are available for breaking down these semicosts into fixed and variable. Three will be discussed:

1. Maximum/minimum calculation
2. Multipoint graph
3. Regression analysis

To set the stage, we will use the income statement of the Model Motel for a year's period (see exhibit 1.14). The Model Motel operates at an average room rate of $20.00 and last year sold a total of 15,300 rooms ($306,000 total revenue divided by $20.00).

EXHIBIT 1.14. Model Motel Income Statement

Revenue		$306,000
Expenses:		
Employee wages	$120,800	
Management salary	20,000	
Laundry, linen, and guest supplies	38,700	
Advertising	7,500	
Maintenance	17,300	
Energy	18,100	
Office and telephone	4,000	
Insurance	4,600	
Interest	8,300	
Property taxes	20,100	
Depreciation	35,000	294,400
Net income		$ 11,600

The first step is to list the expenses by category: fixed, variable, semi-variable (see exhibit 1.15). The owner or manager's past experience about the costs of the Model Motel, or past years' accounting records, will be **Information from past records**

EXHIBIT 1.15. Model Motel Expenses by Category			
	Fixed	Variable	Semi
Employee wages			$120,800
Management salary	$20,000		
Laundry, linen, and guest supplies		$38,700	
Advertising	7,500		
Maintenance			17,300
Energy			18,100
Office and telephone			4,000
Insurance	4,600		
Interest	8,300		
Property taxes	20,100		
Depreciation	35,000		

helpful in this listing. The figures in the fixed column are those that do not change during the year with a change in volume (number of rooms sold). In other words, even though a fixed cost may change from year to year (insurance rates do change, the amount to be spent on advertising can be increased or decreased at management's discretion), such changes are not directly caused by the number of guests accommodated. The items in the variable column are costs that are the direct result of guests using the facilities. For example, if there are no customers, there will be no cost for laundry, linen and guest supplies. The higher the occupancy, the higher will be these costs. The figures in the "semi" column are those we must break down into their fixed and variable components.

To demonstrate the three methods of breaking down a semicost, we will use the wage amount of $120,800. Since much of the wage cost is related to number of rooms sold, we need a month-by-month breakdown of **Monthly breakdown** the units (rooms) sold each month and the related wage cost for each **of costs** month. (This information could be broken down by the week, but a monthly analysis should be sufficiently accurate for all practical purposes.) The units sold and wage-cost breakdown is illustrated in exhibit 1.16. The figures in the units-sold column show number of rooms, but this column could also have been expressed in revenue dollars each month as long as the average rate of $20 was consistent throughout the year.

EXHIBIT 1.16. Model Motel Monthly Units Sold and Wage Cost		
	Units (rooms) sold	Wage cost
January (minimum)	500	$ 7,200
February	1,000	7,900
March	1,300	9,900
April	1,200	10,800
May	1,400	12,200
June	1,500	12,100
July	2,100	13,100
August (maximum)	2,100	13,200
September	1,500	11,800
October	1,000	7,600
November	1,000	7,400
December	700	7,600
Totals	15,300	$120,800

Maximum/Minimum Method

Three steps in max/min method

In exhibit 1.16, the word *minimum* is noted alongside January. In January, units sold and wage cost were at their lowest for the year. In contrast, August was the maximum month. There are three steps in the maximum/minimum method:

Step 1. Deduct the minimum from the maximum figures.

Step 2. Divide the wage difference by the units sold difference to obtain variable cost per unit sold.

Step 3. Use the answer to step 2 to calculate the fixed cost element.

These steps are illustrated in exhibit 1.17. In this exhibit, "units sold" was used. However, we could equally as well have used "dollars of

---

EXHIBIT 1.17.   Calculation of Fixed Costs Using Units

Step 1.   Deduct the minimum from the maximum figures

	Units (rooms) sold	Wage cost
August (maximum)	2,100	$13,200
January (minimum)	500	7,200
Differences	1,600	$ 6,000

Step 2.   Divide wage difference by units-sold difference

$$\frac{\$6,000}{1,600} = \$3.75$$

which is the variable cost per unit sold

Step 3.   Use the answer to step 2 to calculate the fixed-cost element

August:	total wages	$13,200
	variable cost:	
	2,100 units sold	
	@ $3.75 a unit =	7,875
	fixed cost	$ 5,325

---

revenue" and achieved the same result (see exhibit 1.18).

Also, in step 3, we could have used the minimum sales month instead of the maximum to calculate our fixed cost, and would still obtain the same result:

Use maximum or minimum month

Step 3. January — total wages	.	$7,200
— variable cost, 500 units		
sold × $3.75 a unit =		1,875
— fixed cost		$5,325

The calculated fixed cost is $5,325 a month or:

Calculation of fixed cost

$$12 \times \$5,325 = \$63,900 \text{ a year}$$

Referring again to exhibit 1.15, we can now break down our total annual wage cost into its fixed and variable elements:

EXHIBIT 1.18. Calculation of Fixed Costs Using Revenue

Step 1.

	Units sold		Average rate	Total revenue	Wage cost
August (maximum)	2,100	×	$20.00 =	$42,000	$13,200
January (minimum)	500	×	$20.00 =	10,000	7,200
Differences				$32,000	$ 6,000

Step 2.

$$\frac{\$6,000}{\$32,000} = \$0.18\frac{3}{4}$$

which is the variable cost per dollar of revenue

Step 3. August: total wages $13,200
variable cost:
$42,000 revenue ×
$0.18¾ =   7,875

fixed cost $ 5,325

Calculation of variable cost

Total annual wages	$120,800
Fixed cost	63,900
Variable cost	$ 56,900

Graph could be used

The calculation of the monthly fixed cost figure has been illustrated by arithmetical means. The maximum/minimum figures could have been plotted equally as well on a graph as illustrated (see exhibit 1.19), and the fixed cost read off where the dotted line intersects the vertical axis. If the graph is accurately drawn, the same monthly figure of approximately $5,300 is achieved.

The maximum/minimum method is quick and simple. It uses only two sets of figures. Unfortunately, these sets of figures may not be typical of the relationship between revenue and costs for the year. For example, a one-time bonus may have been paid during one of the months selected. Other, perhaps less dramatic distortions may be built into the figures.

Distortions to be eliminated

These distortions can be eliminated, as long as one is aware of them, by adjusting the raw figures. Alternatively, standard costs (rather than

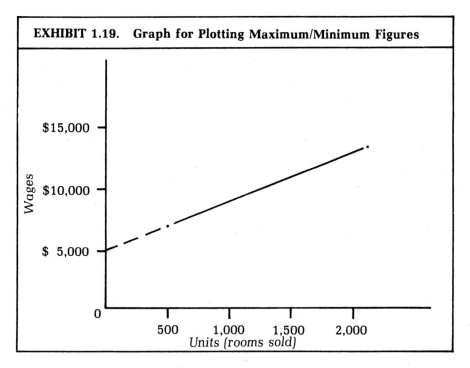

EXHIBIT 1.19. Graph for Plotting Maximum/Minimum Figures

actual costs) could be used for the minimum- and for the maximum-sales months.

Another way to improve on the maximum/minimum method and remove possible distortions in individual monthly figures is to plot the cost and units sold figures for each of the twelve months (or however many periods there are involved) on a multipoint graph.

Multipoint Graph Method

Exhibit 1.20 illustrates a multipoint graph for our sales in units and our wage cost for each of the twelve months. Sales and costs were taken from exhibit 1.16. The graph illustrated is for two variables (units sold and wages). In this case, wages are identified as the *dependent variable* and are plotted on the vertical axis. Wages are dependent on, or vary with, sales. Sales, therefore, are the *independent variable*. The independent variable is plotted on the horizontal axis. Once each of the twelve points are plotted, we have what is known as a scatter graph—a series of points scattered around a line which has been drawn through them. A straight line must be drawn. There is no limit to how many straight lines could be drawn through the points. The line we want is the one which, to our eye, seems to fit best. Each individual doing this exercise would probably view the line in a slightly different position, but most people with a reasonably

Dependent versus independent variable

good eye would come up with a line that, for all practical purposes, is close enough. The line should be drawn so that it is continued to the left until it intersects the vertical axis (the dependent variable). The intersect-point reading is our fixed cost. Note that, in exhibit 1.20, our fixed cost reading is $4,500 (approximately). This is the monthly cost. Converted to an annual cost, it is:

$$\$4,500 \times 12 = \$54,000$$

Our total annual wage cost would then be broken down into:

Fixed	$54,000
Variable	66,800
Total	$120,000

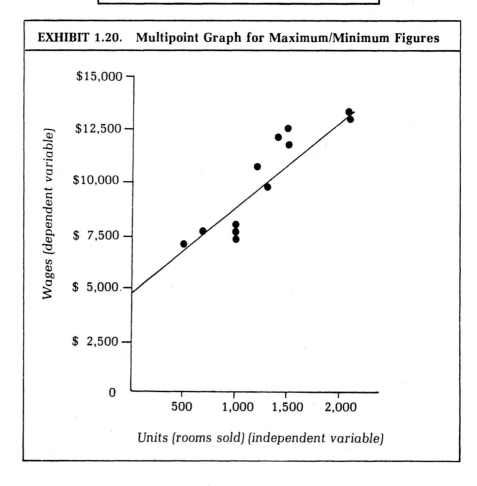

EXHIBIT 1.20. Multipoint Graph for Maximum/Minimum Figures

Note that, in drawing graphs for the purpose discussed, the point where the vertical and horizontal axes meet should be given a reading of zero. The figures along each axis should then be plotted to scale from zero. **Plot to scale from zero**

The straight line on a scatter graph can be drawn by eye, and, for most purposes, will give us a fixed cost reading that is good enough. However, the question arises: is there one best line which can be drawn that is the most accurate? The answer is yes. The method used to determine it is called *regression analysis*.

Regression Analysis Method

With the preceding method, the objective was to find a line drawn through the points that would allow us to read off the fixed cost amount on the vertical axis. With regression analysis, we can use an equation that will allow us to calculate the fixed cost amount directly.

Before the equation is used, we have to take the units (rooms) sold and the wage cost information from exhibit 1.16 and develop it a little further, as has been done in exhibit 1.21. In exhibit 1.21, the units-(rooms)-sold column has been given the symbol X for the independent variable. The wage-

EXHIBIT 1.21.	Information for Regression Analysis Equation			
Month	Units (rooms) sold = X	Wage cost = Y	XY = (X × Y)	X^2 = (X × X)
1	500	7,200	3,600,000	250,000
2	1,000	7,900	7,900,000	1,000,000
3	1,300	9,900	12,870,000	1,690,000
4	1,200	10,800	12,960,000	1,440,000
5	1,400	12,200	17,080,000	1,960,000
6	1,500	12,100	18,150,000	2,250,000
7	2,100	13,100	27,510,000	4,410,000
8	2,100	13,200	27,720,000	4,410,000
9	1,500	11,800	17,700,000	2,250,000
10	1,000	7,600	7,600,000	1,000,000
11	1,000	7,400	7,400,000	1,000,000
12	700	7,600	5,320,000	490,000
Totals	15,300	120,800	165,810,000	22,150,000

Regression analysis equation

cost column, the dependent variable, is given the symbol Y. Two new columns have been added: XY (X multiplied by Y) and X² (X multiplied by X). The equation we can use is:

$$\text{Fixed costs} = \frac{(\Sigma\ Y)\ (\Sigma\ X^2) - (\Sigma\ X)\ (\Sigma\ XY)}{n(\Sigma\ X^2) - (\Sigma\ X)^2}$$

Meaning of symbols

Two new symbols have been introduced in this equation:

Σ means *the sum of*, or the column-total figure.

n is the *number of periods*, in our case 12 (months).

Replacing the symbols in the above equation by the column totals from exhibit 1.21, we have:

$$\text{Fixed costs} = \frac{\$120,800\ (22,150,000) - (15,300)\ (\$165,810,000)}{12\ (22,150,000) - (15,300)\ (15,300)}$$

$$= \frac{\$2,675,720,000,000 - \$2,536,893,000,000}{265,800,000 - 234,090,000}$$

$$= \frac{\$138,827,000,000}{31,710,000}$$

$$= \$4,378.02 \text{ a month}$$

Rounding out answer

Our answer could be rounded out to $4,400 a month, which would give us a total annual fixed cost of:

$$\$4,400 \times 12 = \$52,800$$

Comparison of Results

Let us compare the results of our fixed and variable breakdown of the Model Motel's annual wage cost using each of the three methods described. The results are:

	Fixed	Variable	Total	
Maximum/minimum	$ 63,900	$ 56,900	$120,800	Results show differences
Multipoint graph	54,000	66,800	120,800	
Regression analysis	52,800	68,000	120,800	

In practice, only one of the three methods need be used. Regression analysis is the most accurate, and, since today even hand calculators are, or can be, programmed to handle regression analysis, the work involved does not take long. The multipoint graph results are fairly close to the regression analysis figures. Therefore, if the graph is well drawn, the results should be exact enough for most practical purposes. The maximum/minimum results are about 20 percent different from the other two sets of figures. This method should be used with caution, and only if one is sure the maximum and minimum months selected are typical of all periods. This might be difficult to determine.

With reference to the Model Motel figures, we have so far analyzed only the semivariable wage cost figures. The maintenance, energy, and office and telephone figures would have to be similarly analyzed so that we can then have total fixed costs and total variable costs for decision-making purposes.

SUMMARY

One way of increasing net income in a business is to increase revenue. Another way is to control costs. In order to do this, one must understand the type of cost that one is dealing with in making cost-control decisions.

An *actual cost* is what a cost or expense actually was as opposed to a *budgeted cost* that is a forecast of what the actual cost might be. A *direct cost* is one that is the responsibility of, and controllable by, a department head or department manager. An *indirect cost*, sometimes referred to as an undistributed or overhead cost, is not normally allocated to an operating department. All costs are *controllable costs* whether they are direct or indirect. A *joint cost* is one that is shared by two or more departments, or by the organization as a whole. A joint cost could therefore be a direct one (for example, wages) or an indirect one (for example, building maintenance).

A *discretionary cost* is one that is incurred only at the discretion of an individual, usually the general manager. A *relevant cost* is one that needs to be considered in the making of a specific decision. If a cost makes no difference to a decision then it is not relevant. A *sunk cost* is an example of a cost that is not relevant. An expenditure made on an item of equipment five years ago (a sunk cost) is not relevant to a decision to purchase a replacement for that equipment item today.

An *opportunity cost* is the profit foregone by not doing something. For example, a motel could operate its restaurant at a profit or lease it out. If the motel operates the restaurant, the lease income foregone is an opportunity cost. A *standard cost* is what a cost should be for a given level of revenue or number of units sold.

A *fixed cost* is one that does not change in the short run, regardless of the level of revenue. An example of this might be the general manager's salary. *Variable costs* are those that do vary, generally in a linear fashion with revenue. Food cost would be a typical example. However, many costs fall into the category of a *semifixed* or *semivariable cost*. In order to make meaningful decisions, these semicosts must be broken down into their fixed and variable elements. Three methods of doing this were illustrated in this chapter:

1. The maximum/minimum method which, although easy to use, may give misleading results if the maximum and minimum revenue and cost periods selected are not truly representative of all periods.

2. The multipoint graph method, which eliminates the possible problem inherent in the maximum/minimum method. The graph is subject to an element of personal judgment but, in most cases, will give results that are close enough for practical purposes.

3. Regression analysis, which is the most accurate method. It does require time to make the calculations and can probably best be used as a spot check on the results of using one of the other two methods.

DISCUSSION QUESTIONS

1. Differentiate between a direct and an indirect cost.

2. What is a discretionary cost? Give two examples other than those mentioned in the chapter.

3. Define and give an example of a standard cost.

4. Differentiate between a fixed and a variable cost. Give an example of each.

5. Why are some costs referred to as semifixed or semivariable?

6. Why might it be unwise to allocate an indirect cost to various operating departments based on their revenue levels?

7. List what you think might be the relevant costs when considering the purchase of one of a number of competitive vacuum cleaners for the housekeeping department.

8. Explain why you think it sometimes might make sense to sell below total cost.

9. Explain the term *high operating leverage.*

10. In times of rising revenue, would it be preferable to have high or low operating leverage? Explain.

11. With figures of your own choosing, illustrate how the maximum/minimum method can be used to separate the fixed and variable elements of a semicost.

12. Give a brief explanation of how to prepare a graph when using the multipoint graph method of separating the fixed and variable elements of a semicost.

PROBLEMS

1-1. A restaurant owner is considering expanding by purchasing one of two similar, competitive restaurants. Present annual revenue of each of them is $675,000. Rita's Restaurant has annual variable costs of 50 percent of revenue and fixed costs of $300,000, while Rosa's Restaurant has annual variable costs of 60 percent of revenue and fixed costs of $232,500. The restaurant owner thinks that, if she were to purchase Rita's, she could save $15,000 per year on its fixed costs. On the other hand, if she were to purchase Rosa's, she could reduce variable costs to 55 percent. In either situation, she calculates that revenue can be increased by 20 percent per year.

 a. Calculate the present net income of each restaurant.

 b. Given the above assumptions, advise the restaurant owner about which one she should purchase. Support your recommendation with necessary calculations.

1-2. A restaurant complex provides you with the following annual information about its three departments:

	Dining room	Coffee shop	Tavern	Total
Revenue	$368,200	$271,900	$305,600	$945,700
Direct costs	307,500	257,200	255,100	819,800
	$ 60,700	$ 14,700	$ 50,500	$125,900
Indirect costs				104,000
Net income				$ 21,900

The restaurant owner thinks that, in order for him to have a better view of how each department is doing, the indirect costs should be allocated to each department pro rata, according to their square foot area as a fraction of total area. The dining room has 2,400 square feet, the coffee shop 1,680, and the tavern 1,920.

a. Allocate the indirect costs as indicated, and advise the owner about whether or not he should accept an offer from a drug-store operator who is anxious to rent the coffee-shop space for a rental of $1,300 a month.

b. Before making a final decision, the restaurant owner decided that a more detailed analysis of the indirect costs is necessary. This analysis showed what would happen to each cost if the coffee shop were rented out. The information is:

	Present cost	Cost if coffee shop is rented
Administrative and general	$28,400	$27,000
Marketing	19,200	18,200
Property operation and maintenance	9,500	8,800
Energy	7,900	7,600
Insurance	7,300	6,700
Interest	10,700	10,700
Depreciation	21,000	14,200

Further, if the coffee shop is rented out, tavern sales will decline by $26,900 a year, and tavern direct costs will decrease by $20,300. Dining room revenue and direct costs will not be affected. Advise the restaurant owner about whether or not to accept the offer from the drug store. Explain your anwer.

1–3. A restaurant has the following annual revenue and direct costs in each of its three departments:

	Dining room	Lounge	Banquet room
Revenue	$540,300	$452,700	$406,700
Direct costs	458,100	382,800	388,400

Annual indirect costs for the entire operation are $157,100. The restaurant owner wishes to allocate the indirect costs to the three departments on a square-foot basis. The dining room has 3,300 square feet, the lounge 1,500, and the banquet room 1,200. Allocate the indirect costs, and then advise the owner about whether or not she should consider leasing out the banquet room space to a storage company for $20 per square foot per year.

1–4. Before she makes the final decision in problem 1–3, you suggest to the owner that an analysis of the indirect costs be carried out. Analysis shows the following:

Administrative and general	$42,400
Marketing	29,200
Property operation and maintenance	10,800
Energy	15,100
Insurance	10,800
Interest	15,900
Depreciation	32,900

If the banquet room space is leased out, the following changes in banquet-room indirect costs will occur:

Administrative and general. This will be reduced by $2,500 per year.
Marketing. There will be savings of $160 per month.
Property operation and maintenance. This will be reduced by $60 per month.

Energy. The storage company will pay $1,200 per year towards this cost.

Insurance. This cost will be reduced to $10,000 per year.

Interest. No change is anticipated.

Depreciation. Equipment depreciation will be reduced by $10,000 per year.

In addition to these changes, there will be reductions in lounge revenue of $40,000 and in lounge direct costs of $30,000 per year. Dining room revenue and direct costs will not be affected. What would you advise the restaurant owner to do?

1-5. A hotel owner is considering replacing an old piece of equipment with a new one. He has provided you with the following information concerning the three alternative models:

	Model A	Model B	Model C
New equipment cost	$24,000	$23,000	$22,000
Estimated life	5 years	5 years	5 years
Trade-in value at end of life	$ 2,400	$ 2,200	$ 1,800
Training costs (year 1)	1,000	1,100	1,200
Annual maintenance	500	700	400
Annual supplies cost	900	800	700
Annual energy cost	700	700	700
Annual employee wages	24,000	24,000	24,000
Cash received from old equipment sale	1,600	1,800	2,000

Using lowest cash cost over the five-year period as the basis for the decision, advise the operator about which model to buy.

1-6. A hotel has the following breakdown of its revenue and of wages in its rooms department:

	Revenue	Wages
January	$ 96,100	$52,200
February	96,700	44,600
March	102,500	45,000

	Revenue	Wages
April	$ 97,200	$45,300
May	137,200	51,900
June	185,100	75,200
July	213,500	86,600
August	177,900	64,600
September	136,800	60,400
October	122,000	51,300
November	112,500	45,100
December	108,200	45,400

The January wage figure includes a profit-sharing bonus of $7,900, and the July wage figure includes a lump-sum retroactive wage increase of $9,700. Make these adjustments, and then use the maximum/minimum method to calculate the rooms department's fixed wage cost per month.

1–7. Using the figures and information in problem 1–6, plot the twelve sets of figures on a graph to determine the fixed wage cost.

1–8. Given the following revenue and wage cost figures, use regression analysis to calculate the monthly fixed wage cost (figures are in thousands of dollars):

	Revenue	Wages
January	$ 59	$33
February	57	31
March	62	32
April	58	33
May	79	37
June	101	46
July	118	49
August	97	41
September	80	41
October	70	35
November	67	33
December	63	32

Cost Control by Budgeting

2

Objectives

After studying this chapter, the reader should be able to do the following:

- Define the three purposes of budgeting.
- Describe some of the types of budgets such as short-term, long-term, departmental, and fixed versus flexible.
- Briefly discuss some of the advantages and disadvantages of budgeting.
- List and briefly discuss each of the five steps in the budget cycle.
- Briefly explain some of the limiting factors to be kept in mind when budgeting.
- Define the term *derived demand*.
- Explain what information is required to determine budgeted revenue in a restaurant operation and budgeted revenue for guest rooms.
- Prepare budgeted (pro forma) income statements given appropriate revenue and cost information.

PURPOSES OF BUDGETING

Budgeting is used by most firms to aid in controlling costs and to ensure that costs are kept in line with forecast revenues.

Budgeting is planning

Budgeting is planning. In order to make meaningful decisions about the future, a manager must look ahead. One way to look ahead is to prepare budgets or forecasts. A forecast may be very simple. For a restaurant owner/operator, a budget may be no more than looking ahead to tomorrow, estimating how many customers will eat in the restaurant, and purchasing food and supplies to accommodate this need. On the other hand, in a larger organization, a budget may entail forecasts up to five years ahead (such as for furniture and equipment purchases), as well as day-to-day budgets (such as staff scheduling). Budgets are not always expressed in monetary terms. They could involve numbers of customers to be served, number of rooms to be occupied, number of employees required, or some other unit rather than dollars.

Budgets not always in dollars

The main purposes of budgeting could be summarized as follows:

- To provide organized estimates of future revenues, expenses, manpower requirements, or equipment needs, with estimates broken down by time period and/or department

Purposes of budgeting

- To provide a coordinated management policy both long-term and short-term, expressed primarily in accounting terms

- To provide a method of control so that actual results can be evaluated against budget plans and adjustments, if necessary, can be made

TYPES OF BUDGETS

There are a number of different types or kinds of budgets. Some of these are:

Long-term versus short-term budgets. Budgets can generally be considered to be either long-term or short-term. A long-term, or strategic, budget would be anywhere from one year to five years ahead. Such a budget concerns the major plans for the organization (expansion, creation of a new market, financing, purchasing new furniture and equipment, and similar matters). From such long-term plans evolve the policies concerning the day-to-day operations of the business and, thus, the short-term budgets. Short-term budgets could be for a day, a week, a quarter, or a year. Such budgets use the resources of middle management to meet the long-term plans or objectives of the organization.

Short term budgets for day-to-day operations

Capital budget. The capital budget relates to items that appear on the balance sheet. A three-month cash budget for a restaurant would be a capital budget. A five-year replacement schedule for hotel-room furnishings would also be a capital budget.

Operating budget. The operating budget concerns the ongoing projections of revenue and expense items, or items that affect the income statement. For example, a forecast of revenue for a restaurant for a month would be an operating budget. Similarly, in a multidepartment hotel, the forecast of total payroll expense for the year would be an operating budget.

Examples of operating budgets

Department budget. Separate departmental budgets are only prepared in establishments with two or more departments. They would show the forecast revenue and direct expenses for each department. Alternatively, if a department does not directly generate any revenue (for example, the maintenance department of a hotel), a department budget would be prepared showing anticipated expenses in detail. Generally, such department budgets are prepared for up to a year, month by month.

Monthly departmental budgets

Master budget. A master budget is the most comprehensive of all budgets. Generally, a master budget is prepared for a year's period and would include a balance sheet for a year hence and all the departmental income and expense statements for the next year's period.

Fixed versus flexible budgets. A fixed budget is one that is based on a certain level of activity or revenue. Expense estimates are based on this level of revenue. No attempt is made to introduce higher or lower levels of revenue, and thus different expense amounts are in the budget. The disadvantage of such a budget is that, if the actual level differs from budgeted level, because there had been no plan covering this possibility, expenses can only then be adjusted in the short run by guesswork. For example, suppose the rooms-department budget in a hotel is based on an average year-round rooms occupancy of 70 percent. Operating costs (such as payroll, supplies, linen, laundry) are based on this level of occupancy. If actual occupancy dropped to 60 percent because of unforeseen economic conditions, it might be difficult for the rooms-department manager to know, in the short run, what the new payroll level or other expenses should be.

Expenses based on revenue forecasts

On the other hand, a flexible (or variable) budget would be prepared for several levels of activity. In our rooms-department flexible budget, revenue could be forecast for 60 percent, 70 percent, and 80 percent occupancy levels (or as many levels as are appropriate). As the actual year progresses, it can be determined into which level the operation is best go-

Adjustment is easier with flexible budgets

Fixed amounts in flexible budgets

ing to fit, and the appropriate expense amounts will have already been determined. In other words, adjustment is easier. The question could be raised, using the rooms-department example, whether this is truly flexible (variable) budgeting, or whether it is three (or more, if more occupancy levels are used) fixed budgets at three different occupancy levels. The question is academic. The practicality of such a method of budgeting is that management is prepared to adjust when adjustment is required.

Even with flexible budgeting, it is possible for a particular expense item to remain fixed. For example, a budget might be prepared for a restaurant based on a number of levels of revenue. Expenses are calculated based on each different level. However, advertising expense might be left the same (that is, fixed) regardless of the actual level of revenue. In other words, regardless of the volume of sales, a definite, fixed amount is budgeted to be spent on this expense.

BUDGET PREPARATION

Budgets in small operation

In a small, owner-operated restaurant or motel, the owner would prepare the budget. If it were a formal budget, the help of an accountant might be useful. If the budget were an informal one, there might be no written supporting figures. The owner might just have a plan in his mind about where he wants to go, and would operate from day to day to achieve his objective, or to come as close to it as possible.

In a larger organization, a great many individuals might be involved in budget preparation. In such organizations, budgets are prepared from the bottom up. At the very least, the department heads or managers should be involved. If their subsequent performance is to be evaluated on the plans included in the budget, then they must be involved in preparing their own departmental budgets. They, in turn, might well discuss the budget figures with certain employees within their own departments.

Budget committee

Above the department heads would be a budget committee. Department managers might be members of this committee. Such a committee is required for overall coordination of the budget to ensure that the final budget package is meaningful. For example, the rooms occupancy of a hotel determines, to a great extent, the breakfast revenue for the food department. The budget committee must ensure that food breakfast revenue is not based on an occupancy that differs from the rooms-department figure.

The formal preparation of the budget is a function of the accounting department. The organization's comptroller would be a member of the budget committee. His task is to prepare final budget information for submission to the general manager for approval.

The worst form of budget preparation is to impose budgets, without consultation, from the top down, through the accounting department to the operating and other departments. Coordination might be excellent, but the cooperation of the employees where the activity takes place would be minimal.

Worst form of budgeting

When Are Budgets Prepared?

Long-range budgets for up to five years forward are generally prepared annually. Each year, such budgets are revised for the next period (up to five years) forward.

Short-term budgets are prepared annually, for the most part, with monthly projections. Each month, budgets for the remaining months of the year should be revised to adjust for any changed circumstances. Department managers should be involved in such revisions, as well as the budget committee for overall coordination.

Revisions to monthly budgets

Weekly or daily short-range budgets are usually handled internally by the department heads or other supervisory staff. For example, the housekeeper would arrange the room-attendant staffing schedule (which affects the payroll budget) on a daily basis based on the anticipated rooms-occupancy day by day.

Advantages and Disadvantages of Budgeting

A number of advantages accrue to an organization that uses a budget-planning process.

1. Since the budgeting process involves department heads and possibly other staff within the department, it encourages participation and thus improves communication and motivation. The operating personnel can better identify with the plans or objectives of the organization.

Communication and motivation

2. In preparing the budget, those involved are required to consider alternative courses of action. For example, should the advertising budget be spent to promote the organization as a whole, or would better results be obtained if emphasis were placed on one particular department rather than on another? At the department level, a restaurant manager might need to consider increasing the number of customers to be served per meal-period per waiter (increased productivity per waiter) against the possible effects of slower service, reduced seat turnover, and perhaps lower total revenue.

Alternative courses of action

Comparison of actual results with budget

3. Budgets outline in advance the revenues to be achieved and the cost involved in achieving these revenues. After each budget period, the actual results can be compared with the budget. In other words, a standard for comparision is predetermined, and subsequent self-evaluation by all those involved in the operation is possible.

4. In the case of flexible budgets, the organization as a whole, and each department within it, is prepared for adjustment to any level of activity between minimum and maximum levels, assuming that the departments have been involved in developing their budgets within these levels.

Budgets are forward-looking

5. Budgeting forces those involved to be forward-looking. This is not to suggest that what happened in the past is not important and not to be considered in budget preparation; but, from now on, only future revenues and future costs are important to future plans and profits. For example, do menu item selling prices need to be changed to take care of anticipated future increases in food and/or labor and/or other operating costs?

Obviously, just as there are advantages to budgeting, so are there disadvantages. Some of these are:

Time constraints

1. The time and cost to prepare budgets can be considerable. Usually, the larger the organization, the larger the amount of time, and thus the cost, of preparing budgets.

Unpredictable future

2. The future is unpredictable. Budgets are based upon unknown factors (as well as some known factors) that can have a big bearing on what actually happens. (It could be argued that this is not a disadvantage, since it forces those involved to look ahead and prepare for the unknown.)

Confidential matters

3. Top management, for its own reasons, may want to keep some matters confidential. Budget preparation may require that these matters be included in the budget, and they are thus no longer confidential.

Spending to budget problem

4. The "spending to the budget" approach can be a problem. If an expense budget is overestimated, there can be a tendency to find ways to spend the money still in the budget as the end of the budget period approaches. This tendency can be provoked by a desire to demonstrate that the budget forecast was correct to begin with and/or to protect the budget from being cut for the next period.

Therefore, in any decision about whether or not to prepare budgets, one should consider both the advantages and the disadvantages. In most cases, the advantages would outweigh the disadvantages.

THE BUDGET CYCLE

The budget cycle is a five-part process:

1. Establishing attainable goals or objectives
2. Planning to achieve these goals or objectives
3. Comparing actual results with those planned, and analyzing the differences (variances)
4. As a result of step three, taking any corrective action if required
5. Improving the effectiveness of budgeting

Each of these five steps will be discussed in turn.

1. Establish attainable goals or objectives

In setting goals, the most desirable situation must be tempered with realism. In other words, if there are any factors present that limit revenue to a certain maximum level, these factors must be considered. An obvious example is that a hotel cannot achieve more than a 100 percent room-occupancy for overnight purposes. In the short run, room revenue (if a hotel were full every night) can only be increased by increasing room rates. But, since very few hotels do run at 100 percent year-round, it would be unwise, desirable as it might be, to use 100 percent as the budgeted occupancy on an annual basis.

Similarly, a restaurant is limited to a known number of seats. If it is running at capacity, revenue can only be increased, again in the short run, by increasing meal prices or increasing seat turnover (seat occupancy). But, again, there is a limit to increasing meal prices (customer resistance and/or competition often dictate upper pricing levels), and, if seat turnover is increased by giving customers rushed and hurried service, the end result may be declining revenue as customers eat elsewhere.

Other limiting factors are a lack of skilled labor or skilled supervisory personnel. Increased productivity (serving more customers per waiter) would be desirable and would decrease the payroll cost per customer, but well-trained employees, or employees who could be trained, are often not available. Similarly, supervisory personnel who could train others are not always available.

Shortage of capital could limit expansion plans. If financing is not available to add guest rooms or expand dining areas, it would be a useless exercise to include expansion in our long-term budget.

Management's policy, such as a decision concerning the market in which the organziation will operate, may also limit budgets. For example, a coffee-shop department head may propose that catering to bus-tour groups would help increase revenue. On the other hand, the general manager may feel that catering to such large, transient groups is too disruptive to the regular clientele.

Remember customer demand and competition

Finally, customer demand and competition must always be kept in mind when budgeting. In the short run, there is usually only so much business to go around. Adding more rooms to a hotel does not automatically increase the demand for rooms in the area. It takes time for demand to catch up with supply, and new hotels, or an additional block of rooms of an existing hotel, will usually operate at a lower occupancy than normal until additional demand increases with time. A new restaurant, or addition of facilities to an existing restaurant, must compete for its share of business.

2. Plan to achieve goals or objectives

Planning at departmental level

Once objectives have been determined, plans must be laid to achieve them. At the departmental level, a restaurant manager must staff with employees skilled enough to handle the anticipated volume of business. A chef or purchaser must purchase food in the quantities required to take care of anticipated demand, and of a quality that meets the required standards expected by the customers and that allows the food operation to match as closely as possible its budgeted food cost. Over the long term, a budget expansion of facilities might require top management to make plans for financing and to seek out the best terms for repayment to achieve the budgeted additional profit required from expansion.

3. Compare actual results with those planned, and analyze the differences

Most important steps

This is probably the most important and advantageous step in the budget cycle. Comparing actual with planned budget allows one to ask questions such as:

Questions that could be asked

a. Our actual dining room revenue for the month of April is $30,000 instead of the budgeted $33,000. Was the $3,000 difference caused by a reduction in number of customers? If so, is there an explanation (for example, are higher prices keeping customers away? or, did a competitive restaurant open nearby?)? Or is the $3,000 difference a result of reduced seat-turnover (is service slowing down?), or are customers just spending less (a reduced average check, or reduced customer-spending because of belt-tightening by the customer)?

b. Yesterday, the housekeeper employed two more room attendants than were required to handle the actual number of rooms occupied. Is there a communication problem between the front office and the housekeeper? Did the front office fail to notify the housekeeper of reservation cancellations, or did the housekeeper err in calculating the number of room attendants actually required?

c. The annual cocktail-lounge departmental net income was greater than the previous year, but still fell short of budgeted net income. Did the revenue reach the budgeted level? Or did costs increase over the year more than in proportion to revenue? If so, which costs? Was there a change in what we sold (change in the sales mix); in other words, are we now selling less profitable items (such as more beer and wine than liquor, in proportion to total revenue)?

These are just a few examples of the types of questions that can be asked, and for which answers should be sought, in analyzing differences between budgeted and actual performance. It should be noted that differences between actual and budgeted figures do not by themselves offer solutions to the fact that problems may exist. The solutions can only come from proper interpretation, investigation, and, if necessary, corrective action.

Solutions from interpretation and investigation

4. Take any corrective action required

Step three in the budget process points to differences and possible causes of these differences. The next step in the budget cycle necessitates taking corrective action if this is required. The cause of a difference could be the result of a circumstance that no one could foresee or predict (for example, weather, a sudden change in economic conditions, or a fire in part of the premises). On the other hand, a difference could be caused by the fact that selling prices were not increased sufficiently to compensate for an inflationary rate of cost increases; or that the budgeted forecast in occupancy of guest rooms was not sufficiently reduced to compensate for the construction of a new hotel nearby; or that staff was not as productive in number of customers served or rooms cleaned as it should have been according to predetermined standards. Whatever the reason, it should be corrected, if possible, so that future budgets can more realistically predict planned operations. The fact that there are variances between budget and actual figures should not be an argument in favor of not budgeting. For, without a budget, the fact that the operation is not running as effectively as it should and could be would not even be apparent. If the variance were a favorable one (for example, guest room occupancy higher than budgeted), the cause should also be determined because that information could help in making future budgets more accurate.

Unpredictable differences and their causes

Favorable variances provide useful information

5. Improve the effectiveness of budgeting

Improving budget accuracy

This is the final step in the five-step budget cycle. All those involved in budgeting should be made aware of the constant need to improve the budgeting process. The information provided from past budgeting cycles and particularly the information provided from analyzing variances between actual and budgeted figures will be helpful. By improving accuracy in budgeting, the effectiveness of the entire organization is increased.

DEPARTMENTAL BUDGETS

Income statements are basis for all budgets

The starting point in any complete budgeting process is the departmental income statement. The rest of the budgeting process generally hinges on the results of these operating departments. For example, a budgeted balance sheet cannot be made up without reference to the income statements; a cash budget cannot be prepared without knowledge of departmental revenues and expenses; long-term budgets for equipment and furniture replacement, for dividend payments, or for future financing arrangements cannot be prepared without a budget showing what net income will be generated from the internal operation.

Steps in departmental budgeting

The departmental budgets are probably the most difficult to prepare. However, once this has been done, the preparation of any other budgets required is a relatively straightforward process. This chapter will, therefore, only deal with income statement budgets since they are the prime concern of day-to-day management of a hotel or restaurant. In summary, the procedure is as follows:

1. Estimate revenue levels by department.
2. Deduct estimated direct operating expenses for each department.
3. Combine estimated departmental operating net incomes, and deduct estimated undistributed expenses to arrive at overall net income.

Further explanation about each of these three procedures follows:

1. Estimate revenue levels by department

Revision during year

Even though departmental income statements are prepared for a year at a time, they should be prepared initially month by month (with revisions, if necessary, during the budget year in question). Monthly income statements are necessary so that comparisons with actual results can be made each month. If comparison between budget and actual were only made on a yearly basis, any required corrective action might already be eleven months too late. The following should be considered in monthly revenue projections:

Factors to be considered

    a. past actual revenue figures and trends

    b. current anticipated trends

    c. economic factors

    d. competitive factors

    e. limiting factors

For example, suppose the dining room revenue for the past three years for the month of January was:

0001	$30,000
0002	35,000
0003	37,000

It is now December in the year 0003 and we are finalizing our budget for the year 0004, commencing with January. The increase in volume for year 0002 over 0001 was about 17 percent ($5,000 divided by $30,000). Year 0003 increase over year 0002 was approximately 6 percent. These increases were caused entirely by increases in number of customers. Sales prices have not changed on our menus in the past three years, nor has the size of our restaurant been changed. No change in size will occur in year 0004. Because a new restaurant is being opened a block away, we do not anticipate our customer count to increase in January, but neither do we expect to lose any of our current customers. Because of economic trends, we will be forced to meet rising costs by increasing our menu prices by 10 percent commencing in January 0004. Our budgeted revenue for January 0004 would therefore be:

Examples of revenue forecasting

$$\$37,000 + (10\% \times \$37,000) = \$40,700$$

    The same type of reasoning would be applied for each of the eleven other months of year 0004, and for each of the other operating departments. One other factor that, in some situations, might need to be considered in revenue projections is derived demand. In other words, what happens in one department may have an effect on what happens to the revenue of another. An example of this might be a cocktail bar that generates revenue from customers in the bar area as well as from customers in the dining room whose drinks are served from the adjacent bar.

Derived demand

    In budgeting the bar total revenue, the revenue would have to be broken down into revenue within the lounge area and revenue derived from dining-room customers. Similarly, in a hotel, the occupancy of the

Interdependence of departments

guest rooms will affect the revenue in the food and beverage areas. The interdependence of departments must, therefore, be kept in mind in the budgeting process.

2. Deduct direct operating expenses for each department

Many expenses vary with revenue

Since most departmental direct operating costs are specifically related to revenue levels, once the revenue has been calculated the major part of the budget has been accomplished. Historic accounting records will generally show that each expense varies within very narrow limits as a percentage of revenue. The appropriate percentage of expense to revenue can therefore be applied to the budgeted revenue in order to calculate the dollar amount of the expense. For example, if laundry expense for the rooms department of a hotel varies between 4½ percent to 5½ percent of revenue, and revenue in the rooms department for a particular month is expected to be $100,000, then the laundry expense for that same month would be:

$$5\% \times \$100,000 = \$5,000$$

Similarly calculations can be done for all other direct expenses with obvious cost to revenue percentages.

Fixed element of some expenses

In certain cases, however, the problem may not be as simple, because there may not be as direct a relationship between cost and revenue. A good example of this would be labor, where much of the cost does not vary with revenue. In a restaurant, the wages of the restaurant manager, the cashier, and the hostess are generally fixed. Such people receive a fixed salary regardless of volume of business. Only the wages of serving people and busboys can be varied in the short run. In such cases, a month-by-month staffing schedule must be prepared listing the number of variable staff of each category required for the budgeted revenue level, calculating the total variable cost, and adding this to the fixed cost element to arrive at total labor cost for that month. It is true that this requires some detailed calculations, but, without it, the budget might not be as accurate as it could be for effective budgetary control.

Development of staffing schedules

Staffing schedules for each department for various levels of revenue can be developed, based on past experience and on the standards of performance required by the establishment. Then, when revenue levels are forecast, the appropriate number of man-hours or staff required for each type of job can be read directly from the staffing schedule. The number of hours of staffing required or the number of employees needed can then be multiplied by the appropriate prevailing rates of pay for each job category. Staffing schedules or guides will be discussed and illustrated further in chapter 11.

3. Combine departmental operating net incomes, and deduct undistributed expenses to arrive at overall net income

The departmental operating profits budgeted for in steps one and two can now be added together. At this point, certain undistributed expenses must be calculated and deducted. These expenses are not allocated to the departments because an appropriate allocation is difficult to arrive at. Nor are they, for the most part, controllable by, or the responsibility of, the department managers.

Undistributed expenses not allocated

These expenses usually include administrative and general, marketing, guest entertainment, and property operation, maintenance and energy costs. Also included would be other fixed costs such as rent, property taxes, insurance, interest, and depreciation.

Since these expenses are usually primarily fixed, they vary little with revenue; historic records will generally indicate the narrow dollar range within which they fall. To take care of inflation, they might be increased by a certain percentage each year. (A technique known as zero-based budgeting for better estimation of these expenses will be explained in chapter 12.)

Little variation in some expenses

Sometimes these expenses will vary at the discretion of the general manager. For example, it may be decided that a special extra allocation will be added to the advertising and promotion budget during the coming year, or that a particular item of expensive maintenance can be deferred for a year. In such cases, the adjustment to the budget figures can be made at the general manager's level. Usually, these undistributed expenses are calculated initially on an annual basis (unlike departmental revenue and direct operating expenses, which are initially calculated monthly). If an overall pro forma (projected or budgeted) income statement, including undistributed expenses, is to be prepared monthly, then the simplest method is to divide each undistributed expense by twelve, and show one-twelfth of the expense for each month of the year. A three-month budget would show one-fourth of the total annual expense. (Note that it is only the undistributed expenses that are handled in this way. Revenue and allocated direct expenses should be calculated correctly month by month to take care of monthly or seasonal variations.)

Time allocation of undistributed expenses

For example, exhibit 2.1 shows how the undistributed costs could be distributed in a budget prepared on a quarterly basis. Exhibit 2.1 also indicates a budgeted loss in two of the quarters. It is argued that such budgeted losses are misleading because the quarters with low revenue are unfairly burdened with overhead costs, and a fairer way to distribute such costs would be in ratio to budgeted revenue. Such a distribution would be calculated as in exhibit 2.3.

Alternative allocation of undistributed expenses

The revised budget, prepared on the new allocation of these expenses to the various quarters, would be as in exhibit 2.2. The method illustrated in exhibit 2.2 may, as it does in our case, ensure that no period has a budgeted loss. Over the year, however, there is no change in total net income.

EXHIBIT 2.1. Undistributed Expenses Allocated on Quarterly Basis

	Quarter 1	Quarter 2	Quarter 3	Quarter 4	Annual totals
Revenue	$300,000	$600,000	$800,000	$300,000	$2,000,000
Direct departmental expenses	(250,000)	(450,000)	(550,000)	(250,000)	(1,500,000)
	$ 50,000	$150,000	$250,000	$ 50,000	$ 500,000
Undistributed expenses	(75,000)	(75,000)	(75,000)	(75,000)	(300,000)
Net income (loss)	($ 25,000)	$ 75,000	$175,000	($ 25,000)	$ 200,000

EXHIBIT 2.2. Undistributed Expenses Allocated on Revenue Volume Basis

	Quarter 1	Quarter 2	Quarter 3	Quarter 4	Annual totals
Revenue	$300,000	$600,000	$800,000	$300,000	$2,000,000
Direct departmental expenses	(250,000)	(450,000)	(550,000)	(250,000)	(1,500,000)
	$ 50,000	$150,000	$250,000	$ 50,000	$ 500,000
Undistributed expenses	(45,000)	(90,000)	(120,000)	(45,000)	(300,000)
Net income	$ 5,000	$ 60,000	$130,000	$ 5,000	$ 200,000

| | | | EXHIBIT 2.3. | Calculation of Undistributed Expenses Breakdown by Revenue Volume |

Quarter	Revenue	Percent to total revenue	Share of undistributed expenses
1	$ 300,000	15%	15% × $300,000 = $ 45,000
2	600,000	30	30 × 300,000 = 90,000
3	800,000	40	40 × 300,000 = 120,000
4	300,000	15	15 × 300,000 = 45,000
Totals	$2,000,000	100%	$300,000

BUDGETING IN A NEW OPERATION

New hotels and restaurants will find it more difficult to budget in their early years because they have no internal historic information to serve as a base. If a feasibility study had been prepared prior to opening, it could serve as a base for budgeting. Alternatively, forecasts must be based on a combination of known facts and industry or market averages for that type and size of operation.

For example, a restaurant could use the following equation for calculating its breakfast revenue:

$$\text{Number of seats} \times \text{Seat turnover rate} \times \text{Average check} \times \text{Days open in month} = \text{Breakfast total monthly revenue}$$

Equation for forecasting food revenue

This same equation could be used for the luncheon period, for the dinner period, and even separately for coffee breaks. Meal periods should be separated because seat turnover rates and average check figures can vary considerably from period to period. The figures for the number of seats and days open in the month in the above equation are known facts. The seat turnover rates and average check figures can be obtained by reference to published information or from personal observation at competitive restaurants.

Combination of facts and estimates

Once monthly revenue figures have been calculated for each meal period, they can be added together to give total revenue. Direct operating expenses can then be deducted, applying industry average percentage figures for each expense to the calculated budgeted revenue.

In a rooms department, a similar type of equation would be:

Equation for forecasting room revenue

Forecast occupancy percent	×	Average room rate	×	Number of rooms available	×	Days in month	=	Total revenue for month

Again, direct operating expenses can then be budgeted for using industry percentages for the type of hotel.

Beverage figures are a little more difficult to calculate. There are some industry guidelines, such as a coffee shop serving beer and wine generates alcoholic beverage revenue approximating 5–15 percent of food revenue. In a dining room, the alcoholic-beverage revenue (beer, wine, and liquor) approximates 25–30 percent of food revenue. For example, a dining room with $100,000 a month in food revenue could expect to have about $25,000 to $30,000 in total liquor revenue. These are only approximate figures, but they may be the only ones that can be used until the operation can refer to its own historic accounting records.

Difference between food and beverage average check

As for beverage figures in a cocktail lounge, there is no simple equation. An average check figure (such as average spending figure per customer) can be misleading. For example, one customer can occupy a seat and spend $3 on each of five drinks; average spending for that customer is $15. On the other hand, five different customers could occupy the same seat and spend $15 over the same period of time; average spending in this case would be $30. Therefore, the equation used in calculating food revenue may be difficult to apply in a bar setting. One alternative is to use the current industry average revenue per seat per year in a cocktail bar:

Example of beverage revenue forecast

Average annual revenue per seat	×	Number of seats	=	Total annual revenue

To convert to a monthly basis for budget purposes, this figure can then be divided by twelve and added to the already calculated beverage revenue by month generated from the food departments. Direct operating expenses can then be allocated using industry average percentage guidelines.

Although these equations do not cover all possible approaches, they should give the reader some idea of the methods that can be used in budgeting for a new operation.

Improving forecasts based on past records

The equations illustrated are not limited to a new operation. They could also be used in an ongoing organization. For example, instead of applying an estimated percentage of revenue increase to last year's figure for the current year's budget, it might be better to break down last year's revenue figure into its various equation elements and adjust each of them individually (where necessary) to develop the new budget amount. For example, last year, June rooms-revenue was $100,200. This year, we expect a 5 percent increase; therefore, budgeted revenue will be:

$$\$100,200 \times (5\% \times \$100,200) = \$105,210$$

A more comprehensive approach would be to analyze last year's figure in the following way:

Actual occupancy percent	×	Average room rate	×	Number of rooms available	×	Days in month	=	Total revenue for month
83.5%	×	$20.00	×	200	×	30	=	$100,200

Example of room revenue forecast

We can then apply the budget-year trends and information to last year's detailed figures. In the budget period, because of a new hotel in the area, we expect a slight drop in occupancy down to 80 percent. This will be compensated for by an increase in our average room rates of 12 percent. Our budgeted revenue is therefore:

Budgeted occupancy percent	×	Budgeted average room rate	×	Number of rooms available	×	Days in month	=	Budgeted monthly revenue
80.0%	×	$22.40	×	200	×	30	=	$107,520

This approach to budgeting might require a little more work, but will probably give budgeted figures that are more accurate and can be analyzed more meaningfully than would otherwise be the case.

More accurate forecast figures

SPECIAL SITUATIONS

To this point, we have looked at budgeting as a monthly problem. In some situations, however, it might be preferable to budget on a weekly or even daily basis, such as in a food operation that experiences extreme fluctuations in volume by day or by meal period. A statutory holiday or other special day (for example, Mothers' Day) that has an effect on business can be more readily coped with if sales forecasting is handled by day of the week and if the guest count (a simplification of number of seats × seat turnover rate) is the key figure, along with the average check. A form that could be used for this is illustrated in exhibit 2.4. Again, in an ongoing

Extreme volume fluctuations

EXHIBIT 2.4.	Dining Room Weekly Food Sales Forecast						
	Mon.	Tue.	Wed.	Thu.	Fri.	Sat.	Sun.
Breakfast:							
Guest count	150	140	130	140	150	120	100
Average check	4.10	4.10	4.10	4.10	4.10	4.10	4.10
Sales	615	574	533	574	615	492	410
Lunch:							
Guest count	180	180	180	180	180	120	80
Average check	9.25	9.25	9.25	9.25	9.25	9.25	9.25
Sales	1,665	1,665	1,665	1,665	1,665	1,110	740
Dinner:							
Guest count	210	210	200	190	240	240	170
Average check	14.50	14.50	14.50	14.50	14.50	14.50	14.50
Sales	3,045	3,045	2,900	2,755	3,480	3,480	2,465
Total sales	5,325	5,284	5,098	4,994	5,760	5,082	3,615

operation, past history will form the basis for forecasting the guest count, adjusted for the other factors (listed earlier in this chapter) to be considered when estimating budgeted revenue levels.

Catering Department Sales

In the catering (banquet) department, the guest count is not as significant as it might be in a dining room or coffee shop, because of the diversity of groups that one might have from one type of banquet to another (for example, a retirement dinner, an annual bowling club banquet, a weekly club membership luncheon, or a wedding function). Some groups want a much lower cost per customer than others (such as, perhaps, a wedding party) for whom the price per person may be less important.

Forecasting by function

Therefore, banquet sales forecasting must be done function by function, multiplying the forecast guest count by the actual contracted customer spending for that function. This needs to be done day by day for the entire forecast period (for example, a week or a month).

For banquet forecasting that is more than a month ahead, the possibility of some additional functions, as well as the likelihood of some cancellations, must also be built into the forecasts.

SUMMARY

Budgeting is part of the planning process. It can involve decisions concerning day-to-day management of an operation or, on the other hand, involve plans for as far ahead as five years. The main purposes of budgeting are:

- To provide estimates of future revenues and expenses.
- To provide short- and long-term coordinated management policy.
- To provide a control by comparing actual results with budgeted plans, and to take corrective action if necessary.

There are various types of budgets such as short-term, long-term, capital, operating, departmental, master, and fixed or flexible.

In a small operation, budgets can be prepared by an individual. In a large operation, there would normally be a budget committee. In all cases, whether for a day, a year, or some other time period, budgets should be prepared in advance at the start of the period.

Some of the advantages of budgets are:

1. They involve participation of employees in the planning process, thus improving motivation and communication.
2. They necessitate, in budget preparation, consideration of alternative courses of action.
3. They allow a goal, a standard of performance, to be established, with subsequent comparison of actual results with that standard.
4. Flexible budgets permit quick adaptation to unforeseen, changed conditions.
5. They require those involved to be forward-looking, rather than to be looking only at past events.

The budgeting cycle has five parts:

1. Establishing attainable goals (remember the limiting factors).
2. Planning to achieve these goals.
3. Analyzing differences between planned and actual results.
4. Taking any necessary corrective action.
5. Improving the effectiveness of budgeting.

The starting point in budgeting is to predetermine revenue levels. In a large organization, this forecast would be done by department. In forecasting, one must consider past actual revenue levels and trends, current anticipated trends, and the economic, competitive, and limiting factors.

Once revenue has been forecast, direct operating expenses can be calculated based on anticipated revenue, and, finally, indirect or unallocated expenses can be deducted to arrive at the net income for the operation. Once the departmental and general income statement budgets have been prepared, other required budgets (such as balance sheets and capital budgets) can be prepared as required.

If there is no historical accounting information available, which would be the case in a new venture, then the forecasting of revenue and expenses is more difficult, but not impossible.

DISCUSSION QUESTIONS

1. How would you explain budgeting?

2. What are three purposes of budgeting?

3. Explain the difference between a short-term and a long-term budget.

4. Give an example of
   a. A hotel department budget.
   b. A capital budget for a restaurant.

5. Explain the difference between a fixed and a flexible budget.

6. List and briefly discuss three advantages of budgeting.

7. Two of the steps in the budgeting cycle are:
   a. Establishing attainable goals.
   b. Planning to achieve these goals.
   What are the remaining three steps?

8. Discuss three possible limiting factors to consider in preparing a budget for a hotel or restaurant.

9. A cocktail lounge had revenue in May of $40,000. Budgeted revenue for that month was $42,000. List three questions that could be asked the answers to which might explain the $2,000 difference.

10. In projecting the coffee shop breakfast period revenue in a hotel what factors need to be considered?

11. What is derived demand?

12. List the four items that must be multiplied by each other to forecast total annual food revenue for the dinner period of a restaurant.

13. Explain how banquet sales forecasting is done.

PROBLEMS

2–1. Forecast the annual revenue for each of the following situations:

   a. A 300-room hotel with a 70 percent occupancy and an average rate of $75.

   b. A seasonal resort hotel of 150 rooms that is closed for the months of November, December, January, and February. During the months in which it is open, it has an occupancy of 90 percent and an average rate of $95.

   c. A cocktail lounge that is closed on Sundays and on four statutory holidays each year. Assume a 52-week year (rather than 365 days). Average revenue is $17 per seat per day open. There are 72 seats.

   d. A 125-seat coffee shop that is open for all three meals every day of the year. Seat turnover and average check figures are as follows:

	Turnover	Average check
Breakfast	1.5	$ 5.05
Lunch	1.75	8.10
Dinner	1.25	15.20

2–2. Calculate the room revenue for a 40-room motel for the first six months of the year, given the following:

	Room rate	Occupancy
January	$40	70%
February	40	75
March	45	75
April	50	75
May	50	80
June	50	80

2–3. A resort hotel has a dining room that derives its business solely from hotel guests who occupy its rooms. It has 120 rooms and, during the month of August, expects a 90 percent occupancy of those rooms. Because the resort caters to the family trade, there are, on average, three people per occupied room per night. From past experience, management knows that 90 percent of those occupying rooms eat breakfast, 20 percent eat lunch, and 80 percent eat dinner in the hotel's dining room (some of the guest rooms have their own cooking facilities). The dining room is open seven days a week for all three meals. Its average meal prices are: breakfast $5.10, lunch $7.75, and dinner $14.20. Calculate the budgeted dining room revenue for the month of August.

2–4. The restaurant of a 150-room year-round resort hotel depends entirely on its room guests for its revenue. Average annual rooms occupancy is 70 percent. There are, on average, four people per occupied guest room per night. From past experience management knows that 80 percent of those occupying rooms eat breakfast, 25 percent eat lunch, and 50 percent eat dinner in the hotel's restaurant (some of the guest rooms have cooking facilities). The restaurant is open every day of the year. Average check figures are: breakfast $4.60, lunch $9.10, and dinner $16.20. Calculate the restaurant's annual revenue.

2–5. A financial forecast is being carried out for a proposed new 110-seat restaurant. It will be open for both lunch and dinner from Monday through Saturday, and for buffet dinner only on Sunday. For simplicity, assume a 52-week year. Seat turnover and average food check figures are estimated to be as follows:

	Seat turnover	Average check
Weekday lunch	1.5	$ 5.60
Weekday dinner	1.25	10.50
Sunday dinner	1.25	13.00

In addition, the restaurant has a small banquet room, where food revenue is estimated at 1,200 guests per month and an $11.00 average check. In the main part of the restaurant, alcoholic beverage revenue is estimated to be 15 percent of lunch food revenue and 25 percent of dinner food revenue. In the banquet room, alcoholic beverage revenue is forecast to be 35 percent of food revenue. Food cost is estimated to be 35 percent of total food revenue, and liquor cost is estimated to be 25 percent of total beverage revenue. Wage cost for employees on salary is estimated at $294,000 per year. Wages for all other employees are forecast to be 15 percent of total restaurant revenue (including banquets). Employee benefits will be 15 percent of total salaries and wages. Other operating costs are estimated at 11 percent of total annual revenue. Fixed costs for administration, marketing, energy, and other items are expected to be $131,000 per year. Prepare the restaurant's budgeted income statement for the first year. Round all calculated figures to the nearest dollar.

2–6. A 130-seat restaurant is open Monday through Saturday for both lunch and dinner. On Sundays and holidays (which total 60 days during the year) it is open for dinner only. For the coming year, it has budgeted the following:

	Seat turnover	Average check
Weekday lunch	1.75	$ 5.40
Weekday dinner	1.25	11.10
Sundays/holidays	1.5	12.00

Attached to the restaurant is a private party room that is expected to generate 1,000 customers per month, each spending $12.00, on average, on food. Alcoholic beverage revenue is 15 percent of weekday lunch food sales and 30 percent of weekday dinner sales. There are no alcoholic beverage sales on Sundays and holidays. In addition, beverage revenue in the private party room will be 30 percent of food revenue in that area. Food cost averages 40 percent of overall food revenue, and beverage cost averages 25 percent of overall beverage revenue. Fixed wages for salaried personnel are estimated to be $300,000 next year. The balance of total salaries and wages is a variable wage cost that averages 15 percent of overall restaurant revenue from all sources. Employee benefits are 15 percent of total salaries and wages. Other operating costs are expressed as a percentage of total revenue from all sources. These costs are as follows:

China, glass, silver, linen	1.8%
Laundry	1.3
Supplies	3.4
Menu and beverage lists	1.0
Marketing	2.5
Repairs and maintenance	1.4
Miscellaneous operating costs	0.8

Rent expense will be $7,000 per month, and other annual fixed costs are as follows:

Administrative and general	$24,200
Licenses	14,800
Equipment depreciation	73,100

Prepare the restaurant's budgeted income statement for next year. Round all calculated figures to the nearest dollar.

2–7. A 150-room hotel forecasts its average room rate to be $65 next year, with an 80 percent occupancy rate. The rooms department's fixed wage cost is $348,000 per year. The variable wage cost for rooms department guest room cleaning employees is $5.00 per hour, and it takes half an hour to clean a room. Employee benefits for rooms department employees are 15 percent of total fixed and variable wages. Linen, laundry, supplies, and other variable room costs are $10.50 per occupied room per night. The hotel also has a 90-seat dining room. Breakfast revenue is derived entirely from guests who have stayed in the hotel overnight. On average, 60 percent of rooms occupied are occupied by one person, and the remainder are double-occupied. On average, 75 percent of overnight guests eat breakfast, with an average check of $6.10. Lunch seat turnover is 1.25, with an average check of $9.40. Dinner seat turnover is 0.75 with an average check of $16.30. The dining room is open 365 days per year for all three meal periods. Direct dining room operating costs (food, wages, supplies, and other items) are 80 percent of dining room revenue. Indirect costs (administration, marketing, energy, and other items) for the entire hotel are estimated at $1,750,000 for next year. Calculate the hotel's budgeted net income for next year. Round all calculated figures to the nearest dollar.

Purchasing and Inventory Cost Control

3

Objectives

After studying this chapter, the reader should be able to do the following:

- List and briefly discuss the five major steps in the purchasing cycle.
- Define the term *specifications* and list some of the advantages of preparing them.
- Discuss centralized purchasing and the factors to consider when selecting a supplier.
- Describe the various types of purchasing arrangement such as open market and one-stop buying.
- Describe two types of standing order.
- Explain how perpetual inventory cards and requisitions are used.
- Use the three costing methods (most recent price, first-in/first-out, and weighted average) for valuing inventory and costing requisitions.
- Describe value analysis.
- Solve problems concerning purchase discounts, and differentiate between a rebate and a discount.
- Use the economic order equation to aid in quantity ordering.

COST INCURRENCE

Effective
purchasing
increases profits

When the decision to purchase goods or to contract for services is made, a cost is incurred. It would therefore seem that, to minimize costs, more attention should be paid to the purchasing function than is probably the case for most hospitality enterprise operators. Perhaps one of the reasons for this is that to have a part- or full-time person on the payroll responsible for purchasing is an added cost that erodes profits. However, many larger enterprises have entire purchasing departments on their payroll with several employees involved in purchasing. Such companies do not consider a purchasing department to be a cost center but rather a department that contributes to net income through effective purchasing. Effective purchasing is generally considered to reduce overall company costs.

THE PURCHASING DEPARTMENT

Role of purchasing
department

The purchasing department's role is to make sure that supplies, equipment, and services are available to the operation in quantities appropriate to predetermined standards, at the right price, and at a minimum cost to meet desired standards. Generally, those responsible for purchasing have the authority to commit the establishment's funds to buying required goods or services. Sometimes, a maximum dollar amount for any individual purchase may be established, beyond which a higher level of authority is required before proceeding with the purchase. Those responsible for purchasing may have authority to question individual purchase requisitions with reference to the particular need or the stipulated specifications. They may also be required to prepare reports for management, to design necessary control forms, to ensure that there is smooth cooperation with operating departments, and to establish fair practices with suppliers.

Applying effective
purchasing in small
operation

Even though a smaller enterprise may not be able to afford, nor would it need, a separate purchasing department, the person responsible for purchasing, whether it be the chef (in the case of certain food purchases), the storekeeper (in the case of other food purchases and general supplies), or the general manager (in the case of capital items such as furniture and equipment) can all benefit from applying some of the purchasing practices and procedures discussed in this chapter. This benefit was particularly valuable for the last few years when shortages of many products arose and high prices resulted.

Purchasing pitfalls

By following established purchasing procedures, an operation can avoid many purchasing pitfalls such as panic buying, over- or short-purchasing, buying by price rather than by a combination of quality and price, pressure buying, or, what is probably quite common, satisfied buying. With the latter, the purchaser operates under the assumption that no improvements in either quality or price can be achieved.

THE PURCHASING CYCLE

There are a number of steps in the purchasing cycle. The major ones are:

1. Recognizing the need to purchase goods or services
2. Preparing specifications, if necessary
3. Selecting a supplier
4. Ordering the goods or services
5. Receiving the goods or services

Each of these will be discussed.

Steps in the purchasing cycle

Recognizing Need

Generally, the authority to request a needed item is vested in those responsible for running specific departments. For example, the chef, since he is generally responsible for establishing daily menus, would have the authority to request needed food supplies. The bar manager would have the authority to request alcoholic beverages and other supplies to replenish his bar stock. The housekeeper is in the best position to recognize the need to replenish housekeeping items such as linen and guest supplies. In many cases, these same individuals may be responsible for actually ordering the items. However, in larger operations, where purchasing is centralized in one individual, or in the purchasing department, it is necessary that these individuals communicate their needs to purchasing department personnel. This is generally handled by way of purchase requisitions. Purchase requisitions may take many different forms, but a basic format that would cover the needs of most establishments is illustrated in exhibit 3.1.

Who has purchasing authority?

Preparing Specifications

Wherever practical, it is recommended that purchasing specifications be completed for major items of expenditure. Obviously, for many items purchased in a hospitality enterprise specifications may not be practical or necessary. This might apply in the purchase of items required on an everyday basis, such as dairy or bakery goods. But food specifications should be encouraged for major food purchases such as meat, fish, and poultry items that can account for as much as fifty cents out of each food purchase dollar. They would also be recommended for other major purchases such as housekeeping linens or kitchen equipment. A specification is a carefully written description of the item desired. In a smaller operation, the specifications may be drawn up by the department head who has the authority to purchase the item. In other cases, the specifications may need to be prepared by a number of people, possibly in conjunction with an

Items requiring specifications

EXHIBIT 3.1. Purchase Requisition

#4964

Date _____

Department _____

Date required _____

Requested by _____

Department head checked _____

Purchasing manager approved _____

Note: Please use a separate purchase requisition for each item or group of related items.

Description	Quantity	Purchase order number	Suggested supplier

employee of the purchasing department who has experience in that area. It might be useful to prepare guidelines for those responsible for preparing specifications. These guidelines would list the points to be covered for all the items for which specifications must be prepared from time to time. Exhibit 3.2 illustrates guidelines for two possible items. Sufficient copies of

Guidelines for specifications

EXHIBIT 3.2. Specification Guidelines

Beef
Quality or grade, weight, degree of aging, amount of fat, cutting instructions, state of refrigeration (chilled or frozen).

Carpets
Type of construction, width, yarn and yarn weight per square yard, pile density and height, type of backing.

---

specifications should be prepared so that one copy may be sent to each potential supplier and copies distributed to appropriate personnel such as the purchasing manager, the department head involved, and the person responsible for receiving the goods. The language of the specifications must be sufficiently precise so that there is no misunderstanding between supplier and establishment. However, this does not mean that, once prepared, specifications cannot be changed. Indeed, as market conditions or the needs of the establishment change, new sets of specifications should be prepared.

Changing specifications

In summary, specifications should include the following items:

- The name or description of the item required
- The specific quality required
- The frequency with which the item is required
- Where it is important, the size, weight, amount, or number of the items required
- Where it is important, the form that the items should take (for example, whether an item of food should be fresh, frozen, or canned)

In other words, it is up to the buyer, in the specifications, to determine the intended use of the items required, and this will normally dictate the specifications. To illustrate, a specification for prime rib might be as follows:

Intended use of items

Item: Prime rib
       bone in
       oven ready

Grade: USDA choice
    upper half
Weight range: 18 lb min. – 22 lb max.
    average 20 lb (9 kg)
State of refrigeration: chilled when delivered
    not previously frozen
Fat limitation: 0.25 – 0.75 inch (average 0.5) on outside
    moderate marbling
Color: light red to slightly dark
Quantity requirement: approximately 300 lb per week
    (15 roasts)

The main advantages of specifications are that they—

1. Require those who prepare them to think carefully and document exactly what their product requirements are.

2. Leave no doubt in suppliers' minds about what they are quoting on, thus reducing or eliminating misunderstandings between supplier and establishment.

Advantages of specifications

3. Eliminate, for frequently purchased items, the time that would otherwise have to be spent repeating descriptions over the telephone or directly to salespersons each time the product is needed.

4. Permit competitive bidding.

5. Allow the person responsible for receiving to check the quality of delivered goods against a written description of the quality desired.

Selection of Supplier

There are many types of suppliers, such as manufacturer, wholesaler, retailer, and local producer or farmer. Depending on the product to be purchased, a different type of supplier may be contacted. For example, in the case of an item of capital equipment, it might be the manufacturer or his wholesaler representative. In the case of a food product, it might be the meat packer or the local farmer. The important consideration is to con-

Obtaining market quotations

tract as many suppliers as is practical to ensure that enough quotations are received so that the right quality of product is purchased at the lowest possible price. A minimum of three market quotations are recommended, although this may not be necessary or possible in every case, to ensure that competitive pricing prevails. In some cases, these quotations would be in writing because detailed specifications were prepared. In other cases, particularly in the case of food and beverage items purchased on a daily basis for which specifications might be impractical, these quotations might be taken over the telephone and simply summarized on a market quotation sheet. For an illustration of such a form see exhibit 4.1 in chapter 4 on food purchasing.

Large firms can often take advantage of their size through centralized purchasing. Some large firms do not use centralized buying, however, because they feel that the costs of centralization outweigh the benefits. Where centralized purchasing does occur, the degree of centralization can vary. The most highly centralized type of operation would be a commissary-based system, where all items (including perishable foods that need to be kept frozen or refrigerated) are purchased. In some commissaries, the food may even undergo some processing before distribution to individual outlets.

Centralized purchasing

Less centralized would be a distribution center that purchases and distributes to individual units all nonfood items—and perhaps nonperishable or even frozen food items—but lets individual units do their own direct purchasing of perishable foods.

Even more decentralized would be, for example, individual units of a chain or franchised operation that buy whatever they need from local suppliers as long as the local supplier has head-office approval for quality and price of products.

Some centralized buying only occurs in the arranging of a contract for products at a reduced price between the head office and a national manufacturer. The head office agrees that all units will use the product, in return for a volume discount; but the units do the purchasing directly from the local wholesalers or distributors, who have had the discount passed on to them. The question to be raised is, can the individual units buy from other local sellers if their price is better?

Chain operations can frequently benefit from lower price quotations for most items, except, perhaps, perishable foods that have to be purchased daily and locally by each unit. This is achieved by individual units making known their requirements in advance to the chain's central purchasing office. As a result of bulk purchasing, lower cost prices can usually be obtained, thus benefiting each individual unit in the chain.

Chain operation advantages

Other advantages are that the central purchasing office may be able to contact a greater number of suppliers, and that larger overall inventories of certain items can be maintained, thus reducing cost prices and ensuring a constant supply to individual units in the chain. Centralized purchasing may mean, however, that the individual unit must accept the quality dictated by the central purchasing office. This may also preclude the individual unit from taking advantage of local supplies at a low price or other "specials."

Problem of centralized purchasing

The following factors may be involved in the selection of suppliers:

- The quality of the products offered. The "top" quality is not always the "best" in a particular situation. Consider, for example, the requirement for a vegetable to be used in a soup.

Here, appearance might not be an important factor requiring the purchase of a top-quality item; if the same vegetable were to be served as an accompaniment to an entree item, however, quality of appearance would be important.

- The prices of the items. Again, the highest price may not be the "best" price to pay, depending on the quality actually needed.

Supplier's reliability

- The supplier's reliability and services, including such matters as whether or not its prices are in line with those of its competitors, the promptness and frequency of its deliveries, the consistency of its product quality, the degree to which it provides information about new products on the market, and its concern about its own reputation as a supplier.

- Sanitation, where important. This could be critical, for example, on the premises of a supplier of perishable food items.

Number of suppliers

The question also arises about how many suppliers to deal with. In some cases, the purchaser, by using as few suppliers as possible, becomes a more important customer to each supplier and can use this as a form of price leverage to lower prices. In other cases, there may only be one or two suppliers for specific products, and these suppliers can maintain a monopoly, or near monopoly, and not reduce prices. This would be the case in a government-run liquor operation, where the government is the sole supplier. It would also prevail in a situation where a licensed liquor supplier has the sole distributorship for a particular popular product that an operator must have because of customer demand.

Where there are many suppliers for a product, the purchaser has more ability to shop around and may be able to lower prices by playing one supplier against another. This would probably work when there is a large quality and price variance among suppliers for a particular product. It is in this situation that market quotations play an important role. Most food suppliers are in this very competitive situation, as are some liquor suppliers.

Purchasing Arrangements

There are a number of different types of purchasing arrangements possible. Some of these are:

Most used purchasing method

Competitive or open market buying. Under competitive buying, quotations are received by telephone, in person directly from a salesperson, or in writing through the mail. Wherever possible, written quotations are preferable, but they are not always practical when items are required within a day or so. Probably the majority of purchases made by the typical hospitality enterprise are bought through competitive or open market buying.

In some situations, because of the time and cost involved in competitive or open market buying, an operator will select only one or two suppliers. This situation is most likely to prevail in small, independent enterprises. The important consideration is that these suppliers must be carefully selected, on the basis of the factors previously outlined. This type of purchasing usually works best in areas where there is not a constant wide fluctuation in prices, and where the time to obtain several market quotations would not yield savings worth the time and cost.

Time and cost involved

Single-source buying. This would only be common when the product required is unique, and there is only one manufacturer/supplier. In such cases, the purchasing establishment may have little control over the cost of the item.

Contract buying. This form of buying might be useful for a product or products that must be purchased in relatively large quantities over a fairly long period (for example from three months to a year), and the price can be guaranteed by the supplier during this period. However, contracts might be written allowing for possible price changes during that period within a specified range of prices. Government and other institutional feeding operations frequently purchase on a contract basis. Chain operations might also use this purchasing method for certain products.

Users of contract purchasing

Sealed bid buying. This form is generally used only by large organizations or institutions. This method requires that the requirements for a product, with detailed specifications, be prepared and suppliers requested to make sealed bids on the item(s). This method eliminates the problem of frequent pricing and purchasing. It may also have the advantages of reducing prices of products and eliminating supplier pressure on an individual establishment. The disadvantage may be that the individual establishment may not be able to benefit from subsequent local price advantages as they occur since sealed bid buying generally requires that a contract be signed between the organization and the successful bidder.

Disadvantage of sealed bid buying

Cost-plus buying. With this arrangement, the establishment makes an arrangement with a supplier to purchase all of its requirements for a product or products at a specific percentage markup over the supplier's cost. The advantage to the purchaser is that this markup would generally be smaller than would otherwise be the case. Time that would be spent dealing with a variety of suppliers is also reduced. The problem with this buying method is that it may be difficult, if not impossible to verify the supplier's "cost." Cost-plus buying would probably not be used by the typical individual hospitality-industry enterprise.

Problem of determining seller's cost

Demand for audit

Where it is used, however, the markup is usually 10 to 15 percent over cost. An alternative to using cost-plus on a percentage basis might be to have cost plus a fixed fee per delivery. But what is "cost," and does the purchaser have the right to audit the supplier's books to determine "cost"? It is likely that a purchaser could impose a demand for an audit only if it were a major or chain operation. For example, a motel chain that decided to purchase all its guest room furniture and/or linen requirements from a single supplier might be able to insist on an audit. This arrangement could also be used when a firm or fixed price contract is not possible but the purchaser wants a contracted guaranteed delivery and is willing to pay whatever the prevailing price is at the time of delivery. For example, a restaurant that wants to feature an unusual special item on its menu may obtain a guarantee from the supplier that it will be available and in return may agree to pay the prevailing price and simply adjust the menu selling price from time to time as necessary.

Only one supplier

One-stop buying. This involves the purchase of all items of a particular type (for example paper and cleaning supplies) from one supplier. There is only one order required, only one delivery, and only one invoice to be paid. Theoretically, this reduces purchasing costs. However, since there is no competitive bidding, the financial advantages of one-stop buying would have to be carefully weighed before using this purchasing method.

The important ingredients in one-stop buying are careful selection of the supplier and periodic price comparisons to ensure that the supplier's prices are still in line.

One-stop buying may provide an overall cost advantage to the purchaser, even though the costs on some items may be higher than they would be if purchased elsewhere. These higher costs on some items are more than compensated for by reduced costs on others and/or by the supplier's willingness to offer a volume discount on the total purchase cost of all items.

Large suppliers that offer one-stop buying may also have product specialists on their payroll who can give the operator detailed information on both longtime and new products available.

Risk involved

The big risk with one-stop buying is that the purchaser becomes too dependent on the supplier and fails to stay alert to prices that are out of line or to newer products or additional services that have been introduced by the supplier's competitors.

In some situations (particularly for large-volume purchasers), it might be feasible to use a system that combines competitive pricing with one-stop buying within a particular group of products. For example, a beverage operation might have five licensed suppliers from whom it purchases alcoholic beverages. Over time, it has found that suppliers A, B, and E consistently offer the best prices for distilled products, so they will be asked to bid competitively each time a purchase is to be made. These three suppliers know that they are in a good position to receive a certain amount of the purchaser's business and will thus stay competitive in price, service, and quality. Supplier C can only compete on imported beer supplies (since it specializes in them), but it always offers the best overall prices and is given all imported beer orders without competitive bidding. Meanwhile, supplier D is consistently best in variety of wines offered and in wine prices, and it is given all wine orders without competitive buying. Suppliers C and D must be made aware of the fact that, if their prices, service, or quality and availability of product slip in any way, they may lose the business to their competitors.

Cooperative buying. Cooperative buying occurs when a group of operators join together to purchase products. The operators benefit from quantity-discount prices as the result of mass buying. Although not common in the hospitality industry for purchase of food, beverages and other operating supplies, it could occur, for example, if a group of hotels joined together to contract for the purchase of the same standard of bed linen from one supplier or manufacturer.

Group purchasing

Negotiated buying. Negotiated buying occurs when seller and buyer agree on the price to be paid for a good or service through a bargaining process. Obviously, such an arrangement would only take place in unusual circumstances, such as the purchase of a special commodity on a nonrepetitive basis. The purchaser hopes, through negotiation, to obtain concessions or additional services that he would not otherwise obtain without bargaining. Such negotiations would normally only occur with larger hospitality enterprises or institutional establishments. Those involved in negotiations must be highly skilled.

Unique purchasing method

Volume buying and warehousing. In some situations, a purchaser may be able to buy in large quantity and obtain a major discount. In such cases, the supplier may be able to store or warehouse the product, with or without an additional cost. Alternatively, the purchaser may be responsible for making storage arrangements off the premises (if there is not enough space there) and for paying the costs. In the case of certain food items, refrigerator or freezer space may be required. This type of arrangement usually entails having the purchaser pay in advance for items and either pay in advance for storage or pay the storage fee monthly. In all these situations, the purchaser must balance the purchase cost savings against the costs incurred by paying for storage and by losing interest on the money tied up in inventory.

Prepaying for purchases

A variation of volume buying and warehousing is an agreement between purchaser and supplier according to which the supplier agrees to deliver a contracted amount of a product over time and agrees to pay all warehouse and storage costs until the goods are delivered to the purchaser's establishment. This arrangement is sometimes used for items such as paper products, cleaning supplies, and linens.

Lowest Overall Cost

Purchasing objective

The real goal in purchasing is to purchase products at the lowest possible total cost, not at the lowest price per se. This has implications in the purchase of unprocessed foods, where the on-site labor can add considerably to the total costs. Few restaurants do their own butchering any more, and thus many have been able to eliminate a significant labor cost. Instead they purchase preportioned, pre-prepared individual cuts of meat (so-called convenience or prefabricated foods) that require little or no butchering. The total cost of purchasing such foods is lower, and the approach also provides better inventory control (again creating a reduction in costs). Consequently, in contracting for purchases, all other possible costs should be considered—not just the quoted price of the goods.

ORDERING GOODS

Distribution of purchase orders

Where an organization is large enough to warrant a formalized system of purchase requisitions and specifications, the ordering procedure should be similarly formalized with the use of purchase orders. A purchase order describes the product, gives the specifications or refers to the specification form number, and states the quoted price. Three copies of the purchase order are required—one for the supplier, one for the person responsible for receiving, and one for the accounting office, to be attached to the invoice when it is received for payment. A sample purchase order is illustrated in exhibit 3.3. Note that, for control purposes, this purchase order number should be cross-referenced to the purchase requisition number, and vice versa.

Impracticality of purchase order

In many cases in the hospitality industry, particularly where it involves day-to-day food and supplies ordering, a system of purchase orders is just not practical since most orders are placed at short notice and by telephone. In such cases, special procedures and forms will prevail. These will be discussed and illustrated in chapter 4 (on food purchasing), and chapter 7 (on beverage purchasing).

How much to order?

One question that does arise in the ordering process is the quantity to order. This is often left to the discretion of the department head involved, either because he has authority to order directly what is needed, or because he is in the best position to advise the purchasing department of required quantities. In the case of items purchased only occasionally, the quantity required is not too difficult to determine from past experience. In some cases, for example, equipment purchases, a purchase might occur

EXHIBIT 3.3. Sample Purchase Order

Franklyn Hotel
1260 South St., Manchester
Telephone: (261) 434-5734

PURCHASE ORDER   #653

(The purchase order number must appear on all invoices,
bills of lading, or correspondence relating to this
purchase. Invoice must accompany shipment.)

Department _____   Purchase requisition # _____

Purchase order date _____   Delivery date _____

To supplier:

Description	Quantity	Price

Purchasing manager's signature _____

only once in ten years. On the other hand, there are many items purchased by hospitality enterprises that are required very frequently and often tens or hundreds of these different items may be required each day for restocking depleted inventories. One method for dealing with this problem is to have standing orders.

Standing Orders

Two types of standing orders

A standing order is an arrangement with a supplier to provide a predetermined quantity of a particular item or items on a daily or other periodic basis without contacting the supplier each time. One type of standing order would be that a supplier deliver, at an agreed price, a fixed quantity of a specific item each day. For example, a daily supplier might be asked to deliver each day a specified number of dozens of eggs. This same quantity would remain fixed until there is a need to change the quantity. Another type of standing order requires the supplier each day to replenish the stock of a certain item up to a predetermined or par level. The par stock level would be established for each item handled this way, according to the needs of the establishment. To prevent replenishing beyond the par level, a par stock form is recommended. This form requires a designated employee to take stock of each item covered by this system each day in order to calculate the quantity required and so advise the supplier. A form that could be used for this is illustrated in exhibit 3.4.

Use of par stock form

EXHIBIT 3.4. Par Stock Form			
Item	Par stock	On hand	Required
Apples, cooking			
Apples, baking			
Apples, crab			
Apples, table			
Apricots			
Bananas			

Although these two methods of standing orders are most commonly used for perishable food supplies, there is no reason why they could not be used for other items (for example, cleaning or paper supplies) that are used in large quantities and need replenishing on a daily, or at least weekly, basis. For example, the paper supplies used in a fast-food restaurant might well be replenished in this way.

Perpetual Inventory Cards

For items carried in storerooms that are under the control of an authorized person, a system of perpetual inventory cards is recommended. A separate set of individual perpetual inventory cards should be maintained for each separate storage location. For example, the housekeeper would have a set of cards for linens and other supplies required in the rooms department, and the steward would have a set of cards for the items he has under lock and key in the food storeroom.

Separate cards for each location

An individual card is required for each type and size of item carried in stock. A sample card is illustrated in exhibit 3.5. The In column figures are taken from the invoices delivered with the goods. The figures in the Out column are recorded from the requisitions (to be discussed later in this chap-

EXHIBIT 3.5. Perpetual Inventory Card for a Single Item				
Item _____ Supplier _____ Tel. # _____				
Minimum _____ Supplier _____ Tel. # _____				
Maximum _____ Supplier _____ Tel. # _____				
Date	In	Out	Balance	Requisition cost information

Cards and inventory control

ter) prepared and signed by persons in the department served by that particular storage location. Obviously, if all In and Out figures are properly recorded on the cards by the person in charge of the storeroom, the Balance column figure should agree with the actual count of the item on the shelf. Thus the cards aid in inventory control as a double check. They are also useful for accounting purposes, since the cards carry the purchase prices of the items and allow the requisitions to be costed out; this ensures that each department is correctly charged with its share of the costs.

Cards aid stock level control

The cards also help ensure items are not overstocked or understocked, since they can show the maximum stock for each individual item and the minimum point to which that stock level can fall before the item needs to be reordered. Without having to count quantities of items on the shelves, the person responsible only has to go through each of the cards in turn once a week, or however frequently it is practical to reorder. At that time, he lists all items for which the balance figure is at or close to the minimum point and then orders the quantity required to bring the inventory up to par stock, keeping in mind possible delivery delays. Note that the cards can also be designed to carry the names and telephone numbers of suggested suppliers.

When establishing par stock and reorder levels, the consumption rate of the item and the time lag between ordering and delivery must be considered.

Example of par stock ordering

For example, suppose the housekeeping department normally used twenty-one gallons of bleach a week (or three a day) and reordered every two weeks. Normally, therefore, forty-two gallons would be ordered each time. However, a safety or minimum level of six gallons for that item has been established. Therefore, par or maximum stock would be forty-eight gallons, and minimum stock six. If, on a particular order day, there were nine in stock and two days are required for delivery, then forty-five gallons should be ordered, since that will be the amount that will bring the par stock up to forty-eight gallons two days hence.

In some establishments, management prefers to use a single form to summarize all perpetual inventory records, as in exhibit 3.6. On this form, a series of columns are dated across the top, with each column representing a day of the month. Each item in stock is represented on a single line. The boxes for each item are divided by a diagonal line. Quantities are entered on either side of the diagonal line, or actually on it. The figure to the upper left of the line identifies the balance of that item on hand. A figure straddling the line shows the quantity of an item received, according to purchase records. The figure to the lower right of the diagonal line shows the quantity of the item issued. At the end of each day on which a delivery and/or an issue is made, the balance is recalculated and carried forward to the upper left of the diagonal line in the next large square. For example, on day 1 there were three on hand of item #1, as indicated to the left of the diagonal line. During the day, twelve were received (the circled figure on the line) and two were issued (the figure to the right of the diago-

EXHIBIT 3.6.	Perpetual Inventory Card for Multiple Items					
	1	2	3	4	5	6
Item 1	3 / (12) / 2	13				
Item 2						
Item 3						

nal line). This left a balance on hand of thirteen to be carried forward to the left of the diagonal on day 2.

This simplified system of perpetual inventory control can be reserved for especially high-cost items such as steak or lobster. It also provides a quick daily overview of what needs to be purchased of these items. With this form, a box for each item controlled is needed for each day of the month—even if none of that item has been received or issued that day.

Use for high-cost items

The advantages of perpetual inventory cards for inventory control and time saving in reordering are obvious. The major disadvantages are the time and cost to keep the cards up to date. Each establishment must weigh the costs against the benefits for its own operation in order to decide whether or not to use them.

Requisitions

Whether or not perpetual inventory cards are used to control items in stock and aid in ordering, requisitions should be used in order to allow authorized people to receive items from the storeroom and to ensure that the various departments are correctly charged with their share of the costs. A sample requisition is illustrated in exhibit 3.7.

Requisitions used in cost allocation

Blank requisitions should only be made available, preferably in duplicate, to those authorized to sign them. The original, listing items and quantities required, is delivered to the storekeeper. Duplicates are kept by the person ordering so quantities received from the storeroom can be checked.

EXHIBIT 3.7.   Sample Requisition

#6329

Department _____   Date _____

Quantity	Item description	Item cost	Total

Authorized signature_____

Costing requisitions from cards

If perpetual inventory cards are used, they should carry the current price of the item in stock. Perpetual inventory card Out column figures can be recorded from the requisitions (and the Balance column figure adjusted) and the price of the item can be taken from the card and recorded on the requisition in the Item Cost column. Frequently, the same item in stock may have been received with a different delivery date and price. In this case, a number of different methods are available for keeping track of the various prices on the perpetual inventory cards. These methods include the most recent price, first-in/first-out, and the weighted average.

Illustration of most recent price method

Most recent price.   The simplest method is to use the most recent price paid for an item in stock as the price for all of that item in stock. In other words, if there were five items in stock at $1.00 and twelve new items were purchased at $1.10, then $1.10 would be recorded on requisitions as the cost for any of those seventeen items subsequently requisitioned. If, before the seventeen were issued, a new order of that item were received, the new order price would again prevail. For example, suppose stock on hand dropped to two and eighteen were received at $1.05; it would now be assumed that the twenty items in stock would have a price of $1.05 each.

This is a simple method to use, but, in times of wildly fluctuating purchase prices, it can be inaccurate. The first-in/first-out and weighted average methods take more time but are both more accurate.

First-in/first-out. With first-in/first-out pricing, it is assumed that proper stock rotation is in effect (this should be the case regardless of the requisition costing method) and that, as the items purchased earliest are issued first, they are issued at the price that was paid for them. Using the figures from the most recent price method already discussed, you will recall that we originally had five items on hand at $1.00 and twelve more were purchased at $1.10. If six items were then requisitioned, five would be costed on the requisition at $1.00, and one at $1.10. Since we have now used all the first group of items at $1.00, the $1.10 price would prevail on requisitions until a further shipment arrived at a new price. It is obvious that the related perpetual inventory card must have recorded on it, in the Requisition Cost Information column, how many of that balance are at each price. Alternatively, as items are received, the price can be handwritten onto the case or carton or, if necessary, onto each separate can, bottle, or package.

Illustration of first-in/first-out method

Weighted average. The weighted average requires some simple arithmetic calculations as each new delivery is received. Let us again use the quantities and prices we are already familiar with:

5 items on hand at $1.00	=	$ 5.00
12 received at $1.10	=	$13.20
17 items total	=	$18.20

The weighted average price would be $18.20 divided by 17 = $1.07 (rounded to the nearest cent), and that would be the cost recorded on all requisitions until another shipment is received. Assume that, just prior to the next shipment, we still have two items on hand at $1.07 and that eighteen new items were received at $1.05:

Illustration of weighted average method

2 items on hand at $1.07	=	$ 2.14
18 received at $1.05	=	$18.90
20 items total	=	$21.04

The new weighted average price would drop from $1.07 to $1.05 ($21.04 divided by 20). Regardless of the pricing method used, it is suggested that item prices always be rounded to the nearest cent. For all practical purposes, this will give results that are accurate enough.

Rounding cost prices to cent

If perpetual inventory cards are not in use, the easiest method of recording item costs on the requisitions is simply to write the price of the item, taken from the invoice at the time of delivery, on the container, case, can, or package. Alternatively, pricing machines, such as those used in supermarkets, could be used. Recording the item price on the case, con-

Alternative method of costing items

tainer, can, or package then makes it easy to transfer this price to the requisition as the requisition is completed. This pricing method also has a psychological control advantage in that each person handling the items is made aware of their cost.

Requisitions, once costed out, can then be later extended and totalled so that at the end of each accounting period each department can be charged with its proper share of expenses. Issuing to each department **Color coding** blank requisitions of a different color will aid in departmental identifica-**requisitions** tion. If necessary, for control purposes, requisitions could also be numbered.

Of course, where establishments are large enough to support computerized inventory records, much of the paper work that would otherwise be required with perpetual inventory cards and requisitions can be handled directly by the computer including, for example, a daily printout of all items whose level has dropped to the reorder point, and cost information for inventory on hand.

RECEIVING GOODS

Who receives goods?
The last step in the purchasing cycle is the receiving of goods. The person designated for receiving must be knowledgeable about the products being delivered. In smaller establishments, it might be the person responsible for requesting and ordering the supplies (the housekeeper for housekeeping supplies, the chef for meat deliveries, for example). In a larger establishment a separate receiving department will be responsible for checking all deliveries before distributing the items to the individual departments or storerooms.

What should be checked when goods are received?
In all cases where purchase orders have been prepared, a copy of the purchase order should be on hand while receiving. Where specifications have been prepared, they, too, should be available, so that delivered goods can be checked in detail against the specifications. In particular, quantities received should be checked against quantities ordered and invoiced. Wherever items are purchased by weight (as is the case with certain food products), then weighing scales of an appropriate type should be provided so that weights received can be verified against invoiced weights.

Finally, prices on invoices should be checked against the quotation references or against the purchase order. In some cases, a department head may be asked to verify the quality of an item if the receiver is in any doubt. It is also not uncommon for the chef to be asked to check the quality of all meat, fish, and poultry items as they are delivered.

More specific receiving control procedures will be outlined in chapter 4 (for food) and in chapter 7 (for beverages).

Use of receiving reports
Receiving reports. Receiving reports are recommended for summarizing information about items received. Receiving reports are particularly

useful for cost control of food and alcoholic beverages. Specialized types of receiving reports have been developed by the industry for these two major cost items. These receiving reports will be discussed in chapter 4 (for food) and chapter 7 (for alcoholic beverages).

Receiving stamp. All invoices, whether they are recorded on a receiving report or not, should be stamped, and the stamp should be initialed in the appropriate spots to indicate that the checking has been completed. A typical receiving stamp is illustrated in exhibit 3.8. Insisting that employ-

---

EXHIBIT 3.8.   Typical Receiving Stamp

Date received _____

Quantity checked by _____

Quality checked by _____

Prices checked by _____

Listed on receiving report by _____

---

ees responsible for checking deliveries stamp each invoice and initial where necessary is a form of psychological control.

Dummy invoices and credit memoranda.   It is generally preferable that suppliers provide invoices, or copies of them, with each shipment of items. Without an invoice, it is difficult for a receiver to check certain details. If an invoice is not received, then it is useful for the receiver to prepare a "dummy" invoice from other records (the purchase order or other type of order record) so that it can be later matched with the actual invoice sent later by the supplier to the accounting office.

Goods without invoices

In some cases, goods are invoiced but not received. On other occasions, they are delivered and then returned to the supplier because they were not of acceptable quality, or for some other reason. In these cases, a credit memorandum or credit invoice should be prepared, preferably in duplicate, by the establishment. This memorandum will carry necessary details, including an explanation of why the credit memorandum has been prepared. It should be signed by the delivery driver so the establishment has proof that the goods were indeed returned. One copy should go to the supplier. The other copy remains with the establishment to ensure that proper credit is received from the supplier. Exhibit 3.9 is a sample credit memorandum.

Use of credit memorandum

Blind receiving.   Although not common in the hospitality industry, some establishments do practice blind receiving. In this situation, the supplier is advised not to send an invoice with the goods but to send it through the mail to the accounting office. Instead of the invoice, a shipping, delivery, or packing slip accompanies the goods. This slip will show no weights or

Delivery slips and blind receiving

EXHIBIT 3.9. Sample Credit Memorandum

Supplier _____   Date _____

Please issue a credit memorandum for the following:

Quantity	Item description	Unit cost	Total

Reason for request for credit:

Delivery driver's signature_____

---

counts of the items. In this way, the receiver is forced to count or weigh each item and record the weight or count on the slip, thus ensuring that this important aspect of receiving is carried out.

Delivery hours. The hours during which suppliers are instructed to deliver goods may not matter in a large establishment, since there is always a receiver on duty during normal business hours. However, in a smaller establishment, the person responsible for receiving may combine this function with another job, such as storekeeping. Also, there may be nobody to replace him during lunch and coffee breaks. In such cases, sup-

Advising supplier of delivery hours

pliers should be given specific hours when deliveries can be made to ensure that the receiver will be able to properly receive goods.

VALUE ANALYSIS

Value analysis is an important and useful technique for making effective purchases. Value analysis attempts to eliminate unnecessary material or

High quality not always required

parts of a product that would incur an additional cost. If a high quality of a food or supply item, a piece of equipment, or a service is not required, then the product is costing more than it should. Even though every product in an establishment can be analyzed for value, generally it would only pay to analyze those on which larger amounts of money are spent. But even an individual food purchase item can be analyzed critically. For example, does one need the same quality of tomato if it is to be used in a soup, stew, casserole, or similar dish compared to the standardized size and quality required for a grilled tomato to accompany a steak? Obviously, uniformity of size and appearance are considerably less important in the former, and, therefore, one should purchase that type of tomato at a lower cost.

Another example might be the purchase of new calculators for the accounting office. One would first need to analyze the exact features required on the calculators. Do they need floating decimals and square root functions? If yes, do they all need them, or are those optional features only necessary at one or two work stations? Do they need both electronic display and tape printout? Is the equipment really required or only desirable? What alternative models might be available? Are more sophisticated models available that will allow reduction in labor costs? These are only some of the questions one might ask in that particular instance of value analysis.

Example of value analysis

PURCHASES AND PAYMENTS

Wherever possible, an establishment should take advantage of a supplier's billing practices. Most purveyors supply goods as required during each month, and, within a few days of the month-end, mail a statement to the purchaser.

Suppliers' billing practices

Timing

Suppose that a hotel buys a month's supply of items from a supplier at the beginning of each month, using the items as required during the month, and that the terms of the supplier's statement are 2/10, net 30. In other words, there is a 2 percent discount off the total month's purchases if the statement is paid within ten days of the month-end; otherwise, the statement is payable within thirty days without discount. The hotel thus has the use of the supplier's credit for forty days if it takes advantage of the discount, otherwise for sixty days. The hotel can then use this "free" money to advantage, even if all the hotel does is collect bank interest on it.

Discount terms

On the other hand, suppose the hotel purchases from the same supplier but habitually buys at the end of each month sufficient items to carry it through until the end of the next month. In this case, it will have use of the "free" money for only ten days, if it takes advantage of the discount, and otherwise only for thirty days.

Short-term use of "free" money

These two cases are extremes, but they do point out that a wise purchaser can take advantage of a supplier's billing practices in order to increase his own company's net income.

Purchase Discounts

Example of purchase discount

Whenever a purchase discount is offered, the advantage of taking the discount must be considered. For example, suppose on a $1,000 purchase the terms are 2/10 net 60. On a $1,000 purchase paid within ten days, this would save $20. This may not seem a lot of money, but, multiplied many times over on all similar purchases made during a year, it could amount to a large sum. However, in the example cited, the company may have to borrow the money ($980) in order to make the payment within ten days. Let us assume the money were borrowed for fifty days (sixty days less ten days) at an 8 percent interest rate. The interest expense on this borrowed money would be:

$$\frac{\$980 \times 50 \text{ days} \times 8\%}{365 \text{ days}} = \$10.74$$

Discount saving exceeds interest

In this case, it would be advantageous to borrow the money, since the difference between the discount saving of $20.00 and the interest expense of $10.74 is $9.26.

Rebates

A rebate should be differentiated from a discount. With a rebate, the purchaser pays the full invoice amount but has some cash returned at a later date. The amount of the rebate may vary depending on the volume of purchases made during a period of time (for example, a month or a quarter), which is why the invoice is not discounted at the time of payment—since the percentage rebate (discount) will not be known until the end of the period. Rebates are really just a particular form of discount that allows the supplier greater flexibility. They are quite legal (except in jurisdictions that do not allow them to be offered in connection with the purchase of alcoholic beverages), as long as the rebate is given to the purchasing organization, is fully documented, and is not paid to an individual within that organization for favoring a specific supplier. If rebates are given directly to an individual (for example, a purchaser) without any documentation, they are termed *kickbacks* and are illegal.

Legality of rebates

Another form of kickback occurs when a supplier bills an establishment a higher price than is equitable for a product, and the difference between that higher price and the real price is paid to the person approving the invoice. This can occur in small establishments where the purchaser, receiver, and invoice-approving person are one and the same, and in operations where there is no management supervision. It is unlikely to occur in larger establishments where several people are involved in the purchasing, receiving, and invoice-approval system, since collusion (and sharing of the kickback "profits") would have to occur. **Collusion required**

A more subtle form of kickback occurs when noncash payments are given by suppliers to those involved in purchasing. This type of kickback takes the form of free products or other gifts given to the employee, even to the extent of their being delivered directly to the employee's home. The line between what is an ethical token of gratitude or esteem and what may be a bribe from a supplier is thin, and for this reason many establishments maintain a policy disallowing any gifts at all or any gifts above a nominal value from suppliers.

ECONOMIC ORDER QUANTITY

There are costs involved in carrying an inventory of supplies of any kind. These costs include the cost of money that is either borrowed to carry the inventory or that is tied up by the firm and thus not available for other purposes. There are also costs associated with having to store the inventory, such as the necessity to include storage areas in the building (thus increasing the building costs), inventory insurance, labor costs (storekeepers and other personnel), and the cost of control forms (for example, perpetual inventory cards and requisitions). These costs could generally vary from 10 to 30 percent of the value of the inventory. **Costs associated with inventory storage**

The economic order quantity equation can be used, where appropriate, to minimize the costs associated with purchasing and carrying inventories. The equation is:

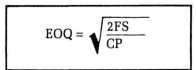

$$EOQ = \sqrt{\frac{2FS}{CP}}$$

where EOQ = Economic order quantity

> F = Fixed cost of placing an order (bookkeeping and other costs)
> S = Annual sales or usage in units
> C = Carrying costs (insurance, interest, storage) as a percent of the dollar amount of the inventory
> P = Purchase price per unit

Let us assume the head office purchases case-lots of hamburger bags for all of its drive-in restaurants in the city. Normal annual sales of ham- **Illustration of use of EOQ equation** burgers would require 1,000 cases of bags per year. Carrying cost of the inventory is 15 percent of inventory value. The purchase cost per case or unit is $12.00, and the fixed cost of placing an order is $8.00. Substituting these values in the equation, we obtain:

$$
\begin{aligned}
EOQ &= \sqrt{\frac{2 \times \$8.00 \times 1{,}000}{15\% \times \$12.00}} \\[2mm]
&= \sqrt{\frac{\$16{,}000.00}{\$\quad 1.80}} \\[2mm]
&= \sqrt{8{,}888} \\[2mm]
&= 94 \text{ cases (to the nearest} \\
&\qquad\qquad\qquad \text{whole number)}
\end{aligned}
$$

Number of orders per year

Therefore, to minimize purchasing and carrying costs, ninety-four cases should be ordered each time. If we wished to know how many orders a year were to be placed, we divide annual usage by the economic order quantity:

$$
\frac{1{,}000}{94} = 10.6
$$

or approximately every 34 days (365 divided by 10.6). If consumption of the hamburger bags were consistent throughout the year (not, for example, affected by seasonal variations), then orders should be spaced at this interval.

Consider lead time required

In ordering, one needs to consider the lead time for delivery and, if necessary, to carry a safety quantity in stock to take care of possible delivery delays. We can also calculate our average inventory of this item simply by dividing the order quantity by 2:

$$
\frac{94}{2} = 47
$$

Add safety margin

If we wish to carry a safety margin for this item in inventory, we simply add the desired safety margin to the average inventory figure. Multiplying the average inventory figure (plus the safety margin, if desired) by the purchase price per unit will give us the average dollar amount tied up in inventory for this item. Similar calculations can be made for each of the various items carried in inventory.

In this example, we assumed that, since 94 was the economic order quantity, that is the quantity we would order. If the supplier only delivers in multiples of 5, our order would be increased to 95; if in multiples of 10, then our order would be 90 or 100. In these latter cases, our costs are going to be increased slightly over the economic order quantity cost level.

Also, if the supplier offered a discount for larger orders, we might also wish to consider this. Suppose that, with the facts set out above, we calculate 94 to be our economic order quantity, but that the supplier will offer us 2 percent off the purchase price if we buy in batches of 150. **Consider quantity discount**

If we accept the supplier's offer there will be a saving of:

> 2% × $12.00 = $0.24 per case
> or 1,000 cases × $0.24 = $240.00 a year

Discount saving calculation

, However, there will be an additional carrying cost since we shall, on average, be carrying more items in inventory at any one time. In fact, we shall be carrying 150 divided by 2 = 75 units in inventory on average, rather than the previous 47. The difference of 28 units means that the additional carrying cost will be:

> 15% × 28 units × $11.76 ($12.00 less $0.24) = $49.39

Additional carrying cost calculation

To offset the additional carrying cost, there will be a saving on ordering costs, since fewer orders will now be placed. Previously, there were 10.6 orders a year. The new number of orders will be 1,000 divided by 150 = 6.7. This means a reduction in number of orders of approximately 3 (10.6 – 6.7). The saving on ordering costs will therefore be:

Saving on ordering costs calculation

> 3 × $8.00 = $24.00

The saving on ordering costs ($24.00) is less than the increase in carrying costs ($49.39). The net increase in costs is about $25.00. However, in this case the offer should be accepted, because the saving of $240.00 on the purchase price more than covers the net increase in costs.

SUMMARY

Since costs are incurred at the time of ordering or purchasing, effective purchasing is therefore important in order to control costs. In fact, most large organizations have purchasing departments whose sole responsibility is the purchasing function. In small enterprises, this function would probably be vested in one person who combines it with other responsibilities.

The first step in the purchasing cycle is the recognition of the need to purchase goods or services. In a larger enterprise, this recognition is often formalized by having department heads responsible documenting their needs on purchase requisitions. The second step in the purchasing cycle is to prepare written specifications wherever this is practical. A specification is a carefully written description of the item desired. Copies of the specifications are sent to potential suppliers so they have no doubt about the goods to be supplied.

The third step in the purchasing cycle is the selection of the supplier or suppliers. In each case where there is more than one possible supplier, quotations should be received to elicit competitive pricing and to ensure that the right quality of product will be purchased at the lowest possible price. Large firms can often take advantage of their size through centralized purchasing. Centralized buying can occur in several different ways. In the selection of an actual supplier, a number of factors must be considered to ensure that the supplier meets certain standards; the pros and cons of using only one or several suppliers must also be weighed. Several different types of purchasing arrangements are possible. These include competitive or open market, single-source, contract, sealed bid, cost-plus, one-stop, cooperative, negotiated, and volume buying and warehousing.

The fourth step in the purchasing cycle is the ordering of goods or services. Large establishments may use a formal system of written purchase orders. However, purchase orders are not practical in the ordering of many of the items needed on a daily basis in the hospitality industry. Standing orders are frequently used. One type of standing order is to have a fixed quantity of an item delivered each day. Another type is to have delivered the quantity that would raise the amount on hand up to a par stock level each day. For items carried in lockable storerooms, perpetual inventory cards are useful for control. These cards can show a running, or perpetual, balance of the quantity of each item in stores. They can also show the minimum and maximum quantities that should be on hand, and they can also carry pricing information that is useful for costing requisitions. Requisitions are used to allow authorized employees to order goods from the storeroom. A number of different pricing methods are available for costing requisitions. Three were discussed in this chapter: the most recent price, first-in/first-out, and weighted average.

The final step in the purchasing cycle is the receiving function. Designated employees who are knowledgeable about products should be made responsible for this. Quantities received must be checked against quantities ordered and invoiced. Prices invoiced must be verified. Finally, quality of all items received must be carefully checked. In many establishments, receiving reports are used to summarize daily purchases. All invoices for goods received should be marked with a receiving stamp. Where necessary, dummy invoices and credit memoranda may need to be prepared by the receiver.

A useful technique in effective purchasing is value analysis, which attempts to eliminate unnecessary material or parts of a product that would incur an additional cost. Also valuable in effective purchasing is the timing of purchases and payments for purchases. If discounts are offered by suppliers for prompt payment, taking this discount should be considered as a way to reduce purchase costs. Rebates are another form of discount. Finally, using the economic order equation to reduce purchasing and inventory carrying costs can be advantageous.

DISCUSSION QUESTIONS

1. List the five steps in the purchasing cycle.

2. What is a purchase requisition?

3. Define the term *specifications* and list three advantages of using them.

4. Of what value are market quotations?

5. Discuss centralized purchasing, when it might be used, and what its pros and cons are.

6. List the major factors about a supplier to consider when selecting a supplier for an item.

7. List three types of purchasing arrangements that are commonly used in the hospitality industry, and briefly describe each of them.

8. What is a purchase order? Why are purchase orders sometimes not practical in the hospitality industry?

9. What is a standing order? Briefly describe two types of standing orders.

10. Explain how a perpetual inventory card is used, and list the purposes it serves.

11. Explain how requisitions are used in conjunction with perpetual inventory cards.

12. Describe how the weighted-average pricing method for costing storeroom items and requisitions works.

13. What is a credit memorandum, and when is it used?

14. What is the meaning of the term *value analysis*?

15. Differentiate a discount from a rebate, and discuss the problem of kickbacks.

PROBLEMS

3–1. For each of the following three situations, calculate the quantity of each item to be ordered:

Item	Consumption rate	Ordering frequency	Safety level	Present stock	Delivery time
1.	14 per week	every 2 weeks	3	6	2 days
2.	7 per week	weekly	1	1	1 day
3.	10 cases per month	monthly	1 case	3 cases	1 week

(Note that this item can only be ordered in full cases.)

3–2. On January 31, the perpetual inventory card for a particular item showed that there were 25 on hand at a cost of $1.48 each. Purchases of this item were made as follows during February:

February 8	3 cases @ $9.12 per case
February 12	2 cases @ $9.24 per case
February 19	4 cases @ $9.48 per case
February 25	1 case @ $9.12 per case

Note that there are six items in each case. The following quantities of that item were requisitioned during February:

February 2	12
February 4	3
February 7	5
February 11	10
February 16	8
February 18	12
February 21	8

February 24	3
February 26	6
February 28	5

a. Prepare a blank perpetual inventory card and record on it in the In and Out columns the purchases and issues quantity information. Calculate and record the Balance amount after each purchase and/or issue.

b. Using the most recent pricing method (rounding figures where necessary to the nearest cent), record on the card after each purchase the cost information required for requisitions.

c. For each date that there was a requisition, calculate the total cost figure that would have appeared on the requisition for that date.

d. Calculate the February month-end total value of that item still in inventory.

3-3. With reference to the information in problem 3-2, repeat parts b, c, and d using the first-in/first-out pricing method.

3-4. With reference to the information in problem 3-2, repeat parts b, c, and d using the weighted average pricing method.

3-5. You are the manager of a hotel with fifty guest rooms, a ninety-seat dining room, and a banquet room capable of handling lunches or dinners for up to 200 persons. The sales representative of your local coffee supplier has approached you today with an offer. Coffee that you have been buying at $3.75 per pound is due to increase next week by 15 percent according to this supplier. However, he says he can let you have all he presently has in stock, about 500 pounds, for the current $3.75 price. He must have your answer today, otherwise he will make the offer to a competitive hotel. List all the factors that you would consider both for and against this offer. How would you decide? Justify your decision.

3-6. You have made a purchase costing $500. The supplier's terms are 2/10, net 60. Assume that, to take advantage of the discount, you were to borrow the money from the bank at 10 percent on the day the invoice is to be paid. The bank would be repaid by you thirty days later. Would you take advantage of the discount?

3-7. On June 5, a restaurant purchased a new item of equipment costing $3,200. A 1 percent purchase discount is offered by the supplier if the invoice is paid by June 15; otherwise the invoice is payable in full by July 31. Should the restaurant borrow the money from the bank at a 12 percent interest rate on June 15 (to be repaid July 31) to take advantage of the purchase discount? Would your decision change if the amount to be borrowed were only $1,500, the balance coming from the restaurant's current bank account?

3-8. A catering company uses 3,000 cases of paper napkins per year. Fixed costs of placing an order are $10 per order. Cost per case is $10, and carrying costs are 12 percent.

a. Calculate the economic order quantity to the nearest case.

b. Suppose the supplier offered a discount of ½ of 1 percent off the purchase price if deliveries were made in five-hundred-case lots. Should this offer be accepted?

Food Purchasing, Receiving, and Inventory Control

4

Objectives

After studying this chapter, the reader should be able to do the following:

- Distinguish between perishable and nonperishable food items and the purchasing thereof.
- Describe a market quotation sheet and an order form.
- Explain the value of food tests.
- List at least five common methods by which suppliers and/or delivery drivers can profit from an operation's poor receiving practices.
- List at least six standard practices for effective receiving.
- Distinguish between direct and storeroom purchases.
- Complete and explain the use of daily food receiving reports.
- List in two or three sentences the main points of storeroom layout and the inventory-taking procedure.
- Reconcile actual inventory with book inventory.
- Explain and calculate open stock inventory.
- Explain and calculate inventory turnover.

This chapter is the first of three on food cost control. It covers food purchasing, receiving, and inventory control. Chapter 5 covers food production controls, and chapter 6 discusses methods of evaluating food cost results.

FOOD PURCHASING

Knowledgeable purchaser required

The first step in effective food purchasing is to have a knowledgeable person, or persons, responsible for this function. As is the case with most products purchased, for any food product there can be wide extremes in quality. Food purchasers must, therefore, know what quality they need. This does not always mean buying the highest quality if a lower quality at a lower price will suit the needs. Food purchasers must also be very familiar with the availability and seasonality of products. They must be aware of weather and transportation problems that can affect product supply and cost. Finally, they must be alert to new products that are introduced on to the market.

Perishable and Nonperishable Items

Example of perishable items

Store nonperishables separately

Generally, food products can be classified into either perishable or nonperishable items. Perishable items are those that have a relatively short storage life, such as dairy and bakery goods, fresh fruit and vegetables, and fresh meat, poultry, and seafood products. Perishable food products are generally put into production and consumed within a day or so of being purchased. Nonperishable items, on the other hand, have a much longer shelf life that could, conceivably, run into years (although investing money in food inventory for several years ahead may not be wise from an opportunity-cost point of view). Nonperishable items are frequently also called groceries, or staples, and are received in sealed cans, packages, or other types of containers. Even certain frozen products could be classified as nonperishable. Since most nonperishables are not usually put immediately into production, they can be stored in a separate, lockable storeroom, and can be controlled with a system of perpetual inventory cards and requisitions (see chapter 3).

Who Orders?

In a small establishment one person, the manager or the chef, might be responsible for all ordering. As establishments grow larger, the ordering might be split between two or more individuals. For example, the chef might be responsible for some or all of the perishable items, since he is usually most knowledgeable about freshness and other important qualities, while the storekeeper might order nonperishable items that she is responsible for controlling in the storeroom. Alternatively the chef might delegate the ordering of certain perishables, such as dairy and bakery goods, to the storekeeper or another qualified assistant. In a fairly large establishment, the chef might be too busy with other important tasks to use up her time ordering and checking perishables. In such cases, all perishable ordering will have to be delegated to an assistant. In an extremely large organization, with a separate purchasing department, the responsibility for all food purchasing and ordering might be centralized in that area along with all other products and services needed by the company.

Delegation of ordering function

Therefore, as can be seen, the responsibility for ordering can vary widely depending on the size or type of establishment. The important point is not who does the purchasing, but rather that that person be knowledgeable about products.

Purchasing Perishables

Since the purchasing of perishables is usually handled on a daily basis, it is recommended that, for most establishments, a system of standing orders be used for bakery, dairy, and fresh fruit and vegetable products. Two methods of standing orders were discussed in chapter 3. Where there are large fluctuations in daily volume of business, or where banquets and similar functions are served, it would probably be necessary to adjust the daily standing orders to take care of these fluctuations. One way to do this would be to establish a minimum par stock or standing order for each item and to order each day the additional quantity required for that day's business. Good internal communication is necessary. For example, the person doing the ordering must know what special functions are being held each day and must be familiar with daily fluctuations in normal volume caused by the day of the week, special events, holidays, or the weather. Sales forecasts based on historical records are useful for this purpose.

Use of standing orders

Consider special functions

Purchasing Nonperishables

Purchasing nonperishables is somewhat simpler than ordering perishables. Since nonperishables do not have to be ordered daily, the ordering process can be limited to once a week or once every two weeks. However,

EXHIBIT 4.1. Market Quotation Sheet

Date ____February 2____

Item	Quantity required	Suppliers			
		Jang	Tobin	Louie	
CHEESE American	25 lb.	(2.10)	2.30	2.28	
Bel Paese					
Camembert	2 lb.		(4.20)	4.30	
Cheddar, Mild	10 lb.	2.22	(2.22)	2.15	
Cheddar, Medium					
Cheddar, Strong	5 lb.	2.50	(2.50)	2.60	
Cottage					

Reduction of ordering frequency

whenever the frequency of ordering is reduced, it means that more of each item must be ordered and carried in inventory. The opportunity cost of carrying a large inventory must be considered.

Whenever an establishment has a storekeeper, even if only part-time, to receive nonperishable items into the storeroom and later issue them out by requisition, perpetual inventory cards (discussed in chapter 3) are highly recommended. As will be seen later, these cards are very useful for food inventory control, but they are also extremely valuable because they considerably reduce the time required to determine how much of each item to order. Without them, each item on the storeroom shelves would have to be counted on each order day and compared with a par stock list to find out how much to reorder.

Market Quotation Sheet

Regardless of the method of ordering and who actually does the ordering, a market quotation sheet is necessary. Market quotation sheets can be individually designed, or, alternatively, standard quotation sheets are available at stationers who deal with the hotel and foodservice business. The standard forms usually have space on them to list the special requirements that an individual establishment may have. Specialty operations that purchase a lot of unusual food products may have to design their own form. A partial market quotation sheet is illustrated in exhibit 4.1. It is recommended that, wherever possible, a minimum of three quotations be obtained for each item desired. It is common industry practice to circle, on the market quotation sheet, the quoted price from the supplier from whom the product is ordered (see exhibit 4.1).

Three quotations preferable

With all ordering, whether for perishables or nonperishables, one should purchase from the supplier who can meet the specifications (if they have been drawn up for that product) and provide the quality desired at the lowest price. However, one may not always buy at the lowest price. Reliability of the supplier and frequency of shipping can be a consideration. Also, if a supplier's quotation is the lowest only for one item, he may not be willing to pay for the shipping cost if his order would only total a few dollars.

Order Form

Since the person receiving the food items ordered may not be the same as the one doing the ordering, it is often useful to summarize all items ordered each day on a food order form. A sample order form is illustrated in exhibit 4.2. Even if all ordering and receiving is carried out by the same person, an order form can still be a useful control form since it can show whether or not the goods were actually received, and, if not, a note or explanation can be put into the Comment column for later reference or for reordering on the next day. Where the receiving function is quite separate from the ordering function, it is very important for the receiver to be given a copy of this form each day so that he knows what should be delivered, at what prices, and in what quantities.

Value of ordering form

Food Deliveries

If it is necessary to restrict hours when shipments can be received (this would likely be the case where the receiving function is combined with some other job), these limited delivery hours should be made known to suppliers. In a large establishment with a full-time receiver or receivers, this

EXHIBIT 4.2. Sample Order Form

Order Date _____ February 2 _____ Delivery Date _____ February 3 _____

Item	Supplier	Quantity ordered	Price	Total	Received	Comment
American	Jang	25 lb.	2.10	52.50	✓	
Camembert	Tobin	2 lb.	4.20	8.40	✓	
Cheddar, Mild	Tobin	10 lb.	2.22	22.20	✓	
Cheddar, Strong	Jang	5 lb.	2.50	12.50	✓	

would not be a problem. Suppliers should also be advised to provide fully-priced invoices with the goods since, as will be seen in the next section, these invoices are required for preparing a daily food receiving report. Blind receiving is not a common practice in food purchasing.

Priced invoices with goods

Food Tests

Value analysis tests can be carried out on food products to ensure one is getting value for money spent. Such analysis might include canned food tests to ensure that the best net weight yield is obtained after the liquid in which the food is packed is drained. The count, uniformity and quality of the canned food items should also be analyzed. If the liquid is to be used, its quality might also be important. Similar tests can be made on packaged products that are not packed in liquids. Fruit and vegetable tests ensure that the best weight or count of product is received for money spent. Another important area of value analysis is the butchering and cooking test carried out on meat, poultry and seafood items. This area of control will be covered in some depth in chapter 5.

Examples of food tests

FOOD RECEIVING

There are various methods suppliers or delivery drivers can use to defraud a hotel or restaurant when they observe that control procedures for receiving are not being used. These methods include the following:

Methods of fraud in food deliveries

1. Failing to meet specifications. Suppliers will sometimes fail to meet required specifications in order to increase their own profit or to compensate for having deliberately underbid in order to obtain the business (in which case they can only now make a normal profit by doing such things as failing to meet size or trim specifications). For example, a supplier could deliberately leave more fat on a roast than the specifications require, charge for boneless cuts and deliver cuts still containing the bone, include preportioned cuts that are short weight, or send a shipment that is incomplete (short weight or count). To control these problems, qualified and trained receiving employees must be on hand to verify quality against specifications and against purchase order quantities and to prepare credit memoranda for short count or short weight shipments.

With size specifications, some tolerance may be allowed. For example, if specifications call for 10-oz prime rib, bone-in steaks, individual steaks may be allowed to vary from 9.5 to 10.5 oz, as long as the overall average is 10 oz. Where these items are shipped by weight and by count, they should be taken out of their cases to be counted and weighed. For example,

Tolerance allowed

100 10-oz steaks = 1,000 oz/16 oz = 62.5 lb. There should be both 100 items and 62.5 lb of steak in this delivery.

2. *Watering and icing products shipped by weight.* Another fraudulent method suppliers may employ is to water moisture-retaining vegetables (for example, head lettuce) excessively or to use excessive packing ice for items (such as poultry) that are shipped in crushed ice. Receiving personnel must examine goods for excessive watering (a water-stained container may signal this) and must weigh items after first taking them out of their ice packing. In all situations where items are shipped by weight, verifying the weight should be a matter of routine.

Weigh goods without packaging

3. *Invoicing high-quality items for low-quality items delivered.* A supplier may invoice at a quoted price but deliver goods of a lower quality than the price calls for. Again, a qualified receiver will be able to catch this type of fraud. Some suppliers, however, have been known to pack a case with correct quality on the top to cover up lower-quality items underneath. Spot checking the entire case is necessary to control this. Alternatively, one or more cases could be opened and inspected from the bottom! Quality, as well as count and weight, of packed goods should always be verified against the actual goods—not against what is printed or stamped on the outside of the case. Suppliers have been known to repack a complete case with lower-quality goods, or goods of short weight or count, when they notice that only the case-printed information is verified by the receiver. A supplier might also open boxes or cases prior to delivery, remove some of the items, reseal and deliver the partially full boxes or cases, and charge for full ones.

Verify quality

4. *Shipping overweight or over count.* A supplier may ship more goods than were ordered, to add to its sales and profits. Accepting more goods than were actually desired can lead to excessive inventories and eventual spoilage of goods. Goods not ordered should be returned to the supplier, accompanied by a supporting credit memorandum.

5. *Invoice overcharging.* Normally, food suppliers are requested to send a priced invoice with delivered goods. In this way the priced invoice can be compared with prices on market quotation sheets and/or purchase orders or order forms. Any overpricing should immediately be corrected on the invoice by the receiver, and a credit memorandum should be prepared forthwith. Where suppliers only mail an invoice some time later, particular care should be taken to verify prices at that time to ensure that a supplier is not deliberately attempting to overcharge; if any invoice prices have been changed, these changes should also be carefully checked. Such suppliers should be instructed to send a priced invoice with the goods in the future.

Invoices with goods

6. *Bulk weighing.* A supplier noticing that certain orders are bulk-weighed may be tempted to defraud by substitution. This could occur with a meat order where various cuts are delivered and are weighed in total rather than by individual cut. For example, a delivery may call for 100 lb of meat, broken down into 50 lb of hamburger at $2.00 per lb (total $100) and 50 lb of sirloin at $4.00 per lb (total $200) for a total invoice cost of $100 + $200 = $300. If these two items are not separately weighed, the supplier could actually ship 55 lb of hamburger (total $110) and only 45 lb of sirloin (total $180), for a total value of $110 + $180 = $290, while still invoicing for $300 and thus making an extra $10 profit. Bulk weighing by a receiver should never be allowed, particularly with expensive items such as meat and seafood.

Disallow bulk weighing

7. *Putting goods directly into storage areas.* It should be a basic rule that no goods are to be put into storage areas by delivery drivers, either before or after the goods have been inspected by the receiver. If direct storage is allowed, a driver may eventually bypass the inspection and fail to deliver the proper quantity or quality of merchandise.

8. *Delivering goods outside normal receiving hours.* A delivery driver who is allowed to deliver outside the hours when the qualified receiver is available may simply obtain the signature of another employee acknowledging that the goods have been received, without any count, weight, or quality checks. Indeed, the driver may simply leave the goods without having anybody check them at all. In both these cases, fraud is encouraged.

Standard Practices

To eliminate these possible causes of losses, a set of standard receiving practices should be prepared in writing so that all employees involved in receiving goods will be aware of them. A set of standard receiving practices could include the following:

Use written practices

1. Count each item that can be counted (number of cases or number of individual items).

2. Weigh each item that is delivered by weight (such as meat). Appropriate weighing scales must be provided for this purpose. Scales are available that print out a tape showing the weight of each item. Tapes should be attached to the related invoices to indicate that this important aspect of receiving has been properly carried out.

Value of print-out weighing scales

3. Check the count or weight figure against the count or weight figure on the invoice accompanying the delivery. If purchase orders are used, the invoice information should also be verified against that.

**Checking
specifications**

4. Confirm that the items are of the quality desired; if specifications were prepared and sent to the supplier, check the quality against these specifications. Specifications should also state acceptable production or quality expiration dates on perishable goods. These dates should be checked by the receiver to ensure that they are not being breached by a supplier. In this regard, wherever possible, all items received should be dated with the date of receipt. New stock must be put behind old stock. Dating allows this process to be verified, and ensures proper stock rotation. For perishable produce that is sensitive to temperature, receipt at the proper temperature should be verified. For example, items to be received frozen should be completely frozen, not partially thawed.

Checking dates

5. Spot check case goods to ensure they are full and that all items in the case are of the same quality.

6. Check prices on invoices against prices quoted on the market quotation sheet, or against the purchase order if purchase orders are used.

7. If goods were delivered without an invoice, prepare a memorandum invoice listing name of supplier, date of delivery, count or weight of items, and, from the market quotation sheet, the price of the items.

**Use of credit
memorandum**

8. If goods are short-shipped or if quality is not acceptable, prepare a credit memorandum invoice listing items returned and obtaining delivery driver's signature acknowledging he has taken the items back or that they were short-shipped. Staple this credit memorandum to the original invoice.

9. Store all items in proper storage locations as soon after delivery as possible.

10. Send all invoices and credit memoranda to the accounting office so that extensions and totals can be checked and then recorded.

**Carry out spot
checks**

In addition, control office spot checks should be carried out to ensure that the receiver is performing all his duties. Complete checking of all deliveries cannot be emphasized too much. When a delivery driver notices that weighing scales are not used or that quantities are not counted, he may be tempted to short-ship deliveries. If he notices that quality is not checked, he can substitute a lower quality.

**Types of loss from
receiving and
storage areas**

Even with all these safeguards in effect, losses can also occur from employees in and around receiving and storage areas, such as:

1. The receiver working with a delivery driver and approving invoices for deliveries not actually made to the establishment

2. The receiver working with a supplier and approving invoices for high quality merchandise while a low quality is actually delivered

3. The storekeeper removing items from a controlled storeroom and changing perpetual inventory card balance figures to hide the fact

4. Employees pocketing items from storage areas or smuggling them out the back door in garbage cans

The necessity for constant management supervision and observation to prevent such abuses is thus obvious.

Distribution of Food

Once food items have been properly received and checked, they must be allocated to the appropriate areas. Generally the perishable items are put into storage rooms, refrigerators, or freezers as close to the kitchen production areas as possible. In some cases, some items might be sent directly to sales areas — for example, luncheon rolls might be sent directly to the dining room each day. Nonperishable items are usually sent immediately to the storeroom. This storeroom should also, wherever possible, be close to the kitchen area to reduce time spent in movement of goods.

Allocating received items to storage areas

Items that are put directly into production (either in the kitchen or sales area) are usually referred to as direct purchases. Items that are put into a controlled storeroom are referred to as storeroom purchases. To simplify the next step in the food cost control process, the receiver should be instructed to note on each invoice, where it is not obvious, that an item went either into a direct or into a storeroom location. This information is useful for compiling the daily food receiving report.

Direct versus storeroom items

Daily Food Receiving Report

A daily food receiving report summarizes each day's invoices. An illustration of a daily food receiving report is shown in exhibit 4.3. It is not necessary to list on the receiving report each individual item on each invoice, since this detail can always be obtained if it is needed later by referring to that particular invoice. One line on the receiving report should suffice for each invoice. The important point is to allocate the purchase-cost figures from each invoice to either the Direct Purchases column or the Storeroom Purchases column. (For this reason, the suggestion in the preceding paragraph about noting the distribution area on the invoice should now be apparent). In some cases, an invoice may have on it nonfood

How to complete receiving report

Handling credit entries

items. In that case, the dollar amount of those items is entered in the Other Purchases column. In other cases, food items may be received that are not intended for the food department. An example of this might be fruit (such as limes) purchased specifically for the cocktail lounge. Since one of the main reasons for having a daily food receiving report is to aid in calculation of daily food cost, the food cost should not be charged with purchases for the bar. In such cases, the cost of those items should also be entered in the Other Purchases column. All invoices for each day should be entered on the receiving report. Note, with reference to exhibit 4.3, how the credit memorandum from Atlantic has been recorded as a deduction. Once all invoices have been entered, the columns should be totaled and cross-footed to ensure a balance; in our case:

Cross-balancing report

$$\$216.20 + \$157.92 + \$13.28 = \$387.40$$

Accounting office responsibilities

At the end of each day, the person completing the receiving report should forward it to the accounting office together with the related invoices and purchase orders (if they are in use). The accounting office should then verify that—

1. All invoices have been extended and totaled properly by the supplier. If any errors are discovered, the receiving report figures should be corrected and the supplier notified.
2. Invoice amounts have been properly entered on the daily food receiving report.
3. Invoices have been matched with purchase orders (if they exist), and prices on invoices have been checked against purchase order prices.

Later in this chapter we shall see how the daily food receiving report figures can be used for storeroom inventory control. In chapter 5, we shall see how the figures can also be used for determining a daily food cost percentage.

Purchase Analysis by Category

Breaking down purchases

Larger organizations sometimes design the receiving report so that it not only breaks down food purchases into either direct or storeroom, but further breaks down all food purchases into several different categories. One of the reasons for doing this is that, by totaling up the dollars spent on each separate category over a period of time (such as a week or a month), com-

EXHIBIT 4.3. Sample Daily Food Receiving Report

Date ___ February 3

Supplier	Items	Direct purchases	Storeroom purchases	Other purchases	Invoice total
Jang	Cheese	65.00			65.00
Charlton	Groceries		113.20	13.28	126.48
Atlantic	Fresh fish	48.16			48.16
Atlantic	Fresh fish	(12.39)			(12.39)
J.G. Packing	Groceries		25.19		25.19
Totals		216.20	157.92	13.28	387.40

parisons can then be made with dollars spent on those same categories in previous periods. The dollars spent on each category are divided by the dollars spent on all categories for that period so that the breakdown of the purchase dollar can be expressed as a ratio or percent. In this way, relative changes can be more readily observed. By comparing these percentages over time, trends may become evident that might be useful for indicating such things as changing consumer preferences resulting in a higher or lower food cost, and possibly for indicating the need for changes in menus. Exhibit 4.4 illustrates a type of receiving report that permits this type of cost analysis by category.

Detecting purchase trends

INVENTORY CONTROL

Storeroom design features

Locating goods in storeroom

It goes without saying that nonperishable food items placed into a lockable storeroom should be kept under ideal conditions to reduce spoilage, wastage, or other nonrecoverable costs. Food should not be stored directly on the floor. Temperature, ventilation, and sanitation must be a consideration in storeroom location and design. The storeroom should be on the same level as the kitchen wherever possible to reduce movement of goods. For the same reason, proximity to the kitchen would be ideal. Food items should be placed in sectionalized compartments that can be labeled for easy product identification. Heavy items that are issued in bulk (sacks of flour or sugar, for example) and items that are frequently used should be closest to the door. Once items have been placed in specific locations, those locations should be changed as infrequently as possible. Permanent locations mean increased efficiency in placing items in their locations and issuing them when needed. It also means that month-end inventory sheets can be preprinted in the same order as the items are located on the shelves, thus speeding up stocktaking and minimizing the possibility of overlooking items. As items are received and put in their right location on the shelf, it might be useful to date-stamp them to ensure proper stock rotation.

A system of perpetual inventory cards and requisitions should be used for controlling the inflow and outflow of goods in the storeroom (see chapter 3). The cards are useful for keeping track of what is, or should be, in the storeroom, and for charging each department with the cost of food it has received by means of requisitions from the storeroom.

Dispensing with Perpetual Inventory Cards and Requisitions

Since only a proportion of food items purchased can be controlled under a supervised storeroom situation, it is sometimes suggested that it wastes time and money to pay someone to control the storeroom and to complete

DAILY RECORD OF PURCHASES AND ISSUES

HOTEL _____

DEPT. _____ DATE _____ 19____ DAY OF WEEK _____

			STOCK TO STOREROOM				BAR				
PURCHASES												
1	2	3	4	5	6	7	8	9	10	11	12	
NAME OF FIRM	AMOUNT OF INVOICE	DIRECT ISSUES TO KITCHEN	MEAT FISH AND POULTRY	STAPLES	FRUITS & VEGETABLES	DAIRY PRODUCTS	LIQUOR	BEER	WINE	MIXES SODA	CARTAGE	

A   TODAY'S PURCHASES

B   BALANCE FORWARD from Yesterday

C   TOTAL TO DATE THIS MONTH

13	14	15	16	17	18	19	20	21	22	23	24	25
					DIRECT ISSUES							FOOD COST 14 TO 24
	MEAT	FISH	POULTRY	FRUITS	VEGET.	DAIRY PRODUCTS	BAKERY PRODUCTS	STAPLES	COFFEE	BUTTER	EGGS	

DIRECT ISS

STORES ISS

TOTAL ISS.

FWD. BAL

TOTAL M D

I   BEGINNING INVENTORY-LAST MONTH END

J   STOCK TO STORE ROOM C4 to 7

K   STORE ROOM ISSUES E 14 to 24

L   I + J - K: BALANCE ON HAND

M   PHYSICAL INVENTORY

N   +L OR -M: ADJUSTMENT $

O   IN% to M: ADJUSTMENT   %

P   SALES M: INVENTORY TURNOVER

5c

21 to 25

EXHIBIT 4.4.   Receiving Report Permitting Cost Analysis by Category

Cost/benefit considerations

perpetual inventory cards and cost-out requisitions. This may be true, except that, generally speaking, the benefits of paying a storekeeper to carry out these functions (even if it is only during limited hours each day so that the storekeeping tasks can be combined with some other job) would probably outweigh the costs. It is better to control, let us say, 50 percent of purchases that are eventually put into production through a storeroom, than to have virtually no control of 100 percent of purchases (both direct and storeroom items). When a storeroom is left unlocked with no supervision, it is very easy for any employee to pocket small items (for example, cans of caviar) that have an extremely high cost per unit.

Limited use of storeroom key

Despite this, it must be accepted that, in quite small establishments, there is just no practical way in which a storeroom can be completely supervised. In such cases, perpetual inventory cards have to be dispensed with. Only one person (such as the chef) should have a key to the storeroom so that other employees are not tempted to remove items for personal use.

Use of single master requisition

In small establishments, it may also be impractical to use requisitions, but it may still be desirable to know what has been taken out of the storeroom. This can be accomplished by having the person with the key record on a sheet each day a list of items and their unit costs issued from stores. The unit cost would have to be recorded on the case, carton, package, can, or bottle at the time the goods were received and put into the storeroom. At the end of each day, this master requisition can be extended (quantity of each item times item cost) and totaled, and this figure can then be added to the direct purchases for the day (from the daily food receiving report) to arrive at total food cost for the day. This topic will be discussed further in chapter 5.

Storeroom Inventory

Inventory taking procedure

Normally, in foodservice operations, inventory is taken monthly, although it can be taken more frequently if desired. A person other than the storekeeper should take inventory. In larger establishments, it is easier and faster if two people (preferably from the accounting office) perform this task. One person counts the quantity of each item on the shelves and the second person verifies that this count agrees with the perpetual inventory card balance. If the figures do not agree, a recount should be made. If they still do not agree, then the figures recorded from invoices and requisitions on the cards should be traced back to the related invoices and requisitions and the arithmetical accuracy of the card balance should be checked. However, this checking of items whose count does not agree should not be done during the actual inventory-taking since it slows down the entire process. If discrepancies between actual counts and card counts cannot be resolved, then the card balance figure should be corrected to the actual figure so that it is correct from that point on.

Discrepancies between card and actual count

EXHIBIT 4.5. Inventory Sheet			
Month of _____ July _____			
Item	Quantity	Unit cost	Total
Balance forward			$3,164.38
Carrots, #10	25	$1.43	35.75
Carrots, baby, 24 oz.	12	0.85	10.20
Corn, creamed, #10	4	1.12	4.48
Corn, kernel, #10	8	1.05	8.40
Total			$4,218.76

Discrepancies between actual count and card balance can also occur if deliveries have been made to the storeroom on that day but have not yet been recorded on cards, or if the invoice information has been recorded on the cards but the items have not yet been put into the storeroom. Similar situations can arise with items requisitioned on stocktaking day. These possibilities should preferably be checked and corrected before inventory is taken. **Month-end adjustments required**

To speed the inventory-taking process, perpetual inventory cards and the listing of the items on the inventory sheets, should be in the same order as items on the shelves. This reduces the possibility of missing items and is, obviously, more efficient. Exhibit 4.5 illustrates a partial inventory sheet.

If the storekeeper is also the same person who completes the perpetual inventory cards from invoices and requisitions, then it would be possible for him to purposely fail to record certain information on the cards, remove items from the shelves for personal use, and still have the card balance figure and the actual count agree. Cards should be spot-checked against invoices and requisitions by control-office personnel to eliminate that practice.

If perpetual inventory cards are not in use, then stocktaking is simply a matter of recording the actual count of items directly on the inventory sheets. The process is faster and easier, but an element of control is lost. **Simplified stocktaking**

Once all items are listed on the inventory sheets, each item must be extended (item quantity times item cost) and the total inventory added up.

Book Inventory versus Actual Inventory

Use of inventory control form

With a daily food receiving report and an accurate system of costing requisitions, we can, at each month-end (or more frequently if desired), check the reliability of our food storeroom inventory control. To do this, we need a food storeroom inventory control form (see exhibit 4.6). At the beginning of the month, the Opening Inventory figure of $2,242.16 is the same as the actual inventory figure from the previous month-end.

EXHIBIT 4.6. Food Storeroom Inventory Control Form

Month _____ February _____

Date	Opening inventory	Storeroom purchases	Storeroom issues	Closing inventory
1	2,242.16	163.19	58.17	2,347.18
2	2,347.18		112.24	2,234.94
3	2,234.94	157.92	182.01	2,210.85
4	2,210.85	42.12	107.60	2,145.37
30	2,406.19	118.70	42.16	2,482.73
31	2,482.73	90.16	116.04	2,456.85
Totals		3,612.40	3,397.71	
Actual month-end inventory				2,443.20
Difference				13.65

Calculating book inventory

Each day, the Storeroom Purchases figure can be copied from the daily food receiving report. For example, the amount of $157.92 on February 3 would have been copied from the Storeroom Purchases column of that day's daily food receiving report (see exhibit 4.3). The Storeroom Issues figure is simply the total of all requisitions, costed, extended, and totaled, each day. A running balance of the closing or book value of storeroom inventory can thus be calculated each day: Opening Inventory plus Storeroom Purchases less Storeroom Issues equals Closing Inventory. The term *book inventory* is used for this figure since it may not be entirely accurate. In fact, it would be surprising if it were accurate, since the pricing of items in the storeroom is rounded to the nearest cent, and the requisition costing system used will frequently create inaccuracies, as would storekeeping errors in costing out requisitions.

At any time, the closing or book value figure from the food storeroom inventory control form can be compared to the actual inventory figure. Normally, this would only be done at month-end, but, if weekly checks were desired, it could be done weekly.

At the month-end, we can make a quick reconciliation to ensure the arithmetical accuracy of our last day's closing or book inventory figure. First, we add the Storeroom Purchases and Storeroom Issues columns. Then the day one Opening Inventory plus Storeroom Purchases column total minus Storeroom Issues column total should equal the last day's Closing Inventory figure. In our case:

Month-end reconciliation of accuracy

$$\$2{,}242.16 + \$3{,}612.40 - \$3{,}397.71 = \$2{,}456.85$$

The difference between the book inventory and actual inventory figures should normally be no more than 1 percent of total issues for the month. In other words, in our illustration (see exhibit 4.6), the difference should be no more than 1 percent of $3,397.71 or about $34. Our difference of $13.65 is well within that figure. Differences greater than 1 percent of issues would likely be for reasons other than those already mentioned. These other reasons might include issuing items without requisitions, employees helping themselves to items without requisitions, or outright theft. Possible causes should be investigated so that they can be prevented in the future.

Amount of difference allowed

Taking an actual inventory each month-end is an integral part of ensuring that accurate income statements are produced for the food operation. In addition, comparison of this figure with the book figure is a check on the effectiveness of the food receiving, storing, and issuing procedures of all items controlled through the storeroom.

Open Stock Inventory

The storeroom inventory is not, however, the only food inventory to be taken into consideration to ensure that income statements are as accurate as possible. In any food operation, there are direct purchases and

Items comprising open stock

storeroom issues that have not yet been used up, as well as stocks, soups, sauces, and other menu items that are in a state of preparation. This is true of month-end as well as on any other day. There are also unused food products such as condiments, sauces, nonalcoholic beverages, and many other similar items in dining room, coffee shop, and banquet areas. All of these items are part of inventory, and their value must be calculated each month-end. This part of the inventory is usually referred to as open stock.

To obtain an accurate open stock inventory, each item should be physically counted, listed on an inventory sheet, and costed out. In some cases, a cost is difficult to determine for products that have already been combined into other items (soups, sauces). In these cases, an estimate must be made, preferably with the help of the chef, to value them.

Simplifying open stock valuation process

It may not be necessary to repeat this work every month. Perhaps it need be done only quarterly. In the interim months, an estimate could then be made as to how much the current month's open stock is above or below the base period. In most cases, it would be safe to assume that the bulk of open stock items does not fluctuate from month-end to month-end in total dollar value. What might fluctuate are the key items that constitute the major part of the food-purchase dollar such as meat, poultry, and seafood items. Therefore, why not use only these items? Taking an inventory of them is relatively easy, and that amount can be used as the basis for adjusting our total open stock for each interim month. Let us look at an example.

Assume that an accurate physical inventory of all open stock is taken in month one and the total is $5,400. Out of this total, $2,500 is for meat, poultry, and seafood items, and $2,900 is for all other items. In month two, an accurate inventory of the meat, poultry, and seafood items gives a new total of $2,750. This is $250, or 10 percent ($250 divided by $2,500, and multiplied by 100) more than in month one.

Choice of alternative methods

At this point, there are two alternatives. With alternative one, we assume that the entire open stock value has increased from month one to month two by 10 percent:

10% × $5,400 = $540 and $5,400 + $540 = $5940 open stock month 2

With alternative two, we assume that the value of open stock items other than meat, poultry, and seafood, have remained the same as in month one, or $2,900, and that the 10 percent increase applies only to the meat, poultry, and seafood part of our open stock. In this case, the total open stock value would be:

$2,900 + 2,750 = $5,650 for month 2

The difference between the two alternatives is $290. Whether or not this is a large difference would have to be decided on the basis of how it might affect the food cost percentage. Perhaps the dilemma can be solved by suggesting that, if the 10 percent increase in meat, poultry, and seafood items were the result of overall market price increases, then it might be logical to assume that all market prices have gone up and therefore we should use alternative one. On the other hand, if the meat, poultry, and seafood open-stock increase were the result of carrying more of these items in stock than might normally be the case, then alternative two might be more realistic.

When to use each method

One final consideration is that open stock is normally higher if the month-end falls on a Friday because additional purchases would have been made to carry the operation through the weekend. If the month-end falls at the end of a long weekend or holiday period, the reverse is generally true. Under normal circumstances, with daily delivery of most food items, one would expect to see the value of open stock equal to about one-and-a-half day's normal food cost. In other words, if an operation's food cost for a typical month were $30,000, or about $1,000 a day, then open stock would probably be about $1,500.

How much open stock?

Inventory Turnover

Finally, in this section on inventory control, we come to the matter of inventory turnover. It has already been mentioned that, to avoid tying up too much investment in inventory and thus losing interest (the opportunity cost) that could otherwise be earned on these funds, it is important not to carry too much in inventory. It is also important not to have too few items and risk running out. This can be controlled by recording maximum and minimum quantities on perpetual inventory cards, adjusting them from time to time as the need arises, and ensuring with control office spot-checks that the storekeeper is keeping within these limits. Without drastically increasing the total value of items carried in inventory, items of individual small value can normally be ordered in larger quantities, thus increasing maximum levels to reduce the frequency of ordering. These items generally also take up little storage space. The reverse would generally be the case with higher value items.

Maximum and minimum inventories

A useful control over the entire inventory is to calculate periodically (monthly) the food inventory turnover rate. The equation is:

Inventory turnover equation

$$\frac{\text{Food cost for the month}}{\text{Average inventory}}$$

How to calculate food cost

Food cost can be calculated using the following general formula:

> Beginning of the month inventory
> plus
> Purchases during month
> minus
> End of the month inventory
> equals
> Food cost for the month

How to calculate average inventory

Average inventory is calculated as follows:

> Beginning of the month inventory
> plus
> End of the month inventory
> divided by
> 2

Assuming the following figures:

Beginning of the month inventory	$7,000
End of the month inventory	8,000
Purchases during month	24,500

Example of inventory turnover calculation

Our calculation of the inventory turnover rate would be:

$$\frac{\$7,000 + \$24,500 - \$8,000}{(\$7,000 + \$8,000) \div 2} = \frac{\$23,500}{7,500} = 3.1 \text{ times}$$

Traditionally, the food industry food inventory turnover ranges between two and four times a month. At this level, the danger of running out of food items is minimal; on the other hand, there is not an over-investment in inventory tying up money that could otherwise be put to use earning interest or profit. However, despite this range of two to four times a month, there may be exceptions. Perhaps of more importance to an organization is not what its actual turnover rate is, but whether or not there is a change in this turnover rate over time and what the cause of the change is. For exam-

Detecting turnover trends

ple, let us assume that the figures $23,500 for food cost and $7,500 a month for average inventory, giving a turnover rate of 3.1 were typical of the monthly figures for this operation. If management noticed that the figure for turnover changed to two, this could mean that more money was being invested in inventory and not producing a return:

$$\frac{\$23,500}{\$11,750} = 2 \text{ times}$$

Alternatively, a change in the turnover rate to four could mean that too little was invested in inventory, and that some customers may not be able to get certain items listed on the menu:

$$\frac{\$23,500}{\$ 5,875} = 4 \text{ times}$$

In some establishments, the turnover rate may be extremely low (less than two). For example, a resort property in a remote location may only be able to get deliveries once a month and thus be forced to carry a large inventory. On the other hand, a drive-in restaurant that receives daily delivery of its food items from a central commissary and carries virtually no stock overnight could conceivably have a turnover rate as high as thirty times a month. Each organization should establish its own standards for turnover and then watch for deviations from those standards.

Special turnover ratio situations

SUMMARY

Of major importance in effective food purchasing is the appointment of a knowledgeable person to the purchasing position. Generally, food items can be categorized into perishable and nonperishable items. Perishable items are put into production and consumed shortly after purchase. Nonperishable items have a longer shelf-life and their usage is usually controlled through a lockable storeroom. Standing orders are frequently used for the purchasing of perishables on a daily basis. For perishables not purchased through standing orders and for nonperishables, market quotation sheets should be used so that prices from several suppliers can be obtained. Each day, the list of items to be ordered can be summarized on an order form. To control the quality of food items being purchased, value analysis by way of food tests should be carried out from time to time.

In food receiving, one should be alert to the many ways in which less than honest suppliers or delivery drivers can defraud an establishment. To combat these possibilities, a list of standard practices should be prepared in writing so that employees responsible for receiving goods can conform to these practices. Each day's purchases can be summarized from accompanying invoices on a daily food receiving report. In larger establishments, receiving reports are frequently designed so that purchases can be listed by category for subsequent category-trend analysis.

Food storeroom control is an important aspect of food cost control. For this reason, storeroom design and layout should be well planned. Storeroom items are usually controlled by way of perpetual inventory cards and requisitions. However, in smaller establishments, it is still possible to have effective control and not be burdened with the extra paper work required with cards and requisitions. Food storeroom inventory should be taken at least monthly so that a reconciliation between the book inventory and actual inventory can be made. It is considered satisfactory if the difference between the two sets of figures is no more than 1 percent of total food storeroom issues for the month. In addition to the food storeroom inventory, open stock inventory should also be estimated or calculated so that total inventory can be arrived at. Finally, monthly food inventory turnover can be calculated. The equation for this is:

$$\frac{\text{Food cost for the month}}{\text{Average inventory}}$$

Generally this turnover rate ranges between two and four times a month, but each establishment should determine its own standard for later comparison of actual turnover with that standard.

DISCUSSION QUESTIONS

1. Differentiate between perishable and nonperishable food items.

2. Discuss whether or not an establishment with a daily fluctuation in volume can use a system of standing orders for purchasing perishables.

3. Describe how a market quotation sheet is used.

4. Of what value is an order form?

5. Explain the value of food tests.

6. Why should suppliers be instructed to have invoices accompany deliveries?

7. List as many ways that you can think of by which suppliers and/or delivery drivers can defraud an establishment that does not have good receiving procedures.

8. List as many standard practices that you can think of to help insure good receiving procedures.

9. What would be appropriate column headings on a simple daily food receiving report?

10. Of what value is it to analyze food purchases in detail by category?

11. List the main points about storeroom design and layout.

12. Explain why it is normal to have some difference between the book and actual inventory figures.

PROBLEMS

4-1. Prepare a blank daily food receiving report and then complete it from the following invoice information:

County Products	$34.68 for fresh dairy products. On this invoice $4.25 was for cream for the cocktail bar.
Hubbard Bakery	$68.20 for fresh bakery products.
Atlantic Fish	$124.52 for seafood products. Of this amount $83.51 was for fresh fish and the balance for canned seafood items put into the storeroom.
Miller Flour	$72.12 for bulk flour put into the storeroom.
Pacific Packers	$148.20 for fresh meat items.
City Suppliers	$46.80. Of this amount $24.10 was for canned items put into the storeroom and the balance for items put directly into production.
Greenland	$32.15 for fresh fruit and vegetables. However, the quality of some of these items was not acceptable. A credit memorandum in the amount of $8.20 was prepared and the goods returned to the supplier.

4-2. Past records indicate that the purchase-dollar breakdown for a restaurant had been as follows:

Meat	16.9%
Fish	6.1
Poultry	5.8

Produce	10.2
Groceries	19.3
Frozen food	2.7
Bakery products	12.1
Dairy products	15.0
Butter and eggs	9.8
All other items	2.1

For the current period, purchases were as follows:

Meat	$904
Fish	204
Poultry	327
Produce	449
Groceries	747
Frozen food	107
Bakery products	539
Dairy products	771
Butter and eggs	348
All other items	30

Compare the current period's purchase-dollar breakdown with that of the past, and comment about any significant differences.

4-3. Items in a food storeroom are controlled with perpetual inventory cards. There is one card for each item in the storeroom. Purchase entries from invoices and requisition entries on the cards are made by the storekeeper who also calculates the running or perpetual balance of items. At the end of each month, a person from the accounting office takes each card in turn, calls out the name of the item, asks the storekeeper to count the quantity of the item on the shelf, and then compares the storekeeper's count with the figure on the card. In this way, inventory is taken and checked. Comment about this situation from a control point of view.

4-4. For a food storeroom the opening inventory figure on January 1 was $1,642. For the months of January, February, and March you have the following information:

	Storeroom purchases	Storeroom issues	Actual month-end inventory
January	$2,321	$2,211	$1,827
February	2,598	2,619	1,831
March	2,518	2,506	1,943

For each of the three months, compare the book and actual inventories and state which sets of figures would not normally be acceptable. Why? Explain what you could do to correct unacceptable situations in any month or months.

4-5. The open stock inventory of a restaurant was estimated to be $1,620 on November 30. Included in this amount were meat, poultry, and seafood items valued at $520. On December 31, the meat, poultry, and seafood items had a value of $572.

   a. On the assumption that the increase in meat, poultry, and seafood items was the result of general market price increases for all food items, calculate the open stock inventory at December 31.
   b. On the assumption that the increase in meat, poultry, and seafood items was solely the result of carrying more of these items in stock at the end of December, calculate the open stock inventory at December 31.

4-6. You have the following information: January 1 total food inventory $3,050; purchases during January $9,475; January 31 total food inventory $2,750. Calculate the inventory turnover rate to one decimal place.

4-7. A restaurant provides you with the following information:

Opening food inventory	$22,600
Food purchases for month	67,200
Closing food inventory	21,400

   a. Calculate the food inventory turnover for the month.
   b. Assume that management allowed the food inventory turnover rate to vary between two and one-half and three and one-half times per month. Calculate the minimum and maximum levels of average inventory that would have been permitted for this month.

The Food Cost Percent

Objectives

After studying this chapter the reader should be able to do the following:

- Calculate a food cost percent and discuss it as a control measure.
- Explain where certain figures are obtained that appear on the daily food cost form.
- Calculate the daily and accumulated food cost percent figures that appear on the daily food cost form.
- Adjust the month-end accumulated food cost for the two types of inventory difference.
- Define *standard recipes* and *portion costs*.
- Calculate menu item portion costs and portion cost factors.
- Solve problems relating to purchases of meat yielding by-products.
- Calculate menu item selling prices given item costs and the desired food cost percent.

TRADITIONAL COST CONTROL

The processing of food items through a foodservice operation can be compared in some ways to a manufacturing concern (with the additional problem that the foodservice operator has to clean up after the customer has consumed the product). However, traditional manufacturing cost control methods cannot be easily applied in a foodservice operation. Some of the reasons for this are that:

1. In most foodservice operations, there are daily fluctuations in individual menu items demanded.

Variation in daily demand

2. The total daily demand can also vary considerably from day to day, and it is not always feasible to prepare products and hold them in inventory until demand catches up, since many products have to be purchased and prepared while they are fresh and of high quality.

3. Most products are processed in anticipation of an expected daily demand, and, if this demand does not materialize, menus may have to be changed the following day to make use of leftovers.

4. The initial product purchased may end up as a component of a number of different menu items.

Large variety of products at hand

5. Since a kitchen, at any one time, may have hundreds of different food products in a raw, semiprocessed, or finished-goods state, it is not difficult to envision the impossibility of trying to trace each individual product through from start to finish. The cost of the labor required to do this would exceed the benefits derived (although computers may eventually help resolve this problem).

For these reasons, the concept of food cost percentage was developed to measure how well the cost of food was being controlled in light of the company's objective. The equation for calculating food cost percent is:

Food cost percent equation

$$\frac{\text{Cost of food sold}}{\text{Revenue}} \times 100$$

The reason for using a percent is that cost and revenue are compared on a common basis. For example, it is difficult to compare the relative change from month one to month two if one has only the following information:

	Month 1	Month 2
Revenue	$140,000	$120,000
Food cost	63,000	52,000

Converted to a percent, comparison is much easier:

	Month 1	Month 2
Food cost	45.0%	43.3%

Present figures are an aid in comparison

However, it should be emphasized strongly at this point that, even though the food cost percent has been the traditional yardstick for measuring food operation results, and even though it continues to be a major measuring device, it should not be the only one. As will be illustrated in chapter 6, emphasizing a low food cost percent may be the complete opposite of what one should be doing. Sometimes a higher food cost percent can be more profitable in terms of higher gross profit (revenue less cost of food sold) and thus net income.

Food cost percent and gross profit

CALCULATING A DAILY FOOD COST PERCENT

Many operators like to have a daily food cost percent calculated. With this, they can see over a month the trend of the percent, rather than waiting until the end of the month to calculate only a single overall monthly percent. With a system of daily food receiving reports categorizing purchases of food into either direct or storeroom, and with a system of properly costed requisition for items issued for stores, it is relatively easy to calculate the food cost percent daily. A form that will allow this is illustrated in exhibit 5.1. A brief explanation of how each of the columns on this report is completed follows:

Use of daily food receiving report

Direct purchases. This amount is the total of the Direct Purchases column of the daily food receiving report for that day. For example, compare the February 3 figure on exhibit 5.1 with exhibit 4.3.

Storeroom issues. This is the total amount of food issued from the storeroom according to the requisitions for that day. Note, however, that this figure should only include requisitions for the cost of items to be charged to the food department. If there are any requisitions for other nonfood departments (for example, the cocktail lounge frequently requisitions food items from the storeroom: olives, cherries, sugar, to name only a few), these requisitions should be excluded in calculating the figure for this column.

Excluding certain requisitions

EXHIBIT 5.1. Sample Daily Food Cost Form   Month February

Date	Direct purchases	Storeroom issues	Transfers In	Transfers Out	Employee meals	Cost of food sold Today	Cost of food sold Accumulated	Revenue Today	Revenue Accumulated	Food cost percent Today	Food cost percent Accumulated
1	134.92	42.08	8.16	(4.11)	(24.50)	156.55	156.55	611.95	611.95	25.6	25.6
2	116.20	84.22		(3.20)	(27.00)	170.22	326.77	650.40	1,262.35	26.2	25.9
3	216.20	176.12	9.05	(6.64)	(26.50)	368.23	695.00	994.25	2,256.60	37.0	30.8
30	118.70	42.16		(3.64)	(29.00)	128.22	6,482.20	375.50	19,446.60	34.1	33.3
31	90.16	101.90	11.08		(30.00)	173.14	6,655.34	510.75	19,957.35	33.9	33.3

Storeroom inventory adjustment   13.65

Open stock inventory adjustment   (150.00)

Month-end adjusted food cost   6,518.99

32.7

EXHIBIT 5.2. Sample Transfer Memo

Transfer from_____Bar_____

Transfer to _____Kitchen_____   Date___Feb. 3_____

Quantity	Item	Item Cost	Total Cost
2 bottles	Casa Bello red	3.15	6.30
1 bottle	Domestic dry sherry	2.75	2.75
		Total	9.05

Requested by_____G. Jacobs—Exec. Chef_____

Transfers in.   Frequently, in an operation with more than one department, items in one production area are transferred to another. In order to authorize such transfers, a transfer memo should be completed showing the details of the movement of these goods. Exhibit 5.2 illustrates such a form. As this form shows, the kitchen requested wine (originally purchased and delivered to the cocktail bar) for cooking purposes. Obviously, the food department should be charged with this cost and the bar credited. **Use of transfer memos**

Transfers out.   A transfer out from the food department occurs when food items are sent from the food production areas to nonfood departments. For example, it would not be necessary for the bar to purchase directly each day the small quantities of such items as eggs and cream that it needs. The food operation buys these items in bulk and the bar simply requests what it needs daily by means of a transfer memo. The food department, originally charged with this cost from the invoiced amount recorded in the Direct Purchases column of the daily food receiving report, must now be credited by entering the amount in the Transfers Out column of the daily food cost form. **Transfers to other departments**

Employee meals.   In order to have a meaningful food cost percent, it is important to separate the revenue and cost of employee meals. If this is not done, then comparison of the food cost percent with the standard food cost percent is difficult, since employees who pay for their meals would not normally pay the same markup over cost as would a regular customer. If there is a separate cafeteria where all employees eat their meals, it is relatively easy to separate the revenue and cost. However, employees sometimes eat in the regular dining areas and pay a reduced price for their meals. In such cases, there is normally a sales check for each meal from which the cost can

Alternative methods of employee meal cost calculation

be calculated by the control office. In other cases, employees, particularly those working in food production areas, are entitled to meals without paying for them. There may, or may not, be a written record of such meals. If there is a written record, the cost can be calculated. If not, the general practice is to estimate the average cost of an employee meal and multiply it by the number of employees each day who were entitled to a meal or meals.

Clearly, it is preferable to have a written sales check to record each employee meal. Where there is a separate employee cafeteria, a detailed written record of every employee meal is not necessary, since the cost of employee meals can be determined by costing out the food actually transferred to this cafeteria. To authenticate meals in an employee cafeteria, employees may be issued food coupons or meal tickets, or may be required to sign a register or the register tape receipt for each meal.

In order to obtain a true food cost, therefore, one must invest some effort each day in costing the total value of employee meals so that the food cost can be credited with this total.

Handling promotional meals

Promotional meals. Promotional meals should be handled in the same way as employee meals. Employees who are authorized to give away free meals to good customers or potential customers should be instructed always to sign a sales check to indicate this. In other situations, customers may have promotional coupons that allow two meals for the price of one. In all these cases, the cost of these "free" meals should be deducted from the cost of food sold and be shown as an advertising expense so as not to distort the records for food actually sold in the normal pattern of business. In an establishment where promotional meals are a factor, an additional column (not shown on exhibit 5.1) should be added to take care of this.

Cost of food sold today. This is calculated as follows:

Calculation of today's food cost

$$\text{Direct purchases} + \text{Storeroom issues} + \text{Transfers in} - \text{Transfers out} - \text{Employee meals} = \text{Cost of food sold today.}$$

Accumulated cost of food sold. This figure is simply the sum of today's and all previous days' Cost of Food Sold Today amounts.

Exclude employee meal revenue

Revenue today. This is simply the sum of all revenue for food sold that date, excluding revenue from employee meals (unless of course the employees consumed, and paid, for food as if they were regular guests at normal menu prices).

Accumulated revenue. This is the total of today's revenue plus all previous days' revenue.

Food cost percent today. This is calculated as follows:

$$\frac{\text{Cost of food sold today}}{\text{Revenue today}} \times 100$$

Accumulated food cost percent.   This is calculated as follows:

$$\frac{\text{Accumulated cost of food sold}}{\text{Accumulated revenue}} \times 100$$

Calculating accumulated food cost

Accuracy of Daily and Accumulated Food Cost

It must be stressed that, even though it can be calculated daily, a daily food cost percent can be quite inaccurate. One of the reasons for this is that direct purchases made each day may not all be used that day, yet they are included in the Cost of Food Sold Today figure, thus distorting the daily food cost percent. This might be particularly true on a Friday when large purchases of direct items are made to tide the operation over the weekend. The Accumulated Food Cost Percent figure, particularly after the first seven-day cycle of the month has gone by, tends to average out these peaks and valleys of daily purchases. Therefore, if any comparison is to be made between a standard food cost percent and the food cost percent from the daily food cost form, then this comparison should be made with the accumulated figure rather than the daily one. However, even on the last day of the month, this accumulated figure will need adjusting.

Accumulated food cost more meaningful

Month-end adjustments.   At the month-end, two adjustments would normally have to be made to the Accumulated Cost of Food Sold. The first adjustment is for the difference between the book and actual inventory of food storeroom figures. The second is for the change in the open stock inventory from last month-end to this month-end. Both of these types of inventory were discussed in chapter 4.

Two month-end adjustments required

Book and actual inventory difference.   The rule for this is: If actual inventory is greater than book inventory, the difference is subtracted from accumulated cost of food sold. If actual inventory is less than book inventory, the difference is added. In exhibit 4.6, our actual inventory was $13.65 less than book inventory. This amount has been added in the Accumulated Cost of Goods Sold column in exhibit 5.1.

Storeroom inventory adjustment

Open stock change.   The rule for this is: If this month's open food stock is higher than last month's, the difference is subtracted from accumulated cost of food sold. If this month's open food stock figure is lower than last month's, the difference is added. Assume that January's open stock amount was $600 and February's $750. The difference of $150 has been

Open stock adjustment

subtracted in exhibit 5.1. Once these two adjustments have been made, we can then calculate the adjusted month-end food cost percent.

Accuracy of Daily Food Cost

Impracticality of accurate cost

To reiterate: in any cost control system where food cost is calculated daily, this cost is unlikely to be accurate. It could only be accurate if an inventory of all food in the storeroom inventory, plus all kitchen open stock (raw food, food in process, and finished food unused), were taken every day. This is impractical. Indeed, the calculated food cost can be seriously distorted on any single day and may be misleading.

One might question whether it serves any purpose to have a tightly controlled food receiving, storage, issuing, and production system, if the food cost results from it are inaccurate. If the only reason for these controls were to calculate a daily food cost, the benefits would not be worth the cost. However, the various steps in the control system serve other purposes than to provide an accurate daily food cost. They are intended to control the flow of food in a way that minimizes losses, pilferage, spoilage, and other destructive factors—all of which will affect the food cost not only daily but cumulatively.

Review food cost regularly

Therefore, it is important that the food cost be reviewed regularly and over periods of time that are long enough to cancel out daily random variations but short enough to allow management to take corrective action, where it is needed, before it is too late.

Another problem arises where there is a single food preparation area (the main kitchen) and several separate sales areas (coffee shop, dining room, banquet rooms). Food is issued directly to the main preparation kitchen, rather than to the individual sales areas. In this situation, the main difficulty is not in tracking food to the main kitchen (a relatively easy task), but in tracking it from there to each sales area so that the cost can be matched up with the revenue from the appropriate area. Since many menu items may be prepared jointly for several different sales outlets, the

Complexity of complete control

control problem is quite complex; any cost accounting system capable of providing complete control over the distribution of these food costs may be excessively expensive in relation to the benefits it provides. A relatively simple general method, however, will be demonstrated in chapter 6.

In some situations, such as in a fast-food restaurant, where food usage each day can be very closely matched to sales and where little food inventory is carried overnight, it may be feasible to take inventory at the end of each day and achieve a quite accurate figure for food cost.

WHAT SHOULD THE FOOD COST PERCENT BE?

We now know how to calculate a daily and accumulated food cost percent during the month, and an accurate food cost percent at the end of the month.

It has also been mentioned earlier in this chapter that the calculated food cost percent can be compared with an objective or predetermined standard food cost percent. We have not yet addressed ourselves to the problem of setting this standard percent. This we will now do.

There are certain steps that must be completed before one can develop a realistic standard food cost percent. The three basic steps are:

Steps in setting standard food cost

1. Establish standard recipes and portion sizes.
2. Calculate menu item costs.
3. Determine menu item selling prices.

ESTABLISH STANDARD RECIPES AND PORTION SIZES

A standard recipe is a written formula spelling out the quantities of each ingredient required to produce a specific quantity and quality of a particular menu item. This formula will also describe the cooking method, since that can have a bearing on quality. Standard recipes must indicate the portion size, the portion size being the quantity of that menu item to be served to each customer. The recipe should also include the cooking temperature where it is appropriate, since temperature can affect the quality of the product and the amount of shrinkage in cooking, and thus the cost of the item. Some establishments include color photographs on the individual recipe cards to indicate to employees involved the final appearance of the product. Recipes should be developed by each establishment according to its own standards. Recipes are frequently coded by number for filing purposes and for future reference.

What to include in standard recipe

Standard recipes are required for all menu items, and all those employed in food preparation and service must be instructed to follow these recipes and portion sizes, not only for cost control purposes, but also for consistency of size and quality from the customer's point of view.

Use of portion scales

Portion scales should be provided in cases where they would be helpful, such as in weighing out portions of shrimp for shrimp cocktails, or for slicing cuts of meat. This does not mean that every portion should be weighed, particularly if an employee is experienced. But even an experienced employee should spot check portion weights from time to time to make sure they are not deviating from the correct portion. Casseroles and other cooking and serving dishes or plates that are appropriate to the portion size to be served should be used. Specific ladles, serving spoons, and scoops should be used for portioning such items as soups and sauces. If employees are allowed to use only their own judgement, then the portions may end up being random sizes, and this can severely affect the food cost.

Standard portion utensils

Another advantage of establishing standard portion sizes is that it is easier to calculate purchase quantities. For example, the number of anticipated customers at a banquet can be multiplied by the portion size of main

Portion size list

food items needed at that function. By determining total quantity or weight required, over- or under-buying is less likely to occur.

List of standard portion sizes

A useful control form valuable to employees involved is a list of standard portion sizes of menu items offered. This portion list can be posted in appropriate places in the establishment so that it is easy for employees to use it. A sample of such a portion size list is illustrated in exhibit 5.3. Those involved in food cost control should spot check from time to time to ensure that portion sizes are being followed.

EXHIBIT 5.3. Sample Portion-Size List	Effective date Feb. 1		
Item	Dining room	Coffee shop	Banquet
Tenderloin steak	8 oz.	6 oz.	5 oz.
Boneless top sirloin	8 oz.	6 oz.	6 oz.
Boneless strip loin	8 oz.	8 oz.	6 oz.

The care taken in food production control can all be lost if food is indiscriminately plated or poorly portioned. If an 8-oz steak is overportioned by only $\frac{1}{2}$ oz, this will result in more than a 6 percent increase in food cost. To an individual server, $\frac{1}{2}$ oz may seem very little; but if every steak or every item of food is overportioned by 6 percent, the normal profit margin of almost any food operation will quickly become a serious loss.

Customer perception and satisfaction

Another problem relates to customer perception and satisfaction. If one steak is overportioned by 1 oz and is compensated for by another that is underportioned by 1 oz, the 2-oz difference between them when they are seen side by side is obvious, and the short-portioned customer is going to feel that proper value for money has not been received.

In a buffet or self-serve salad bar, portion control is not easy. The size of plate that the customer is given and the size of ladle provided for salad dressings can be determined by management, but this does little to control how much the customer piles onto a plate or how many repeat visits the customer may make to the serving area. In a self-serve situation, pricing has to be established by management based on what the average person will eat and on how many trips the average person will take to reload. This has to be determined by test observations.

Portion control in fast-food operations

In a fast-food operation, portion control is relatively straightforward, since most items are purchased and inventoried in preportioned units, and since employees have little or no discretion to affect the quantities served. Even in the case of an item such as french fries, the carton's serving size dictates the volume that can be served; and items such as mustard and ketchup can be dispensed through machines that serve a controlled quantity.

The only other problem, then, involves checking suppliers to ensure that preportioned sizes or weights of items purchased conform to specifications and that the operation is not paying full price for undersize or underweight preportioned items (which would also mean that the customer would be paying for value not received).

CALCULATE MENU ITEM COSTS

Once standard recipes have been formulated for each menu item, then those menu items should be costed out. This is simply a case of multiplying the quantity of each ingredient required in that menu item by the cost of the ingredient. At times, it may be necessary to refer to another recipe to obtain the cost of a component. For example, when costing a casserole, it may be necessary to refer to the recipe for the cost of the stock to be used in that casserole. Since it is sometimes difficult to arrive at an ingredient cost for a single portion, it is a common practice to cost out recipes for, for example, 100 portions, and then to divide total cost by 100 to arrive at the individual portion cost. The cost of seasonings and other items used in very small quantities is often estimated or else included in the safety factor. This safety factor may also include an allowance for shrinkage or wastage that may occur. This safety factor might range up to 10 percent of overall recipe cost and is added to total recipe cost before the individual-portion cost is calculated. If menu item ingredient costs change, then portion costs should be adjusted so that one is aware when it might be necessary to adjust the selling price or, alternatively, adjust the portion size to avoid having to change menu prices. If an establishment has only a few items on its menu, then recosting portion costs to reflect changed ingredient costs is not too time-consuming. If an establishment has a large number of items on its menu, or is changing menu items on a cyclical basis, this problem is compounded. Some establishments have reached the point of computerizing their recipes so that the computer can print out portion-cost changes for every menu item with an ingredient in it whose purchase cost has changed. An example of a standard recipe is given in exhibit 5.4.

Safety factor in portion costing

Computerizing recipes

To avoid having to recost menu items frequently because of seasonal price fluctuations, a test of price changes can be made over a year long period. For example, assume that a test of potato prices per pound varied over a year's period as follows:

Jan.	$0.34
Feb.	0.34
March	0.36
April	0.29
May	0.27
June	0.25

EXHIBIT 5.4. Standard Recipe on Recipe Form

Recipe for: Beef casserole
Portion size: 8 oz.
Quantity produced: 100 portions
Recipe # 14

Ingredient	Quantity	Date:	Feb.	Date:		Date:	
		Cost	Total	Cost	Total	Cost	Total
Stew beef	25 lb.	2.10	52.50				
Flour	2 lb.	0.30	0.60				
Tomato paste	½ lb.	1.00	0.50				
Beef stock	1 gal.	0.75	0.75				
Brown stock	1 gal.	0.65	0.65				
Fresh carrots	5 lb.	0.35	1.75				
Fresh onions	6 lb.	0.40	2.40				
Celery	3 lb.	0.20	0.60				
Green peas	5 lb.	0.40	2.00				
Seasonings			0.25				
Total cost			62.00				
Cost per portion			0.62				

Cooking procedure:

1. Brown meat; add flour and tomato paste; mix well.
2. Add beef and brown stocks; simmer for 1 hour.
3. Dice carrots, onions, and celery, and add them, with the peas; cook until tender.
4. Add seasonings.
5. Serve in 8 oz. casserole dish.

July	0.25
Aug.	0.26
Sept.	0.28
Oct.	0.30
Nov.	0.32
Dec.	0.34
Total	$3.60

The average cost over the year would be $3.60/12 = $0.30, and this figure could be used for menu costing purposes. If menu prices were being established for the next year, this cost could be adjusted upward to take into account any anticipated inflationary effect on the price of potatoes.

Adjustment for inflation

Trim and Cooking Loss

The cost of the main ingredient in many menu items can frequently be obtained directly from the invoice or the supplier's current price list. For example, many establishments purchase meat in prepared, preportioned quantities. Steaks and similar items purchased this way, ready to cook, have a definite known cost to which one has only to add the cost of other ingredients served with them to determine the total menu cost for that item.

If butchering is carried out within the establishment, then certain calculations may be necessary to obtain the main ingredient cost. This is particularly true if meat is aged and a weight loss results during the aging process. There could also be weight losses from butchering (deboning and trimming), and even further losses in the cooking process from dripping and evaporation. The true cost of a menu item in this case can only be determined when we know the net yield after all these processes.

Importance of net yield

For example, suppose that we wished to know how many portions could be served from a twenty-pound purchase of meat that in butchering had a 10 percent butchering loss (bones and fat) and a further 15 percent cooking loss. Portion size will be five ounces cooked weight:

Original purchase weight	20 lb.	
Loss 10% + 15% = 25% × 20 lb.	5 lb.	
Yield	15 lb.	
15 lb. × 16 oz.	= 240 oz.	
and $\dfrac{240 \text{ oz.}}{5 \text{ oz.}}$	= 48 portions	

Calculation of number of portions

If the original purchase cost were $1.75 a pound, our cost per portion would be:

Calculation of portion cost

$$20 \text{ lb.} \times \$1.75 = \$35.00$$

$$\text{and } \frac{\$35.00}{48} = \$0.729 \text{ or } \$0.73 \text{ per portion.}$$

In determining losses from trimming and shrinkage from cooking, it would be preferable to purchase a number of twenty-pound portions of this type of meat and subject each purchase to the same butchering and cooking tests so that the results of all tests can be averaged out. In cooking, the temperature and cooking time should be the same for all tests.

Portion Cost Factor

A useful multiplication factor, once a portion cost for a main ingredient menu item has been calculated, is a portion cost factor. Calculating the portion cost factor eliminates the need to retrace all the steps to recalculate a new portion cost if the supplier changes his price. The equation for a portion cost factor is:

Equation for portion cost factor

$$\frac{\text{Our cost per portion}}{\text{Supplier's price per lb.}}$$

In our example, this would be:

$$\frac{\$0.73}{\$1.75} = 0.417$$

Note that this portion cost factor is not a dollar amount but merely a multiplier. If the supplier changes his price, either up or down, we simply multiply his new price by the portion cost factor to arrive at our new portion cost. If the supplier's price increased to $2.00 a pound, our new portion cost would be:

Example of use of portion cost factor

$$\$2.00 \times 0.417 = \$0.834$$

Note that the portion costs that we have calculated are simply for the main ingredient of the menu item. To obtain the entire menu item cost, we would have to add the cost of the other ingredients, such as sauces and vegetables.

Metric Weights

If one is using metric measures or weights, the same approach to portion costing can still be used. Some of the more common metric abbreviations and conversion factors are:

Equivalent metric weights

1 ounce (oz.)	=	28.35 grams (g).
1 pound (lb.)	=	453.59 g.
1 g.	=	0.035 oz.
1 kilogram (kg.)	=	2.21 lb.
1 kg.	=	1,000 g.

Suppose the supplier sells ten kilogram-size cuts for $3.50 per kilogram. If there is a 25 percent shrinkage loss in butchering and cooking, our yield would be 7.5 kilograms or 7,500 grams. We wish to serve 150-gram portions of cooked weight. Our after-cooking yield will be 50 portions (7,500 divided by 150), and our portion cost is:

Illustration of use of metric weights

$$\frac{10 \text{ kg.} \times \$3.50}{50 \text{ portions}} = \frac{\$35.00}{50} = \$0.70$$

Our portion factor can be calculated as follows:

$$\frac{\text{Our portion cost}}{\text{Supplier's price per kg.}} = \frac{\$0.70}{\$3.50} = 0.2$$

If the supplier's price increases to $3.75 per kilogram, our new portion cost will be:

$$\$3.75 \times 0.2 = \$0.75$$

The Problem of By-Products

Some meat products are purchased in bulk, and yield more than one cut of meat. As well as the main meat item, we might also have by-products that will be used in other menu items. How can we calculate the cost of each different meat item when the supplier's price to us is for the entire cut of meat? Let us illustrate a method using two by-products.

Purchasing bulk meat cuts

The supplier's price for an entire cut of meat weighing thirty pounds is $2.00 a pound, or $60 in total. When butchered, the meat yields the following:

> 15 lb. roast
>
> 5 lb. hamburger
>
> 5 lb. bones (used for making stock)
>
> 5 lb. wastage

By-product item cost purchased separately

It would not be correct to divide the twenty-five pounds of usable products into the $60 total cost to arrive at a cost per pound that would be the same for all three items. If we did that, the cost of each of the three items would be distorted. The reason is that, if the three products had been purchased separately (already butchered), there would normally be a spread between the price per pound of bones and the price per pound of roast, with the hamburger price somewhere in between.

Therefore, the usual practice is to deduct from the total cost the value of the usable by-products as if we had purchased them already butchered from the supplier. We can obtain these values from the supplier. Suppose they were one dollar per pound for hamburger and ten cents per pound for the bones, or a total cost of:

> 5 lb. hamburger @ $1.00 = $5.00
>
> 5 lb. bones   @ $0.10 = $0.50
> $5.50

Calculation of main ingredient cost

The cost assigned to the roast beef will then be:

Total cost	$60.00
Less: hamburger and bones	5.50
Roast beef	$54.50

Use of portion cost factors

We can then proceed to calculate the portion cost for roast beef, taking cooking loss and cooked-weight portion size into account as illustrated earlier. We can also calculate a portion cost factor to be used, should the supplier change his price, in exactly the same manner as already shown. For menu costing purposes, the hamburger and bones will have assigned to them the market values of one dollar and ten cents per pound respectively. Once portion costs for these by-products have been calculated, portion cost factors can also be calculated using the same equation illustrated earlier. In calculating the portion cost factors for both main item and by-products, the simplest approach is to use the supplier's original price per pound (in our case, $2.00) in all equations.

To formalize the information for main cuts and by-products, a butchering- and cooking-test form is often used. Exhibit 5.5 is an illustration of such a form.

Lowest Net Cost

One of the advantages of carrying out butchering and cooking tests is that we can analyze products from different suppliers to ensure that we buy from the supplier who can meet the specifications demanded at the lowest net cost. For example, let us assume we wish to buy twenty-pound cuts of a certain type of meat. Supplier A's price is $2.10 per pound, while B's is $2.20. Total cost from each would be:

Analyzing different suppliers' products

EXHIBIT 5.5. Butchering and Cooking-Test Form

Item_Sirloin roast_   Grade_Choice_   Portion size_6 oz. cooked_

	lb.	oz.	Percent	Cost per lb.	Total cost
Original weight	30	0	100.0%	$2.00	$60.00
Trim loss	5	0	16.7		
Net weight	25	0	83.3		
Breakdown:					
Hamburger	5	0	16.7%	$1.00 (market)	$ 5.00
Bones	5	0	16.7	0.10 (market)	0.50
Roast	15	0	50.0	3.63	54.50
Cooked yield:					
Roast	12	0	40.0%	$4.54	$54.50
Shrinkage	3	0	10.0		

Portions: _____ 12 lb. × 16 oz. = 192 oz. divided by 6 oz. = 32 portions

Cost per portion:_____ $54.50 divided by 32 = $1.70

Portion cost factor:_____ $1.70 divided by $2.00 = 0.85

Supplier A 20 lb. × $2.10 = $42.00

Supplier B 20 lb. × $2.20 = $44.00

Calculating net yields

Loss in butchering and cooking from supplier A is four pounds, and from supplier B three pounds. Net yield is therefore sixteen pounds from A and seventeen pounds from B. Net cost per pound, rounded to the nearest whole cent, is:

Supplier A $\dfrac{\$42.00}{16 \text{ lb.}} = \$2.63$

Supplier B $\dfrac{\$44.00}{17 \text{ lb.}} = \$2.59$

Lowest quoted price not always best

Thus it can be seen that the supplier with the lowest quoted price might not have the lowest net cost based on yield.

The butchering- and cooking-test form illustrated in exhibit 5.5 is useful in providing yield weight information from competitive suppliers. It is also useful, with reference to amount of fat and trim losses, in determining if suppliers are meeting specifications.

DETERMINE MENU ITEM SELLING PRICES

Once menu item costs have been calculated, we have some foundation on which to base selling prices. Traditionally, selling prices have been established to yield a desired food cost percentage. Again, the reader is cautioned against placing too much emphasis on food cost percentage (as we shall see in the next chapter), but, at least for purposes of menu pricing, it is a starting point.

Use of overall food cost

Menu prices are initially determined to yield a predetermined overall food cost. For the sake of simplicity, let us assume we wished to have a 40 percent food cost. We would simply take the cost of the menu item (let us say it is two dollars) and divide it by 40 percent to arrive at a five-dollar selling price:

$$\frac{\$2.00}{40} \times 100 = \$5.00$$

Use of food cost multipliers

Alternatively, the menu item cost of two dollars could have been multiplied by 2½ (the 2½ multiplier is simply 100 divided by 40). If a 50 percent food cost were desired, the multiplier would be 2 (100 divided by

50). In fact, the multiplier for any specific food cost percentage can be arrived at by dividing 100 by that cost percent number.

Even though we might desire an overall 40 percent food cost percent for our operation, this does not mean that all menu item costs will be multiplied by 2½ to establish menu prices. Competition and customer acceptance of prices may dictate that some items will be marked up less (using a lower multiplier and giving a higher cost percent), while others will be marked up using a higher multiplier (resulting in a lower food cost percent). The objective is to arrive at a menu that gives a range of prices that will, on balance, result in the desired overall objective. This sounds simple and can often only result from experience and observation of what happens if prices are changed, or if one menu item is substituted for another. A further complication is that the same menu item, with the same cost, may be offered at a different selling price (even though the portion size might be the same) in a different food sales area (for example the coffee shop versus the dining room).

High versus low mark-up items

Menu item selling prices can also be influenced by such factors as the type of clientele, the style of service, the cost of interior decor, location, labor rates, and similar factors. The amount of convenience foods used can also have a bearing. When one uses convenience foods, much of the preparation labor is borne by the supplier, who, in turn, passes on this cost in his selling price. The purchasing establishment thus pays more for the product but benefits from a reduction in its own preparation labor cost. The result is that the food cost percent may be higher, and the labor cost percent reduced, relative to the selling price.

Use of convenience foods

Another complicating factor is the relationship between the selling price for an individual menu item and the volume of sales for that item. Changing the selling price can directly influence the demand for an item. Demand is never easy to determine, but, because most foodservice operators or managers can observe at close hand what happens to demand if a menu item's price is changed (and even what competitive restaurants in the area might do with their menu selling prices as a result), demand/volume changes can be documented to aid in future menu-price determination.

Value of management observation

Therefore, it can be seen that predetermining what the food cost will be for an entire operation can be complicated and is often the result of trial and error. In the next chapter, we shall explore this topic in more detail.

SUMMARY

Food establishments are, in some ways, similar to manufacturing operations. However, there are some major differences insofar as food cost control is concerned. Traditionally, the food cost percent has been used as a measure to control food cost. The food cost percent is calculated by dividing the cost of food sold by revenue and multiplying the result by 100. The cost of food sold figure can be calculated daily as follows: direct purchases + storeroom issues + transfers in − transfers out − employee meals. However, one should be aware that a daily food cost may not be accurate because all of the direct purchases made on any particular day may not have been used on that day. An accumulated food cost tends to even out such possible distortions after the first few days of the month. At the end of each month, the accumulated figure must be adjusted for the difference between the book and actual inventories, and for the change in open stock.

For meaningful control, one should compare the actual food cost with a predetermined standard food cost. The three steps in establishing a standard food cost are:

1. Determining standard recipes and portion sizes.
2. Calculating menu item costs.
3. Establishing menu item selling prices.

A standard recipe is a written formula spelling out the quantities of each ingredient required to produce a specific quantity and quality of a particular menu item. The ingredients can be costed out for each specific menu item once the portion size has been established. If ingredient costs change, then menu item costs should be recalculated. One of the problems arising from menu item costing is trim and cooking loss in meat and similar products. However, a butchering- and cooking-test form is useful for making the necessary calculations in such cases. This form is also useful for recording by-product costs arising from butchering. Portion cost factors are useful in reducing the work involved in recalculating menu item costs as the suppliers' prices change. The portion cost equation is:

$$\frac{\text{Our cost per portion}}{\text{Supplier's price per lb.}}$$

The final step in establishing a standard food cost percent is to set menu item selling prices. Traditionally, menu item selling prices have been set to yield a desired cost percent. For example, if a 40 percent food cost is desired, the menu item cost would be multiplied by 2½ to determine the selling price. However, many other factors than the menu item cost can influence the selling price of a menu item. One must be cognizant of these factors and take them into consideration when establishing selling-price policy.

DISCUSSION QUESTIONS

1. How is the food cost percent calculated?

2. Why is the food cost percent more meaningful than knowing only the dollar amount of food cost?

3. On the daily food cost form, where does the Direct Purchases figure come from?

4. On the daily food cost form, why is it necessary to have Transfer In and Transfer Out columns?

5. On the daily food cost form, how is the Cost of Food Sold Today calculated?

6. Why is the daily food cost not necessarily accurate?

7. At the month-end, what two adjustments are necessary to make the food cost percent more accurate?

8. With what should the month-end actual food cost be compared?

9. How would you describe a standard recipe?

10. Of what value is a portion cost factor?

11. Why is it not always advantageous to purchase meat and similar items at the lowest quoted price?

12. List three reasons why the selling price of all menu items offered cannot be established to yield the same food cost percent for each item.

PROBLEMS

5-1. On July 8, the following figures, among others, appeared on the daily food cost form: Accumulated Cost of Food Sold $1,278.14, and Accumulated Revenue $4,666.25. On July 9, the Direct Purchases figure from the daily food receiving report was $149.52. Total Storeroom Requisitions for that day were $45.21. However, this total included a requisition for items sent to the bar in the amount of $7.56. The kitchen received a bottle of cooking sherry from the bar on July 9 with a value of $4.50 and, on that date, sent fresh oranges and limes to the bar in the amount of $8.15. Employee Meals on July 9 were estimated at $18.50. Revenue was $515.20. For July 9, calculate the following: Cost of Food Sold Today,

Accumulated Cost of Food Sold, Accumulated Revenue, Today's Food Cost Percent, and the Accumlated Food Cost Percent.

5-2. The daily food cost form at the end of a particular month showed that the Accumulated Cost of Food Sold was $18,126, and that Accumulated Revenue was $57,493. The book inventory figure for that same month-end was $4,202 and the actual inventory, $4,299. The open stock at the beginning of the month was $3,250 and at the end of the month, $3,325. Calculate the month-end adjusted food cost and food cost percent.

5-3. On July 30, the following figures, among others, appeared on the daily food cost form: Accumulated Cost of Food Sold $9,115.40, and Accumulated Revenue $23,199.10. On July 31, the daily food receiving report showed that Direct Purchases were $304.16. Total Storeroom Requisitions for that date were $95.90. However, included in that amount was a requisition amounting to $20.46 for items delivered to the kitchen after storeroom inventory had been taken. The date on the requisition was changed to August 1, and that amount will not be considered to be part of the storeroom issues for July 31. Also included in total requisitions for that date was one for the cocktail bar amounting to $14.73. On July 31, Transfers In were $3.75. There were no Transfers Out, but Employee Meals were estimated to be $54.50. The book inventory at the end of July was $1,755.26, and the actual inventory, $1,785.15. However, on checking the daily food receiving report for July 31, you notice that it lists an invoice totaling $35.20 for items received and put into the storeroom after actual inventory had been completed. Adjust the actual inventory figure accordingly. On June 30, open stock was estimated at $1,375 and on July 31 $1,250. Revenue on July 31 was $785.30. For the daily food cost form for July 31, calculate the cost of food sold today, the accumulated cost of food sold, accumulated revenue, the food cost percent today, and the accumulated food cost percent. Also calculate the adjusted month-end food cost and food cost percent.

5-4. The following ingredients, with their cost prices, are required for a particular menu item yielding 75 portions:

Ingredient	Cost
30 lb. boneless beef	$1.75 lb.
2 lb. flour	0.21 lb.

Ingredient	Cost
3 lb. cooking fat	0.43 lb.
2 lb. carrots	0.18 lb.
2 lb. celery	0.24 lb.
2 lb. green peppers	0.55 lb.
½ #10 can tomato puree	1.95 can
2 gals. beef stock	0.95 gal.
10 lb. potatoes	0.14 lb.
seasonings	0.15 total

a. Calculate the portion cost for this menu item.

b. Assuming that other items to accompany this menu item (baked potato, vegetable, and side salad) were costed out to $0.43, what would the selling price have to be to yield a 30 percent food cost?

5-5. A restaurant serves a six-ounce steak (note that this is six ounces before cooking) with potato, vegetable, and side salad. The restaurant purchases sirloins, from which it cuts the steaks, in eighteen-pound weights at a cost of $2.95 per pound. The calculated cost of the potato, vegetable, and side salad is $0.34.

a. How many individual portions can be served from each eighteen-pound sirloin?

b. What is the cost per portion including potato, vegetable, and side salad?

c. Calculate the selling price to yield a 40 percent food cost.

5-6. A restaurant purchases a certain type of roast in forty-pound weights at a cost of $2.15 per pound. Trim loss is 5 percent and cooking loss 30 percent.

a. How many five-ounce cooked-weight portions (to the nearest whole number) can be served?

b. Calculate the cost per portion.

c. Calculate the portion cost factor.

d. Using the portion cost factor, calculate the new cost per portion assuming the supplier's price increases to $2.25 per pound.

5-7. A restaurant purchases a type of roast in forty-pound cuts, at a price of $2.39 per pound. After butchering, it yields twenty-six pounds of roast, five pounds of hamburger, two pounds of stew, and seven pounds of nonusable fat. If the hamburger and stew had been purchased separately, their market prices would have been $1.05 and $1.78 respectively. The roast is subject to a 25 percent weight loss in cooking.

    a. Calculate the cost per portion of roast assuming six-ounce cooked-weight portions are to be served.

    b. Calculate the portion cost factor for roast, and the cost factors per pound for hamburger and stew.

    c. Recalculate your answers to part (b) assuming the supplier's price decreases by ten cents per pound.

5–8. A hotel purchases unbutchered quarters of beef in eighty-pound cuts. When butchered, they yield sixty-three pounds of roasts, ten pounds of stew, and five pounds of hamburger. The rest is trim and fat loss. The quarters cost $1.95 per pound. If the stew and hamburger were purchased separately, their market prices would have been $1.55 and $0.98 respectively. Roasts are subject to a 30 percent weight loss in cooking.

    a. Assuming five-ounce cooked-weight portions of roast are served, calculate the cost per portion.

    b. Calculate the portion cost factor for roast.

    c. Assume that the supplier's price for quarters increases by fifteen cents per pound. Use the portion cost factor to recalculate the portion cost, and then calculate the selling price that will yield a 35 percent food cost assuming that other ingredients accompanying the five-ounce portions of roast total thirty-six cents.

5–9. You wish to buy a certain cut of meat in eight-pound weights, before trimming. Two suppliers have provided a price. Supplier A's price is $2.65 per pound, and supplier B's, $2.70. After trim and cooking, you find that A's weight loss is 12½ percent, and B's, 10 percent. All other things being equal, from which supplier should you purchase? Why?

Evaluating Food Cost Results

Objectives

After studying this chapter, the reader should be able to do the following:

- Calculate a standard cost percent from given information.
- Explain and use a market cost index to update standard cost.
- Explain *sales mix* and calculate the effect a change in the sales mix will have on the cost percent.
- Explain and use a popularity index.
- Explain how certain portion control forms can aid in controlling food cost.
- Allocate actual cost on a departmental basis.
- Define *gross profit.*
- Use gross profit analysis for menu decision-making.

HISTORICAL TEST PERIOD PERCENT

Test period figures used

A most critical aspect of food cost control is comparison of the actual results with the company's objectives. One of the methods of doing this is to compare the current period's actual food cost percent with a standard percent based on a historical test period.

The first step with this method is to take a count of each different menu item sold during a test period. The test period should generally be an entire month, or at least long enough to even out peaks and valleys. At the end of the test period, the quantities of each menu item sold are listed on a test period standard cost form (see exhibit 6.1). Quantities of each menu item sold are then multiplied by their respective cost and selling prices to arrive at Total Standard Cost and Total Standard Revenue. A simple division of overall standard cost by standard revenue, multiplied by 100, gives the standard cost percent. In our case, it is 29.4 percent. From that point on, the actual cost percent for each accounting period is compared with this standard so that deviations can be detected.

EXHIBIT 6.1. Test Period Standard Cost Calculation Form

Item	Item cost	Item selling price	Quantity sold	Total standard cost	Total standard revenue
1	$0.95	$3.00	822	$ 780.90	$ 2,466.00
2	1.22	4.75	1,340	1,634.80	6,365.00
3	2.54	6.75	319	810.26	2,153.25
			Totals	$10,111.98	$34,393.60

Standard cost percent: $\dfrac{\$10,111.98}{\$34,393.60} \times 100 = 29.4\%$

Market Cost Index

Use of index to adjust standard

One of the problems arising from the standard cost percent based on past performance is that, if cost prices of menu ingredients are changed, then new tests must be conducted. Alternatively, an easier method is simply to adjust the standard cost percent by means of a market cost index. A market cost index is composed of a limited number of typical items of major food purchases that, in total dollar value, comprise 20 to 25 percent or more of the total purchase dollar. During the menu test period, the quantities of these items are listed and multiplied by their purchase costs to arrive at a total cost (see exhibit 6.2). In subsequent periods, the same items are listed with their new purchase prices to arrive at a new total cost. The previous standard cost can then be adjusted for comparison with the current period's actual cost with the formula:

$$\text{Test period standard cost percent} \times \frac{\text{Current period total cost}}{\text{Test period total cost}} = \text{Current period standard cost percent}$$

Index equation

In our case, using the appropriate figures from exhibits 6.1 and 6.2, this would be:

$$29.4\% \times \frac{\$10,241.05}{\$\ 9,915.00} = 30.4\%$$

Calculation of adjusted standard

Even though the standard cost is revised in this way, it would still be necessary to confirm the standard cost percent with a complete menu item test from time to time. This would be particularly true if the operation's business were highly seasonal or if the menu were changed.

Generally, with this method, the actual food cost would be allowed to deviate from standard by one percentage point above or below the standard. In other words, if the standard were 35 percent, the actual could vary from 34 and 36 percent. A tolerance is necessary since the standard is based on perfect costing and other factors, and absolute perfection cannot always be expected in practice. Differences could occur for any or all of the following reasons:

Deviation allowed from standard

Possible causes of deviations

1. Poor receiving practices, such as not counting or weighing items, or receiving low quality and paying for high quality
2. Improper storeroom controls resulting in too much wastage or spoilage, or in issuing items to unauthorized personnel for personal use
3. Failure to follow standard recipes and portion sizes, leading again to wastage and spoilage
4. Excessive cost of employee meals
5. Pilferage

EXHIBIT 6.2. Market Cost Index

Item	Quantity used	Test period		New period		New period	
		Unit cost	Total cost	Unit cost	Total cost	Unit cost	Total cost
Salmon	900 lb.	$2.50 lb.	$2,250.00	$2.95 lb.	$ 2,655.00		
Beef hinds	1,400 lb.	2.54 lb.	3,556.00	2.48 lb.	3,472.00		
Lobster	348 ea.	6.25 ea.	2,175.00	6.50 ea.	2,262.00		
Chicken	1,095 lb.	0.95 lb.	1,040.25	0.89 lb.	974.55		
Coffee	325 lb.	2.75 lb.	893.75	2.70 lb.	877.50		
Totals			$9,915.00		$10,241.05		

The Sales Mix Problem

There is one item that can cause a deviation of actual from standard cost percent that has not yet been mentioned, and that is the problem of sales mix. The sales mix is the quantity of each separate menu item that is sold during any period (a meal, a day, a week, or a month). A changed sales mix can cause a considerable change in the cost percent, and is a factor that the owner or manager has very limited control over in most cases. Customers' preferences do change over time, and menu items are sometimes substituted on a seasonal basis or for some other reason. When historical sales mix patterns are used to calculate the standard cost percent, the assumption is made that this sales mix will remain the same, or relatively the same, in the future. This would be highly unlikely in practice, although it is possible that, if the establishment has an extensive menu, changes in the sales mix tend to even themselves out and might have a lesser influence than otherwise.

Limited control over sales mix

EXHIBIT 6.3. Illustration of Sales Mix Effect on Food Cost Percentage

CASE A

Item	Item cost	Item selling price	Quantity sold	Total cost	Total sales	Food cost percent
1	$2.00	$5.00	100	$200.00	$ 500	40.0%
2	3.00	6.00	200	600.00	1,200	50.0
Totals			300	$800.00	$1,700	47.1%

CASE B

Item	Item cost	Item selling price	Quantity sold	Total cost	Total sales	Food cost percent
1	$2.00	$5.00	200	$400.00	$1,000	40.0%
2	3.00	6.00	100	300.00	600	50.0
Totals			300	$700.00	$1,600	43.8%

Illustration of Sales Mix Change

We can illustrate how a change in the sales mix affects the cost percentage using only two menu items. In exhibit 6.3, Case A's overall food cost is 47.1 percent ($800 divided by $1,700 and multiplied by 100).

In Case B, there is a change in the sales mix (with no change in number of customers since 300 items in total are still sold) that causes the cost to

Decreased percent has no effect on gross profit

decrease to 43.8 percent. The reason for this is that we are now selling more of item one, which has a much lower food cost percent, than item two. This change in the sales mix might seem desirable since it has led to a decrease in the food cost percent. However, in fact, it has made absolutely no difference to the operation's net income (as long as all other costs remained constant). In both cases, the gross profit is $900. (Gross profit equals sales less food cost. The importance of gross profit with reference to the sales mix will be explored further later in the chapter.)

PRECOST PERCENT

Forecasts required with precost method

An improvement over the historical standard cost percent has been developed in recent years. It is known as the *precost method*; it bases the standard cost percent on a forecast of what the sales mix will be each day.

Adjusting for special situations

In order to use precost, extensive records must be maintained. This is particularly so where menu items are substituted daily, or when cycle menus are used. Prior to each day, a forecast is made of anticipated sales of each menu item on that day. Most foodservice operations forecast as a matter of course. It is necessary to do this in order to calculate daily purchase requirements and to know how much should be produced of each menu item to avoid over- or under-production. Electronic sales registers make it possible to tally up sales automatically for each menu item by meal period or by day. Thus, much of the paper work previously involved with recording sales of menu items from sales checks to sales tally sheets has been eliminated. However, it still means that someone must predetermine quantities expected to be sold based on past sales and adjust for such factors as day of the week, holidays, special events, weather, house count (in a hotel), and any other pertinent information, combining with the factors a great deal of judgment. These forecasts are not only necessary for precost control, but can also be very useful in such matters as staff scheduling.

EXHIBIT 6.4.   Popularity Index

Item	Quantity sold	Percent
Salmon steak	58	36%
Half chicken	14	9
Prime rib	41	25
Filet mignon	29	18
New York steak	19	12
Totals	161	100%

Popularity Index

A useful technique in forecasting based on past performance is the compilation of a popularity index. A popularity index summarizes, for each menu item, the quantity sold for a particular set of menu offerings. The quantity of each menu item sold is then expressed as a percentage of all menu items sold. For example, in exhibit 6.4, salmon steak represented 36 percent of total items sold in the past when that particular combination of menu items was offered. That percentage is then applied to total forecast sales for the coming day when this menu will again be offered. If 134 items in total that are anticipated will be sold, then salmon steak should sell 36 percent times 134, or 48 portions. Similar calculations are then made for each of the other menu items to be offered that day.

Converting popularity index to percentage

The Production Forecast

One of the advantages of the precost method is that it formalizes the forecasting procedure, and thus aids in purchasing and production with the use of a daily food production worksheet. Exhibit 6.5 is an illustration of such a worksheet. Copies of this worksheet can then be given to those responsible for purchasing, so that required food items will be available, and to those involved in food production. Although the worksheet illustrated only shows a partial list of main entree items, it could be expanded to include entree accompaniments such as potatoes, other vegetables, salads, and also appetizers and desserts. Also, even though this worksheet is prepared a day or more ahead, it should allow for possible last-minute changes because of unanticipated factors. If the establishment also caters to banquets and similar functions, the production requirements for these can also be incorporated on this form.

Forecasting aids in food production

Calculation of Standard Cost

With the precost method, a two-part form is used. The left-hand part is used for calculating the forecast or standard cost percent, and the right-hand part used later for recording actual sales and calculation of the revised standard cost percent. See exhibit 6.6.

Calculating standard cost percent

The quantities expected to be sold of each menu item are recorded in the Forecast Quantity column and then multiplied by their respective cost and selling prices to arrive at Total Standard Cost and Total Standard Revenue. The standard cost percent can then be calculated as illustrated. This is the food cost percent we can now anticipate if our forecast of total meals and breakdown of the sales mix is accurate.

After the meal period or day is over, the right-hand part of the form is then used for recording actual quantities sold. Multiplying each item's quantity by its respective cost and selling price gives the Total Revised

EXHIBIT 6.5. Daily Food Production Worksheet   Date ___February 8___

Item	Recipe #	Anticipated sales	Portion size	Quantity required	Sold	Over- or under-production
Salmon steak	4	48	6 oz.	18 lb.	46	+ 2
Half chicken	16	12	half	6 whole	12	
Prime rib	3	33	8 oz.	16½ lb.	31	+ 2
Filet mignon	32	24	8 oz.	24 portions	20	+ 4
New York steak	7	17	10 oz.	17 portions	20	− 3

EXHIBIT 6.6. Standard Two-Part Cost Analysis Form   Date _____ February 12 _____

Item	Item Cost	Item Selling price	Item cost percent	Forecast quantity	Total standard Cost	Total standard Revenue	Actual quantity	Total revised standard Cost	Total revised standard Revenue
1	$0.75	$2.00	37.5%	42	$ 31.50	$ 84.00			
2	1.25	2.75	45.5	63	78.75	173.25			
3	4.00	6.50	61.5	27	108.00	175.50			
4	2.10	6.00	35.0	80	168.00	480.00			
5	1.50	5.50	27.3	42	63.00	231.00			
Totals				254	$449.25	$1,143.75			

Cost percentages $\dfrac{\$\ 449.25}{\$1,143.75} \times 100 = 39.3\%$

EXHIBIT 6.7.   Completed Cost-Analysis Form   Date ___February 12___

Item	Item Cost	Item Selling price	Item cost percent	Forecast quantity	Total standard Cost	Total standard Revenue	Actual quantity	Total revised standard Cost	Total revised standard Revenue
1	$0.75	$2.00	37.5%	42	$ 31.50	$ 84.00	45	$ 33.75	$ 90.00
2	1.25	2.75	45.5	63	78.75	173.25	60	75.00	165.00
3	4.00	6.50	61.5	27	108.00	175.50	28	112.00	182.00
4	2.10	6.00	35.0	80	168.00	480.00	86	180.60	516.00
5	1.50	5.50	27.3	42	63.00	231.00	44	66.00	242.00
Totals				254	$449.25	$1,143.75	263	$467.35	$1,195.00

Cost percentages

$$\frac{\$\ 449.25}{\$1,143.75} \times 100 = 39.3\%$$

$$\frac{\$\ 467.35}{\$1,195.00} \times 100 = 39.1\%$$

Standard Cost and Total Revised Standard Revenue as illustrated in exhibit 6.7.

The two cost percentages can then be compared. It is inevitable that there will be differences, either because the total meals forecast was wrong, the sales mix forecast was inaccurate, or there was a combination of both. Note, for example, in exhibit 6.7, that nine more total meals were sold than anticipated and that, for each menu item, there is some variation in forecast versus actual quantity, causing a minor variance in our standard and revised standard percentages.

Comparing standard with revised standard

Note that each day both the standard percent and the revised standard percent will change. This is because, even if menu item cost and selling prices remain the same, and even if total meals sold is constant, the sales mix will likely differ.

One of the major advantages of the precost method is that it allows easy comparison of forecast with actual quantities sold. This should lead to improved forecasting in the future and thus improve the effectiveness of the food purchasing and productivity procedures.

Advantage of precost method

Comparison of Standard and Actual on a Daily Basis

Since, with the precost method, we are calculating the revised standard cost on a daily basis, is it feasible to compare it with the *actual* cost on a daily basis? The reader is referred to chapter 5, and to exhibit 5.1, which shows the calculation of actual food cost for each day, both in dollars and as a percentage. Comparisons between the two sets of figures can be made.

Comparison of revised standard with actual cost

However, it should be pointed out that the figures from exhibit 5.1 are raw figures. They have not been adjusted for fluctuations that can be quite large in day-to-day inventories of open stock. Therefore, care should be exercised in interpreting the figures on a daily basis. What would be more practical would be to summarize the actual sales quantity figures over time (a week or a month) and calculate an overall standard cost figure for that period to be compared with an actual cost figure (adjusted for inventory changes) for that same period. This is illustrated in exhibit 6.8.

If a major difference exists between the standard cost percent and the actual cost percent, we can be absolutely sure that it is *not* caused by a change in the sales mix, since we have taken the sales mix into consideration. We also know that it cannot have been caused by a change in menu item selling prices, since any changed selling prices should have been adjusted for in the calculations. The same goes for ingredient cost changes: if these cost changes were major, the menu item cost prices should have been adjusted to compensate for them in the calculations; therefore, any difference that does exist must have been caused by one or more of the factors listed earlier in this chapter, such as poor receiving, storing, and production practices, pilferage, or wastage.

Sales mix not a factor in difference

Under normal circumstances, if we had good control and employees

EXHIBIT 6.8. Comparison of Overall Standard Cost and Actual Cost

Week ending_____ February 17 _____

Item	Item		Actual quantity sold	Total standard	
	Cost	Selling price		Cost	Revenue
1	$0.75	$2.00	143	$ 107.25	$ 286.00
2	1.25	2.75	219	278.75	602.25
3	4.00	6.50	95	380.00	617.50
4	2.10	6.00	305	640.50	1,830.00
5	1.50	5.50	142	313.00	781.00
			Totals	$3,249.00	$8,266.00

Standard cost
$$\frac{\$3,249.00}{\$8,266.00} \times 100 = 39.3\%$$

Actual cost (adjusted)
$$\frac{\$3,275.00}{\$8,266.00} \times 100 = 39.6\%$$

were following procedures properly, this difference would be no larger than one half of one percent. In other words, with reference to exhibit 6.8, our standard cost is 39.3 percent for that particular week. Actual cost could vary between 38.8 and 39.8 percent. Generally, but not invariably, one would expect to see the actual cost above standard cost. The standard cost is based on the assumption that actual menu item costs will turn out exactly as calculated when they are established. Because of wastage and other similar losses in excess of any safety factor built into menu item costs, actual costs would tend to exceed standard costs. Also, the cost of menu items purchased can vary from day to day and it is just not practical to adjust standard menu costs every day.

Actual cost generally above standard

Fixed-Menu Establishments

Problem simplified with limited menus

These days many foodservice operations have limited menus offering only a few items. These items are seldom changed, although sometimes daily "specials" may be offered. Usually, these restaurants have a relatively steady volume of business, and purchase precut, preportioned, and frequently frozen entree and other items that are much less prone to deterioration in the short run. Frequently, these restaurants will only cook to order. For such establishments, the problem of forecasting is minimized, and probably never formalized. They generally carry enough of each item to take care of maximum daily demand, and what is not sold one day is simply carried over to the next with no loss.

For this type of food operation, a system of forecasting, of production worksheets, and of precosting is really not necessary on a daily basis. However, what is useful is a portion control form such as that illustrated in exhibit 6.9. This type of inventory sheet is completed daily. The Quantity Used column is calculated as follows:

Use of portion control form

```
Opening inventory + Purchased − Closing inventory
```

The quantity used is compared with the amount sold to determine any differences. In a smaller operation, this form might be completed by the chef for his own satisfaction so that he can be sure that losses are not occurring. In a larger establishment, the inventory of these items would be stored under lock and key and issued daily by requisition, based on the chef's estimate of anticipated demand. If actual demand is greater than expected, more items can be quickly requisitioned. If less, then unused portions can be returned to the storeroom to be requisitioned again on a future day. In the latter case, the form might need to be redesigned with column headings as illustrated in exhibit 6.10.

Improved inventory control

Even though this type of limited-menu operation may not use precost control, it can still benefit, on a weekly or monthly basis, from a periodic comparison of its standard and actual costs as illustrated in exhibit 6.8.

EXHIBIT 6.11. Banquet Portion Control Form								
Function Construction Association Room Madison Date Feb. 16								
Server number	Appetizers	Soups	Salads	Entrees	Desserts	Guests served	Comment
1	15			15	14	15	
2	14			14	14	14	
3	16			16	13	16	
Totals	428			428	414	428	

Banquet Portion Control

Hotels and larger restaurants that cater to banquets and similar functions can also use a type of portion control. A typical banquet portion control form is illustrated in exhibit 6.11. The figures in the various course col-

EXHIBIT 6.9. Food Inventory Portion Control Form   Date____February 16____

Item	Opening inventory	Purchased	Closing inventory	Quantity used	Quantity sold	Difference	Comment
Filet mignon 6 oz.	18	24	8	34	32	– 2	Customers complained
Filet mignon 8 oz.	22	12	3	31	31		
New York 10 oz.	15	36	7	44	43	– 1	Spoiled

EXHIBIT 6.10. Food Inventory Portion Control—Alternate Form   Date ___February 16___

Item	Quantity requisitioned	Quantity returned	Quantity used	Quantity sold	Difference	Comment

umns can be entered on the form by a person from the kitchen production area as each waiter or waitress leaves that area with trays of menu items to be served to guests. At the end of each banquet, the banquet captain's figure of guests served by each waiter, and in total for all waiters, can be compared with the banquet portion control form figure. This should ensure that servers do not take out of the kitchen more portions than they have guests to serve. This form can also be useful for customer billing purposes.

Allocating Actual Cost to Sales Areas

Comparing actual cost by department

In larger establishments, a number of different food sales outlets may be serviced from a main preparation kitchen, and the overall actual food cost after inventory-taking cannot be identified directly for each sales area. In such cases, it is still useful to be able to compare the actual cost with the standard cost by department. The following method may be used to do this. Let us assume we have the following revenue for a month for three sales areas:

Banquets	$ 30,800
Dining room	82,600
Coffee shop	39,900
	$153,300

Total overall food cost is $49,500 or 32.3 percent ($49,500 divided by $153,300 and multiplied by 100).

According to calculations already made, the standard food cost for this month for each of the three areas is:

Predetermined departmental standard costs

Banquets	28.5%
Dining room	32.0%
Coffee shop	33.2%

Our standard food cost in dollars for each outlet should therefore be:

Calculating standard cost dollars by department

Banquets	28.5% × $30,800 =	$ 8,778
Dining room	32.0% × $82,600 =	26,432
Coffee shop	33.2% × $39,900 =	13,247
Total standard cost		$48,457

We can now calculate a ratio between the total actual food cost (the numerator) and the total standard food cost (the denominator):

$$\frac{\$49,500}{\$48,457} = 1.0215 \text{ (to four decimal places)}$$

This ratio can now be applied to the standard cost percentages by department to arrive at actual percentages by department:

Banquets	1.0215 × 28.5% =	29.1%
Dining room	1.0215 × 32.0% =	32.7%
Coffee shop	1.0215 × 33.2% =	33.9%

Using ratio by department

These actual cost percentages can now be multiplied by the actual sales dollars by department to determine the actual food cost in dollars:

Banquets	$30,800 × 29.1% =	$ 8,963
Dining room	$82,600 × 32.7% =	27,010
Coffee shop	$39,900 × 33.9% =	13,526
Total		$49,499

Final step in cost calculation by department

There is a one dollar difference, from rounding out numbers, between this total and the total actual food cost given earlier of $49,500.

GROSS PROFIT ANALYSIS

The subject of gross profit has been mentioned a number of times. A great deal of emphasis has been placed on food cost percent by the industry in the past. This emphasis will no doubt continue. However, lowering the food cost percent is not necessarily a good thing! This can be easily illustrated by referring to exhibit 6.3, which shows what happens to the food cost percent when the sales mix changes. In this particular case, lowering the food cost, all other things being equal (labor cost, other direct costs, and overheads), would make no difference since, despite the large change in the food cost percent, there is a $900 gross profit in both cases. No one can argue, under these circumstances, that lowering the food cost percent will increase net income. In many cases lowering the percent can *decrease* net income, and vice versa. It is for this reason, the gross profit, that some food establishments can operate with a 60 percent food cost and be very successful, while others may operate at 30 percent and have financial difficulties.

Emphasis on food cost percentage

Food cost percent versus gross profit

EXHIBIT 6.12. Menu Analysis to Determine Gross Profit				

	Item		Average daily quantity sold	Total cost	Total revenue
Item	Cost	Selling price			
1	$1.28	$4.60	75	$ 96.00	$ 345.00
2	2.26	5.95	42	94.92	249.90
3	3.74	6.30	61	228.14	384.30
4	1.78	5.75	99	176.22	569.25
5	1.94	6.25	74	143.56	462.50
Totals			351	$ 738.84	$2,010.95
Gross profit				$1,272.11	
Cost percent				$\dfrac{\$\ 738.84}{\$2,010.95} \times 100 = 36.7\%$	
Average gross profit per guest				$\dfrac{\$1,272.11}{351} = \$3.62$	

Menu Analysis

Ways of increasing gross profit

As discussed in chapter 5, most food menus contain a variety of items covering a range of prices, some with higher markups than others. These prices are dictated by many factors that vary from one restaurant to another. When analyzing menus to improve gross profit, there are a number of alternatives: purchase costs can be reduced by reducing ingredient quality, portion sizes can be reduced, or selling prices can be increased. Alternatively, one can change the entire menu by having on it only items that have a high individual gross profit. However, to make such a drastic move might severely disrupt the restaurant's present clientele and might well result in an imbalanced menu as far as offering a range of prices is concerned.

Substituting menu items

A better way might be to substitute one or two items on the present menu to see what effect this might have on overall gross profit. For example, exhibit 6.12 lists the five entree items presently offered by a restaurant. We are going to substitute for item 5, with a $4.31 gross profit ($6.25 less $1.94), item 6, that has a $4.64 gross profit ($6.40 less $1.76). In anticipation of this change, we expect that a number of customers will switch from one item to another and produce a changed sales mix even though total number of guests will not change. Exhibit 6.13 shows these changed results. If our sales mix predictions are correct, gross profit will increase from $1,272.11

to $1,301.49, or by $29.38 per day on average. In this particular case, the gross profit increase is combined with a decreased food cost percent. Depending on the circumstances, it could also be combined with an increased cost percent. Thus overemphasizing the cost percent and ignoring its effect on gross profit can be misleading.

EXHIBIT 6.13. **Menu Analysis to Determine Gross Profit after Menu Change**

Item	Item Cost	Item Selling price	Average daily quantity sold	Total cost	Total revenue
1	$1.28	$4.60	55	$ 70.40	$ 253.00
2	2.26	5.95	41	92.66	243.95
3	3.74	6.30	65	243.10	409.50
4	1.78	5.75	120	213.60	690.00
5	1.76	6.40	70	123.20	448.00
Totals			351	$742.96	$2,044.45
Gross profit					$1,301.49
Cost percent			$\dfrac{\$\ 742.96}{\$2,044.45} \times 100 = 36.3\%$		
Average gross profit per guest			$\dfrac{\$1,301.49}{351} = \$3.71$		

It is sometimes useful to calculate the average gross profit per guest or customer. This has been done in exhibits 6.12 and 6.13. The average has increased from $3.62 to $3.71. This is to be expected, since overall gross profit has increased and there has been no change in number of customers. If, in substituting menu items, there is an increase in average gross profit per customer but, because of a decrease in total customers, the overall gross profit declines, this would not be a desirable trend.

Average gross profit per customer

Initially, experimental menu changes should be made on paper. Perhaps surveys of customers could also be carried out before changing a menu to improve gross profit. If sales histories have been kept, then popularity indexes as illustrated in exhibit 6.4 could be very useful in forecasting the sales mix from proposed menu changes.

Finally, in evaluating a change to a menu to improve gross profit, one must always be aware of a potential change in total demand for all menu

Other factors to consider

items (particularly if one is removing a popular, but low gross profit, item from the menu), and the potential effect on other costs (such as serving or preparation labor, and cooking time and its effect on energy costs).

SUMMARY

An important aspect of food cost control is comparison of actual results with a standard food cost percent. One of the ways of establishing the standard is to use past information to determine what the food cost percent should be. This standard food cost percent can then be updated from time to time using a market cost index. The equation for this is:

$$\text{Test period standard cost percent} \times \frac{\text{Current period total cost}}{\text{Test period total cost}} = \text{Current period standard cost percent}$$

Some deviation of actual from standard must be expected for a number of reasons, the major one being a change in the sales mix, and another, a change in the quantities of the various menu items that are sold from one period to the next.

An improvement over the establishment of a standard cost percent based on historical records is to use the precost method. With the precost approach, past sales of individual menu items are used to forecast in advance each day how many of each individual menu item will be sold. A popularity index is a useful technique in this forecasting. From the forecast of quantities to be sold, a standard food cost percent can be calculated. At the end of each day, the actual sales mix is used to calculate the revised standard food cost percent. Again, differences between the two percents will probably occur since the total number of meals actually sold, and the sales mix, will probably differ from the forecast. However, over time this should lead to improvement in the forecasting to produce more meaningful results. The standard food cost and revised standard food cost figures so produced should be compared with the actual cost. This can be done on a daily basis, but is probably more useful, and more accurate, if carried out on a weekly or monthly basis after inventory has been taken and any necessary adjustments to the actual food cost made.

Portion control and banquet production control are two other techniques that can be used to control food cost.

Despite the emphasis placed on food cost control and the food cost percent, it should be noted that a high food cost percent is not necessarily indicative of problems. In most situations, what is important is the gross profit (revenue less food cost). Gross profit can frequently be improved by substituting menu items with a low gross profit with those with a high gross profit despite the fact that the latter may have a higher food cost percent.

DISCUSSION QUESTIONS

1. What is a market cost index?

2. Give three reasons why the actual food cost will probably differ from a standard food cost based on past records.

3. How would you explain the term sales mix?

4. What is a *popularity index* and how is it used in food cost control?

5. Explain why, in using the precost control method there might be a difference between the standard and revised standard food costs.

6. With the precost method, will the revised standard cost be the same as the actual cost? Explain.

7. With the precost method, if there is a difference between the revised standard cost and the actual cost, explain why the sales mix cannot be a cause for this difference.

8. Explain how a food inventory portion control form can aid in food cost control.

9. Explain how a banquet portion control form can aid in food cost control.

10. Define *gross profit*.

11. Explain how a menu item can have a low food cost percent and a high gross profit while another menu item can have a high cost percent and a low gross profit.

12. What circumstance could cause average gross profit per guest to increase but total gross profit to decline?

PROBLEMS

6-1. A restaurant has only five items on its menu. Item cost and selling price are as follows, along with the quantity sold figures taken from a test period:

Menu item	Item cost	Item selling price	Quantity sold
1	$0.95	$2.85	1,416
2	1.24	4.65	1,568
3	4.12	8.95	364
4	2.47	6.95	518
5	1.55	5.95	1,112

Calculate the restaurant's standard cost percent.

6-2. A hotel food department's standard cost percent, based on a test period, has been calculated to be 33.2 percent. During the test period, the following quantities of certain major food purchases were consumed with cost prices as shown:

Test Period

Item	Quantity used	Cost price
Beef quarters	750 lb.	$1.55 lb.
Poultry	581 lb.	0.98 lb.
Coffee	510 lb.	2.43 lb.
Eggs	475 doz.	0.95 doz.
Bacon	324 lb.	1.45 lb.

Two months later, current invoices were checked for cost price changes. The new prices were:

Item	Cost price	
Beef quarters	$1.65 lb.	
Poultry	0.99 lb.	
Coffee	2.35 lb.	*1198.50*
Eggs	0.98 doz.	*465.50*
Bacon	1.43 lb.	*463.32*

Calculate the hotel food department's current standard cost percent if the relative quantities used remained unchanged.

6-3. A restaurant features only three entree items on its menu, with the following cost and selling prices:

Item	Cost	Selling price
1	$1.00	$3.30
2	2.20	4.40
3	2.70	6.75

a. For each item, calculate the food cost percent.
b. If fifty of each item are sold each day, what will the standard food cost percent be?
c. If, rather than selling 50 of each, only 25 each of items one and three were sold, and 100 of item two, what effect will this have on the standard food cost percent?

6-4. A popularity index for a certain day of the week indicated the following breakdown of the quantity normally sold of each of the menu items offered:

Item	Sold
1	85
2	32
3	62
4	43
5	48
6	52
7	40

362

Total forecast sales on that day during the current week are for 410 covers to be served. For each of the menu items, calculate, to the nearest whole number, the quantity to be produced.

6-5. A restaurant uses a standard cost approach to aid in controlling its food cost. The following are the standard cost and sale prices, and the quantity sold, of each of the five items featured on its menu during a particular week:

Item	Standard cost	Selling price	Quantity sold
1	$1.80	$3.95	260
2	2.10	4.95	411
3	4.20	8.95	174
4	3.05	6.95	319
5	1.40	3.95	522

Total actual cost for the week was $3,804.10, and total revenue $8,897.70. Calculate the standard and actual cost percentages, and comment about the results.

6-6. The sales records for a dining room that has only six items on its menu show the following quantities sold during the month of January, along with each item's cost and selling prices.

Item	Cost	Selling price	Quantity sold
1	$2.00	$6.00	654
2	1.10	4.50	2,196
3	2.25	7.00	1,110
4	1.75	5.00	990
5	2.25	5.00	295
6	2.00	7.95	259

Actual cost for the month was $9,201, and actual revenue $30,060.05. Calculate the standard and actual cost percentages, and explain whether or not you would be satisfied with the results.

6-7. A hotel's standard food cost percentages are as follows:

Coffee shop	28%
Dining room	36
Banquet department	25

During February, the revenue was as follows:

Coffee shop	$45,590
Dining room	65,811
Banquet department	38,116

Total overall actual food cost for the month was $40,702. Calculate the actual cost percentages and actual cost dollars for each of the three revenue areas.

6-8. A restaurant presently offers the following four items on its menu, with item cost, selling prices, and average daily sales as indicated.

Item	Cost	Selling price	Average daily sales
1	$2.25	$5.20	55
2	1.70	4.80	60
3	1.55	3.55	125
4	2.55	6.00	70

The restaurant is considering replacing the present menu with a new one. Information about the new one is as follows:

Item	Cost	Selling price	Average daily sales
1	$1.80	$5.30	50
2	2.05	5.45	65
3	1.90	3.75	130
4	2.30	5.00	65

a. For each of the menus, calculate the cost percent, the total gross profit, and the gross profit per guest. Which menu would be preferable? Why?

b. On the new menu, suppose item one were taken off and a new item one substituted with a cost of two dollars and a selling price of six dollars. If the substitution takes place and the same quantities are sold, would your answer to part (a) change?

Beverage Purchasing, Receiving, and Storeroom Control

7

Objectives

After studying this chapter, the reader should be able to do the following:

- Differentiate between monopoly and license or open situations for the distribution of alcoholic beverages.
- Discuss the pros and cons of having only one or two suppliers versus having many suppliers, and list some of the factors other than price to consider in selecting suppliers.
- Differentiate between well or house liquor and premium or call liquor, calculate the cost per ounce of liquor, and explain why this measure is of value.
- Discuss the problems of which beverage products to carry and how much to order of each, and describe and explain the purposes of a purchase order.
- Discuss the purchase of nonalcoholic bar supplies.
- Explain the need to break down beverage purchases into three major categories, and be able to analyze costs on this basis.
- Discuss and complete beverage receiving reports.
- Explain the principles of beverage storeroom control.
- Complete a beverage storeroom reconciliation, and calculate and discuss beverage inventory turnover.

What is included in beverages

This is the first of two chapters on beverage cost control. It covers purchasing, receiving, and storeroom control; chapter 8 covers control of beverages at the bar after they have been issued from the storeroom. The word *beverage* in these chapters includes all types of alcoholic beverages, including beer and other malt beverages, wine, and distilled spirits (commonly referred to as liquor). Generally, however, beverage control also includes some types of nonalcoholic beverages—for example, sodas, soft drinks, mineral waters, and juices that are frequently mixed with liquor. Since they become part of the beverage cost of sales, they must be included in overall beverage cost control.

PURCHASING

Consistent product quality

For most bar operations, the purchasing of alcoholic beverages is less of a problem than the purchasing of food items sometimes is for a restaurant. Beverage purchasing and control are simplified because the brands that customers like to drink can be reasonably easily established, the beverages are generally purchased in sealed cases or bottles that are easy to count, the product quality is consistent from one purchase to the next for any particular type or brand of beverage, and most beverages (except for keg beer) have a fairly long shelf life, which means that purchases can be made on a periodic rather than on a continual daily basis. Finally, all beverages can, on receipt, be delivered to a locked, controlled storeroom prior to being issued. This is not the case with food, where the problem of control over direct purchases can be a major one.

Control of Distribution

Government as supplier

In most jurisdictions, the government is the sole wholesaler/distributor, and the prices to the purchaser are controlled and fixed, with few opportunities (if any) for "sales." In such jurisdictions, the government may specify the liquor ordering and invoice paying procedures. In other words, the only supplier offers specific products at a noncompetitive price and requires that specific purchasing procedures be followed.

In the United States, states that have government distribution of liquor are known as "control" or "monopoly" states. The others are known as license or open states. In most of the provinces of Canada, the government also has a monopoly (or control) over the distribution of alcoholic beverages.

Monopoly Situations

In control situations, there is generally only one price for each product, and the bar manager cannot shop around for lower prices. As a result, the product cost is usually higher in control situations than in license situations. There may also be a more limited brand selection, since the government monopoly will usually only carry products that sell well, and since it may be less responsive to purchasers' needs. Nonetheless, some monopoly governments are willing to bring in specialty products for a purchaser if the purchaser is willing to buy them in a specified minimum number of case lots.

Control or monopoly situations

In control situations, the government normally requires purchasers to pay in cash or by certified check at the time of pickup, as well as to arrange and pay for their own pickup and delivery.

Competitive Situations

In most license states in the United States, a monthly list of the names of wholesalers is published, including the products each carries and the prices each charges. The alcoholic beverage purchaser may buy from any wholesaler licensed by the state; in some states, the purchaser may also buy from licensed manufacturers and distributors (distillers, brewers, or vintners). Local laws sometimes override state laws, however, and the regulations for beer and wine sometimes differ from those for distilled spirits. Some manufacturers—for example, breweries—have their own distribution networks and do not sell through other wholesalers or distributors. Wholesalers and distributors may handle the products of many manufacturers and vintners, while importers may handle products from many different countries.

Competitive or license situations

In license situations, prices may be lower because of competition, but this is not necessarily the case on all items. Some manufacturers grant exclusive distribution rights for some products to a particular seller, who then has no competition. Where there is some competition, the sellers may nonetheless be reluctant to compete on the prices of products that a bar must stock. These "must stock" items are the heavily advertised brands that customers virtually demand be available in any bar. Thus, the consumer dictates in most cases what a bar will carry, and to some extent this enables the suppliers to maintain prices even in a competitive situation. Suppliers then compete only on the discretionary products that a bar may wish to carry, or through discounts or other inducements not allowed in government-controlled jurisdictions.

Competition lowers prices

In license situations, the reputable bar operator also has access to supplier credit and will be allowed to pay the invoice by a certain date. In many jurisdictions, if the invoice is not paid by that date, the supplier is required to advise the licensing authorities, who have the discretion to prevent the operator from making further purchases until the bill is paid.

Familiarity with Local Situation

Knowing legal requirements

It is up to the purchaser of alcoholic beverages to be familiar with all the necessary legal requirements and distribution channels in the jurisdiction where the establishment is located; even where the government is the sole supplier, there may still be importers, wholesalers, and dealers, or their agents or sales representatives, trying to influence purchasers to buy their products through the government supplier.

Suppliers are often very useful in advising about local or regional trends in the drinking tastes and habits of customers or potential customers. Of course, suppliers will be anxious to tell purchasers about any new products they have and (where this is allowed) about any discounts or other purchase incentives they are offering. But purchasers must be wary of discounted wines and beers that may have reached the limit of their freshness.

Fixed visiting times

The number of these people that a purchaser has to deal with will depend in large part on the number of products the establishment wishes to carry. Regardless of the number, however, it is a good idea to establish a rule to have them visit only during fixed hours on a specified day each week. Without that restriction, purchasers will be subjected to constant interruptions, impeding their work on the balance of their purchasing responsibilities.

Number of Product Suppliers

Concentrating orders

Finally, in situations where there is a choice of suppliers, it is important for a purchaser to consider how many different purchase sources are desirable to deal with. Concentrating orders with a limited number of suppliers creates larger-sized orders, and the purchaser thus becomes a more important customer of the supplier. In recognition of this, lower prices and/or better supplier services can be expected.

On the other hand, if as many suppliers as possible are dealt with, each one may be forced to compete harder—although with some products, as mentioned earlier, they may be reluctant to do this. In fact, for major-selling products, a purchaser could place an order for each product with a different supplier simply because that supplier currently has the lowest price for the item and meets the quality standards desired.

The opposite extreme would be to place all product requirement orders with a single supplier that—despite having a higher cost on one or two products—provides the *lowest overall cost* on all products. Since this simplifies the overall purchasing, ordering, receiving, storing, and invoicing problem, it is often the best approach. Unfortunately, it is commonly rejected by bar operators and/or purchasers because they think about their purchasing only on a product-by-product basis.

Lowest overall cost

Weekly Purchasing

An effective purchaser tries to limit the purchasing routine, including the completion of purchase orders, to once a week, since this lessens the demands on time, reduces the possibility of errors, and simplifies the paperwork and bookkeeping.

In a small independent bar, the owner should handle the purchasing function personally, since it is a key element in cost control. In certain circumstances, however, the function may have to be delegated, in which case the owner/operator should be alert to the possibility of supplier/purchaser kickbacks or bribes.

Owner handles purchasing

Kickbacks

Kickbacks can take the form of cash or merchandise given to the purchaser for favoring a supplier or agent, even in situations where liquor has to be purchased from a government outlet.

In other cases, the kickback can occur when a supplier sells to the purchaser directly but inflates the price of products, includes items on the invoice that were not actually delivered, or substitutes low-quality products while charging the higher-quality product's price. The "savings" to the supplier are then split with the person doing the purchasing.

Types of kickbacks

These kinds of kickbacks can be spotted through effective management supervision. The manager should watch for a supplier whose products seem to be favored by the person doing the purchasing. The best protection is to ensure that the purchasing and receiving functions are separated and that proper receiving controls are implemented and practiced. Receiving will be discussed later in this chapter.

Supplier Services

Liquor, wine, and beer producers may be allowed in some jurisdictions to provide certain useful services such as supplying an operator with blank purchase orders, bin cards, and other control forms (the use of which will be discussed later). These "free" forms can save an operator money because they help control the purchase, storage, and use of alcoholic beverages.

In some cases, a wine supplier may be useful in helping create wine menus or lists, in training wine service employees, in providing sales and promotion suggestions, and in other matters.

Purpose of purchasing

A beverage operator should not, however, be unnecessarily influenced to favor a particular producer or supplier. Instead, purchasing should serve the purpose of buying the products that, at a reasonable price, will also satisfy the market—that is, the bar's customers.

Other Considerations

Other questions or considerations in purchasing from a particular supplier include the following:

1. What is the frequency of delivery? A supplier that is prepared to deliver daily, even though orders are normally placed less frequently, allows the operator to carry less in inventory and still obtain needed supplies in an emergency.

2. How large a variety of products is offered by the supplier? A supplier with a large and varied inventory is of more use to an operator than a specialist supplier with a limited inventory.

Problem of beer refrigeration

3. For beer supply in particular, does the supplier have a refrigerated warehouse and refrigerated delivery vehicles? It may be a good idea to visit the supplier's warehouse to see how beer and wine are stored (for example, are corked wine bottles stored on their sides?).

4. Where is the supplier's location? If the supplier is remote from the beverage operation, how will this distance affect such things as delivery times? Will travel time and weather affect the product's quality?

5. Does the supplier offer other bar supplies, such as carbonated drinks and drink mixes?

6. What are minimum quantities that must be ordered at any one time?

7. What are the supplier's credit terms?

Order-taker or sales person?

8. Is the supplier's representative an order-taker or a sales person? With the former, an order is simply processed; with the latter, an operator can obtain advice and counsel about products offered.

9. Does the supplier deliver as promised? Undelivered products can translate into lost profits.

Premium and Nonpremium Liquor

In purchasing liquor, the major decision to be made involves the premium and nonpremium liquor brands to be carried.

Most bars serve a house brand (sometimes known as "well" liquor) to customers who do not specify a particular brand but merely the generic type of drink desired (for example, a scotch). On the other hand, premium or "call" liquor refers to specific brand names, such as Chivas Regal scotch.

House or generic brands

Well Liquor

Well liquors are usually the largest-selling items of the basic brands of liquor (rye, gin, rum, scotch, vodka, and bourbon) in a typical beverage operation.

Since they usually provide the best (lowest) cost to the operator, they are also the cheapest for the customer to buy. And since they are generally served with other ingredients, such as a soft drink or other mixer, little taste discrimination by the consumer is possible.

Well liquors are low cost

Despite the fact that a purchaser should seek the best possible price bargain with well liquors, however, some discernment may be needed, since distillers do sometimes produce brands that are simply unacceptable, and since there is a limit to what the customer should be expected to tolerate.

In other words, a purchaser should not purchase Rotgut Rum just because it is 10 cents less per bottle than better brands. Where the government controls the purchase and distribution of liquor, such unacceptable brands are less likely to be available.

A purchaser should select well brands that offer value for money and should stay with those brands for drink consistency. By obtaining a slightly higher-quality product at slightly more money, the purchaser need not pay an appreciably higher cost per drink. For example, consider two well liquors, one costing $10, and the other $9 per bottle, from each of which an operator can obtain 35 drinks per bottle. On the $10 bottle, the cost per drink would be $0.2857; and on the $9 bottle, it would be $0.2571. Thus, the difference is less than 3 cents per drink.

Select value for money

Call Liquor

In the case of premium or call liquor, there is less control over cost, since an operator generally has to carry the brands that customers regularly ask for. Their selling prices will be dictated primarily by what the customer is prepared to pay. And since an operator cannot substitute cheaper brands for call brands, liquor cost cannot be reduced as it can through selection of a bargain in well liquor. However, customers expect to pay more for premium brands.

Rule of thumb

A rule of thumb with call liquors, including liqueurs, is that if it sells it should be carried in inventory; otherwise, it should not. An inventory of unsold call liquors and liqueurs represents money tied up and not earning any income. One good inventory operating method involves never adding a new product without deleting an old one.

It is impossible for most bars to offer every liquor available on the market. At times an operator will be asked for brands not carried. The best that can be done under the circumstances is to offer the closest alternative available. Customers understand that they will not necessarily find their favorite brands in a particular bar. By offering them an alternative (but not substituting it without first asking the customer), an operator will probably keep their patronage.

Sell call brands as house brands

If some type of call liquor is tied up and is just not moving, it might be a good idea to sell this as house or well liquor. At least that way, even if the liquor costs the operator a little more per drink than normal well liquor, money from dead inventory will be freed up.

Since the same selling flexibility is not true of liqueurs, an operator should invest in them as part of inventory only if it is clear that customers want them.

One bar marketing device is to put strict limits on the number of brands carried, and to print a list of those limited brands offered. Most customers will then choose from the list, and the problem of customers' having an open-ended choice disappears.

What to carry depends on the type of bar, the volume of business, the type of clientele, the cash available for investment in inventory, and the customers' preferences over time.

Cost per Ounce

Small difference in cost

The difference in cost price between well and call liquors is not large per drink, but it could amount to a significant difference in total liquor cost if only premium or call brands were served at all times at the well brand's selling price.

Where the government controls the distribution of alcoholic beverages, the price will be the same in every store the government controls. In other jurisdictions, it often pays to shop around to find the best deal on the brands wanted.

In some jurisdictions, quantity discounts (for example, for case lots) are available; these involve sale of the product at a reduced price per bottle from the normal list price. In other jurisdictions, discounts are illegal or may only be allowed if the bill is paid within a certain number of days. In still other situations, a purchaser may have to pay a premium over the list price if less than a full case is ordered.

However, reduced prices—particularly on beer and wine—may indicate a lack of freshness. Question the motive behind such reduced prices. Distilled spirits do not deteriorate in freshness.

Regardless of the situation (discount, list, or premium price) a good costing approach, since the price will vary according to container size, is to convert all prices quoted to a per ounce cost before making the final purchase decision. Good cost control begins with knowing what drinks cost. This is most easily established on a cost-per-ounce basis, since it makes comparisons easier between brands and between containers of different sizes. **Convert all prices to ounce cost**

Generally, the larger the container in which liquor is purchased, the lower the cost per ounce. This is not always so, however, providing another reason to convert the entire container (bottle) cost to a per ounce cost before making the purchasing decision.

Cost per ounce is important for decision making, but it may not be the only factor to consider. Other significant factors include volume of business and availability of a container size that is convenient for pouring. The quantity that an operator is required to buy to obtain desirable savings might necessitate a considerable investment in inventory that may not be used up for several months, or even longer. A purchaser must therefore consider such matters as the resulting loss of interest on money that could otherwise be left in the bank, before making a final decision in such situations. **Other considerations**

Metric Equivalents

It may be necessary to convert metric volumes to an equivalent ounce size. The following table can be used as a guide for distilled spirits:

| | Ounce equivalent | |
Metric size	U.S.	Canada
1.75 liters	59.2	61.6
1 liter	33.8	35.2
750 milliliters	25.4	26.4
500 milliliters	16.9	17.6
200 milliliters	6.8	7.0
50 milliliters	1.7	1.8

Conversion table

For wine bottles, the following table can be used:

		Ounce equivalent	
	Metric size	U.S.	Canada
Conversion table	4 liters	134.8	140.8
	3 liters	101.0	105.6
	1.5 liters	50.7	52.8
	1 liter	33.8	35.2
	750 milliliters	25.4	26.4
	375 milliliters	12.7	13.2
	187 milliliters	6.3	6.6
	100 milliliters	3.4	3.5

ORDERING

A typical bar orders liquor, beer, and wine every week. The biggest decision is about how much to order each week.

For items used in quantity, about 10 days' supply should be on hand after each order is received. Such items are usually ordered in case lots.

For slow-moving items, quantities may be ordered in multiples of bottles—unless the supplier refuses to break open cases, at which point an operator may have to order a full case of an item that may take a year to sell.

Split cases

Alternatively, the supplier may be willing to sell a split case, or a case of several different brands totaling up to a normal case of, say, 12 bottles. In such situations, an operator may or may not be able to benefit from a case price for the 12 bottles.

How Much to Order?

One of the problems in beverage purchase control involves figuring out (without having to take a physical inventory of what is on hand) how much of each product to purchase to carry the bar through until the next order date.

Using perpetual inventory cards

One of the easiest ways to control this situation is to use a system of storeroom perpetual inventory cards. From each card (one for each type and size of product carried in stock), the operator can quickly read what is on hand at any time.

Since each card can also have recorded on it the maximum quantity normally carried of that product, the order quantity is the amount required to increase the present stock to the maximum level, allowing (if necessary) a safety margin for any time delay between ordering and receiving the goods. (Perpetual inventory cards and their use in inventory control were discussed in detail in chapter 3).

It is desirable to develop the ordering system into as precise a mechanism as possible. Liquor is expensive, and when too much is purchased and is sitting idle on a shelf, the money that paid for it is not earning a profit elsewhere. This is an example of an opportunity cost (discussed in chapter 1).

A larger inventory requires more space, more paperwork, and more security, and there may be a problem with deterioration of quality in beer and some wines; in addition, changing customer tastes may leave the operator with inventory that cannot be sold. If a bar specializes in fine wines, however, it may be necessary to buy high-quality wines in large quantities when they are available; otherwise, that opportunity will disappear.

Unsold inventory

Who Orders?

In a small bar, beverage purchasing and ordering will probably be handled by the owner/manager. In a larger operation, particularly one associated with a restaurant or hotel, the food and beverage purchasing might be centralized in one person who has full-time responsibility for this.

Regardless of the situation, the person who does the purchasing must be familiar with the different brands and types of alcohol. The types and brands required (particularly in the case of wine) are often dictated by the demands of customers or by the market served.

Familiarity with brands

For the typical bar, most consumption will be of beverages of the lower-priced brands or types carried (the house brands), as opposed to those of the call brands. The quantity of each type or brand carried will depend on such factors as frequency of ordering, volume of business, and season of the year.

Specifications (detailed descriptions of quality required) are not generally needed, since, for any particular beverage, there may be only one vendor or agent. In fact, for many beverage products, both quality and price remain constant from one purchase occasion to the next. However, the purchaser should be aware of any quantity discounts, sale items, or other specials that are in effect.

Specifications not needed

Order Form

Where many different items are ordered, a purchase order form is useful, since it helps the person responsible for receiving know what is to be delivered from each supplier and at what prices. Exhibit 3.3 in chapter 3 illustrates such a form. An order form is useful in the following ways:

1. It provides the receiver with data for checking deliveries.
2. It provides the accountant with data for checking invoices.

3. It minimizes uncertainty and/or potential misunderstandings between the bar operator and the supplier.

Nonalcoholic Beverages and Other Bar Items

In many cases, the purchase of nonalcoholic beverages to be used in a bar is similar to the purchase of alcoholic drinks. A decision must be made about how many varieties of soft drinks, juices, and mixes (and possibly other nonalcoholic drinks such as coffee, tea, and milk) to carry.

Type of container   A further decision in the case of soft drinks may have to be made as to whether to purchase them by the can, by the bottle, or by the dispensing container. In general, canned and bottled soft drinks offer less profit but more convenience.

Brand Loyalty

Most drinkers of alcoholic beverages who feel a loyalty to a particular liquor brand do not generally have the same loyalty to the soft drink that they may prefer as a mixer. If quality and customer acceptance among soft drink brands is similar, it pays to shop around for the best price. In some cases, by promoting certain brands of soft drink to be used in the bar, an operator may in return obtain a promotional discount from the supplier.

Quality versus price   Generally speaking, the quality and price of soft drinks, like the quality and price of liquor, go hand in hand: the higher the price, the higher the quality, in most situations. For example, a less expensive soft drink may have artificial flavoring or may not hold the carbon dioxide (the gas that gives soft drinks their effervescence) for as long once the container is opened.

Dispensing Equipment

In some cases, the soft-drink supplier may agree to install and maintain the appropriate soft-drink dispensing equipment free, for as long as the operator uses the supplier's particular brands of soft drink. There is nothing wrong with this, as long as the quality satisfies the operator's and the customers' expectations, and as long as the price paid for the product is reasonable in view of the fact that "free" equipment is being used.

Installment purchasing   In some cases, where the equipment is not offered free, an operator may be allowed to purchase the equipment on an installment basis; the cost of the equipment is then added, over a number of years, to the cost of the soft-drink products.

Whenever such an arrangement for the use of equipment is made—

either free or on an installment basis—ascertain how well the distributor will maintain the equipment, and ask for details about the supplier's delivery schedule, ordering procedures, and minimum order requirements (if any).

On some occasions, the choice between suppliers is dictated by the services the supplier provides—such as the "free" dispensing equipment for soft drinks mentioned earlier. Suppliers may also offer free straws, stirrers, coasters, and similar items—sometimes imprinted with their advertising logo. It is a question of management policy whether to accept this form of supplier advertising.

Other free supplies

Ordering and Receiving Nonalcoholic Beverages

In some jurisdictions, ordering and delivery of nonalcoholic beverages may be easier than ordering and delivery of alcoholic drinks, since the operator need not deal with a government agency that dictates its policies and procedures. For the same reason, an operator will probably have more freedom with regard to credit terms and methods of payment.

The main decision boils down to how much to order. Generally, for soft drinks a three- to five-day stock is adequate, although in the case of some perishable products used in bars (such as milk and cream) daily ordering may be advisable.

How much to order?

Most establishments do not try to maintain stringent controls over the purchase and use of nonalcoholic beverages, since controlling them can sometimes cost more than can be saved as a result of the measures. Indeed, employees are often permitted to drink these items for free (a good idea if it stops them from drinking the establishment's alcoholic beverages!!).

Ideally, nonalcoholic beverages should be treated (from a control point of view) in the same way as are alcoholic beverages, but the practical realities of the situation and the cost of controls often dictate otherwise.

One important consideration is to ensure that any deposits paid on returnable empty containers are properly accounted for so that money is not lost on empty containers not returned to the supplier for credit.

Deposits on containers

Other Bar Supplies

Most bars must buy various other supplies such as napkins, stir sticks, limes, lemons, oranges, cocktail onions, olives, and maraschino cherries. These are commonly available from many suppliers; and where the law allows, alcoholic beverage suppliers may offer some of these nonperishable products at a very reasonable price (since the supplier can offer a quantity discount price that might not be available from the local grocery

Deterioration of perishables

dealer), or they may be willing to sell them at little or no profit in order to retain the establishment's alcoholic beverage business.

The most important problem to be aware of in purchasing perishables (milk, cream, and fresh fruit) is deterioration. Buy as frequently as is practical to avoid loss from spoilage. Even nonperishables (such as unopened containers of olives, cherries, and cocktail onions) will not remain fresh once the container is opened. Buying large containers may reduce the cost per item of these products, but the cost saving will disappear if half the contents have to be thrown away because of subsequent deterioration.

RECEIVING

In receiving, it is common practice to break down the goods received into three separate categories: beer, wine, and liquor. Any nonalcoholic beverages received, such as soft drinks, are generally included in the liquor category, since the revenue derived from drinks in which such nonalcoholic beverages are used is generally liquor revenue.

Reason for separating beer, wine, and liquor

The reason for the breakdown into three basic categories is that, since the markup for each category is generally quite different, distortions, false assumptions, and erroneous decisions could result if cost analysis were not made by category. Exhibit 7.1 illustrates this. Notice that, from month 1 to month 2, the overall beverage cost has declined from 36.6 percent to 36.3 percent. On the surface, this might seem desirable. However, analysis of the cost percent by category shows that, in each case, the cost percent has increased, despite the decline in the overall percent. The decline in the overall percent was caused solely by a change in the sales mix. There has been a major shift in month 2 in the amount of beer sold relative to wine (with little change in liquor revenue). Since beer has a lower cost percent than wine, this shift has influenced the overall percent downward even though the cost percent of all three categories has gone up. Only analysis by category will show the underlying trend. Again, as with food cost percentages, beverage cost percentages by themselves can be misleading. For example, in exhibit 7.1, despite the decline in overall cost percent from month 1 to month 2, the gross profit has also gone down from $45,800 to $45,000—and this is not normally a desirable trend.

Standard practices in beverage receiving

Since alcoholic beverages are prone to "evaporation" or removal by unauthorized persons, it is extremely important that the person responsible for receiving and checking be there at the moment of delivery. It may be necessary to instruct suppliers to deliver only between limited hours when a person who combines this beverage-receiving function with some other job is available.

EXHIBIT 7.1. Sales Mix Cost Analysis by Category

	Month 1			Month 2		
	Cost	Revenue	Percent	Cost	Revenue	Percent
Beer	$ 2,400	$ 6,100	39.3%	$ 4,800	$12,100	39.7%
Wine	11,800	24,000	49.2	8,200	16,600	49.4
Liquor	12,200	42,100	29.0	12,600	41,900	30.1
Totals	$26,400	$72,200		$25,600	$70,600	
Overall cost	$\dfrac{\$26,400}{\$72,200} \times 100 = 36.6\%$			$\dfrac{\$25,600}{\$70,600} \times 100 = 36.3\%$		
Gross profit	$\$72,200 - \$26,400 = \$45,800$			$\$70,600 - \$25,600 = \$45,000$		

The receiver should ensure that—

Receiver responsibilities

1. The quantities received agree with the quantities listed on the order form and with the invoice. This requires counting all bottles or other types of container, or counting the number of cases where items have been ordered in case lots. In the latter event, cases should be opened to ensure no bottles have been removed prior to delivery. Alternatively, cases should be weighed where the correct full weight of the case is known. If bottles are sealed, then spot checks should be carried out to ensure seals are not broken.

2. Prices on the invoice agree with prices listed on the order form.

3. The quality of the product is checked (proof of liquor, vintages of wines, freshness of keg beer) where this type of check is appropriate.

Use of credit memorandum

In the event that bottles have been broken prior to receipt, that the wrong product has been delivered, or that items have been short-shipped, then a credit memorandum (see exhibit 3.8) should be prepared by the receiver. If an invoice does not accompany the shipment, then a memorandum invoice should be prepared by the receiver using actual quantities delivered and obtaining pricing information from the order form.

Once all receiving checks have been carried out, each invoice should be stamped with the receiving stamp (see exhibit 3.7) and initialled in the appropriate places. Finally, the beverages should be immediately moved to the locked storeroom.

Beverage Receiving Report

Use of daily receiving report

The final step in the receiving process is the completion, from invoices, of the beverage receiving report. A sample daily beverage receiving report is illustrated in exhibit 7.2. Such a daily report would be used by a large establishment where frequent deliveries, because of the volume of sales, were necessary. In establishments where both food and beverage receiving is the combined responsibility of one person, it might be appropriate to have the daily food receiving report also designed to list daily beverage deliveries. Such a form is illustrated in exhibit 4.4. In either case, the daily beverage totals would be subsequently transferred to the beverage receiving summary form illustrated in exhibit 7.3.

Bypassing daily receiving report

In small establishments, where deliveries are not frequent and, in some cases, might be limited to once or twice a week, it would not be

EXHIBIT 7.2. Sample Daily Beverage Receiving Report

Date___March 2___

Supplier	Beer	Wine	Liquor	Invoice total
Pacific Brewers	$114.60			$ 114.60
Vintage Imports		$125.90		125.90
J. & H. Agency		75.40	$275.48	350.88
Total purchases	$315.95	$461.80	$893.21	$1,670.96

necessary to have both a daily and a summary report. All delivery cost information could be listed directly on the summary form to be later totaled at the end of the control period (a week, ten days, or a month, depending on the policy of the individual establishment).

How this beverage purchase cost information can be used to aid in beverage storeroom control will be explained later in this chapter.

EXHIBIT 7.3. Beverage Receiving Summary Form

Period___March 1-7___

Date	Beer	Wine	Liquor	Total
March 1	$ 72.35		$ 114.10	$ 186.45
2	315.95	$461.80	893.21	1,670.96
Total purchases for period	$1,615.60	$985.46	$2,756.48	$5,357.54

STOREROOM CONTROL

Centralizing beverage storage

In a single bar operation, the beverage storeroom is best located adjacent to the bar. In a food and beverage operation, the beverage storeroom might be part of the food storeroom, although this is not recommended. A separate beverage storeroom, because of the "perishable" nature of the product, would be preferable. In a large hotel with a number of different bars, each bar may have its own small storeroom in addition to the main storeroom. In this case, it is strongly recommended that, for control purposes, all beverage purchases are still routed through the main storeroom before any of the products are distributed to the individual bar storerooms. In some situations, it is not possible to centralize beverage storage. For example, in the case of keg beer that must be kept refrigerated, the storage location may have to be separate from other products. Also, quality wines should be maintained at lower than normal temperatures (about 55°F or 13°C for red and about 40°F or 5°C for white). If properly cooled storage cannot be provided for these wines in the liquor storeroom, then an area elsewhere may have to be set aside for them.

Special requirements for beer and wine

Limited access to storeroom

Regardless of the number and type of beverage storage areas, only one person should have access to them. In a small operation, this might be the bar owner or manager. In a larger operation, it might be the responsibility of the food storekeeper to handle also beverage storeroom responsibilities. In a very large operation, the volume of business might require a separate beverage storekeeper. In order to have control and define responsibility for losses if they occur, only one person should have a key. However, for emergency situations, the pass key of the manager on duty should also open the beverage storeroom door.

Perpetual Inventory Cards and Requisitions

Use of perpetual inventory cards

In chapter three, a system of storeroom control using perpetual inventory cards and requisitions was covered. This material is very relevant to beverages since all beverage purchases should be recorded by item on perpetual inventory cards as the items are placed in storage. Items should be issued only by properly authorized requisitions. First-in/first-out pricing should be used on requisitions. Exhibit 7.4 illustrates a specialized type of beverage requisition that could be used with column headings describing the size of bottle requisitioned, thus reducing the amount of writing required.

EXHIBIT 7.4. Sample Specialized Beverage Requisition Form

Bar _____   Date _____

Bin no.	Item	On hand	Ordered	1.75 liters	1.0 liter	0.75 liter	0.5 liter	0.375 liter	0.25 liter	Unit cost	Total cost

Size

Ordered by _____   Completed by _____

Multibar perpetual inventory card

In situations where an establishment has a number of bars, each requisitioning its own requirements from storage, a specially designed perpetual inventory card is useful. This card will show, for each requisition recorded, the particular bar to which the items were transferred. Exhibit 7.5 is an illustration of such a perpetual inventory card.

Use of bin cards

If, for control purposes, the accounting office decides to record invoice and requisition information on the cards and to cost out requisitions, the beverage storekeeper in that case, for his own purposes, might find it useful to maintain a bin card for each item. A bin card is a simplified version of the perpetual inventory card but without cost information. These bin cards can also be useful when stocktaking if the inventory count of an item does not agree with its related perpetual inventory card. In such a case, comparison of the bin and inventory card In and Out figures might quickly reveal the cause of the difference.

Par Stock

Par stock as control aid

To aid in knowing how much of each item to requisition each day, the bar or bars should be provided with a par stock list. The list shows the person responsible for requisitioning how many of each item should be on hand to start each day's business. These par stock lists must be changed when necessary (for example, if the customers' drinking habits change, as is sometimes the case with a change of season). The lists may also have to be adjusted on any particular day if there is a special event, or for some other reason. Accounting-office personnel should verify from time to time that the par stock lists are being adhered to.

Full-bottle Replacement

Empty bottles with requisitions

It is not usually possible for a bar to replenish its stock each day exactly to the par stock list since there may be partly used bottles in the bar. Therefore, a system of full-bottle requisitioning for each empty bottle on hand is often used. Empty bottles should be returned to the storeroom with the requisitions. These empty bottles should then be destroyed (unless, of course, a refundable deposit is available from the supplier). Some establishments issue full bottles with coding devices that are difficult or impossible to duplicate. Obviously, empty bottles returned for replacement should still have this code on them. This control does not prevent a bartender from bringing in his own privately purchased bottles, selling the contents, not recording the revenue, and pocketing the cash. However, it does reduce that possibility, since spot checks by management will show whether or not all bottles at the bar are properly coded. In that case, management must be alert to a bartender transferring the contents of his

EXHIBIT 7.5. Perpetual Inventory Card for Establishment with Multiple Bars

Item _____   Supplier _____   Tel # _____
Minimum _____   Supplier _____   Tel # _____
Maximum _____   Supplier _____   Tel # _____

Date	In	Out				Balance	Requisition cost information
		Main bar	Bar #1	Bar #2	Bar #3		

privately purchased bottle to an empty, coded one before selling the liquor and pocketing the cash.

Storeroom Inventory Reconciliation

Taking storeroom inventory

Each day, the accounting office should verify that the invoices for beverage purchases have been properly recorded on the daily beverage receiving report (exhibit 7.2) and that each day's total figures are properly transferred to the beverage receiving summary (exhibit 7.3). At the end of each beverage storeroom control period (a week, ten days, or at month-end, depending on each establishment's policy), an actual count of each item in inventory should be taken. The section in chapter 4 concerning the food storeroom describes the procedures for taking food inventory. These procedures would apply equally well to beverage inventory, particularly to reconciling differences between the perpetual inventory card and actual count figures.

Reconciling inventory figures

Once inventory taking has been completed, the final figures for the period can be recorded on the beverage storeroom inventory reconciliation form illustrated in exhibit 7.6. On this form, the Opening Inventory figure is the actual inventory from the previous period. The Purchases for Period amount is transferred from the beverage receiving summary report for that period (see exhibit 7.3). The Requisitions for Period figure is simply the total cost information from all relevant requisitions completed for that period. Opening Inventory plus Purchases for Period less Requisitions for Period provides the Closing Inventory amount. This can be compared with the Actual Inventory for the end of the period. Minor differences between the two sets of figures can be expected because the item cost figures taken from invoiced amounts are rounded to the nearest cent on the perpetual inventory cards and requisitions. Differences of more than a few dollars should be investigated to try to determine the cause.

Complete control of storeroom

With this type of reconciliation in effect, one can be sure that there is good control over the beverage storeroom. The other area of beverage cost control concerns the items once they are issued from the storeroom. This area of bar control will be discussed in the next chapter.

Inventory Turnover

Inventory at the bar

It is appropriate at this point, since we have been discussing beverage storeroom inventory control, to conclude with inventory turnover. As far as beverage inventory is concerned, we have only covered the inventory in the storeroom. At the end of each accounting period, we must include in total inventory the value of all items in each of the bars in the establishment. At the bar, there will be an inventory of items previously requisi-

EXHIBIT 7.6. Beverage Storeroom Inventory Reconciliation Form

Period ___March 1–7___

	Beer	Wine	Liquor	Total
Opening inventory	$ 482.80	$ 611.58	$1,319.20	$2,413.58
Add: Purchases for period	1,615.60	985.46	2,756.48	5,357.54
Deduct: Requisitions for period	1,432.20	1,032.10	2,576.36	5,040.66
Closing inventory	$ 666.20	$564.94	$1,499.32	$2,730.46
Actual inventory	665.14	566.70	1,496.50	2,728.34
Difference	($ 1.06)	$ 1.76	($ 2.82)	($ 2.12)

Beverage inventory turnover rate

tioned from the storeroom that have not yet been used up. Those items should be inventoried and costed. It is normal practice to estimate part bottles in tenths, rather than to spend time measuring contents in exact ounces or, in metric bottles, in centiliters. For example, a half-full bottle would be 0.5. Once all inventory, both in the storeroom and at the bar, has been costed, the inventory turnover for the period can be calculated. The equation for this is the same as that illustrated at the end of chapter 4 for food inventory turnover, except that we substitute beverage inventory for food inventory. The turnover rate in a typical bar will normally range from one half to one time a month, or from six to twelve times a year. Each bar should establish its own standard and then compare the actual turnover with this standard to discern any major deviations.

SUMMARY

For most bar operations, the purchasing of alcoholic beverages is not as big a problem as the purchasing of food items can sometimes be for a restaurant. For example, it is possible to route all beverage purchases through a controlled beverage storeroom before issuing them to the bar(s).

Where the government distributes alcoholic beverages, this is known as a "control" or "monopoly" situation. Where the government licenses others to handle this, it is known as a license or open situation. It is up to the purchaser of alcoholic beverages to be familiar with all the necessary legal requirements and distribution channels in the jurisdiction where the establishment is located. In situations where there is a choice of suppliers, it is important for a purchaser to consider how many different purchase sources are desirable to deal with. The primary objective is to obtain the lowest overall cost on all products purchased.

Purchasing should be turned into a once-a-week routine, in order to reduce the demands on time and paperwork processing. Where the purchasing procedures are delegated to nonmanagement personnel, management should be alert to the possibility of kickbacks.

In selecting suppliers, the purchaser should pose a number of questions related to the particular operation to be supplied.

This chapter differentiated between the purchase of premium (or call) brands and nonpremium (or house or well) brands and suggested that, in comparisons of prices between products, a cost-per-ounce basis should be used.

In ordering beverages perpetual inventory cards are useful for indicating how much of each product to order so as to minimize the amount of money tied up in inventory. An order form for summarizing purchase requirements is desirable.

In receiving, alcoholic beverages are usually summarized and controlled by means of a breakdown into three major categories: beer, wine, and liquor. The reason for this breakdown is that each category generally has a different markup or cost percent; without separate analysis, hidden sales mix charges among the three would not be apparent.

As beverages are received, they should be checked to ensure that the quantities delivered agree with the quantities ordered and invoiced. Quoted prices should also be verified against invoiced prices. Where necessary, quality should also be checked. A beverage receiving report should be completed by transferring invoice cost information by category to the receiving report form. At the end of each day, column totals from the receiving report can be recorded on the receiving report summary.

In the storeroom, beverages can be controlled by using a system of perpetual inventory cards (one for each type or brand carried in stock) and requisitions. Requisitions should be costed on a first-in/first-out basis. A par stock listing should be maintained at each bar so that the quantity of any item requisitioned each day will be sufficient to bring the bar's stock back up to this par level. Each bottle requisitioned should be accompanied by an empty bottle. In some establishments, full bottles issued are coded to help reduce the possibility of bartenders bringing in their own bottles, selling the contents, and pocketing the cash.

At the end of each period, a storeroom reconciliation should be completed. This requires taking a complete inventory of the storeroom and a reconciliation of that actual inventory by category with the book or closing inventory. The closing inventory is calculated as follows:

Opening inventory + Purchases – Requisitions

Finally, inventory turnover of total inventory (storeroom plus what is in open stock at the bar) can be calculated. Normally, inventory turnover for the typical bar will vary from one half to one time per month.

DISCUSSION QUESTIONS

1. In what ways is beverage purchasing easier than food purchasing?

2. Discuss the difference between a control or monopoly situation and a license or open situation for the distribution of alcoholic beverages.

3. Why, in an open situation where there are several suppliers for

the same products, may there not be pricing competition for some of those products?

4. Discuss the pros and cons of having only one or two suppliers for alcoholic beverage needs versus having many suppliers.

5. Explain how kickbacks can occur in liquor purchasing and how they can be controlled.

6. List five factors to consider (other than price) when deciding whether or not to use a particular supplier.

7. Differentiate between well or house liquor and premium or call liquor.

8. Why is it useful to price liquor products on a cost-per-ounce basis? How is cost per ounce calculated?

9. List two factors that you might consider, other than cost, when deciding whether or not to buy a particular product.

10. What factors dictate the quantity of each type or brand of liquor to be carried?

11. What basic column headings are needed on a liquor order form, and what three purposes does this form serve?

12. Why might it not be a good idea to buy low-cost carbonated beverages (soft drinks)?

13. What factors must be considered in buying fresh products (for example, dairy items and fruit) for a bar?

14. In beverage purchasing, what items should be checked when goods are received?

15. Explain how the beverage receiving report is completed.

16. What is par stock in a bar operation?

17. Explain the system of full-bottle replacement. Why are full bottles sometimes coded before being issued from the storeroom to the bar?

18. In reconciling the storeroom inventory at the end of a period, how is the closing inventory calculated?

19. What is the inventory turnover rate in a typical bar operation, and how is it calculated?

PROBLEMS

7-1. A cocktail lounge has the following revenue and cost percent figures for two successive months:

	Month 1		Month 2	
	Revenue	Cost	Revenue	Cost
Beer	$10,212	45%	$12,815	50%
Wine	8,405	60	8,214	65
Liquor	48,622	30	51,675	29

a. Calculate, for each month, the overall beverage cost percent and comment about the changes that have occurred from one month to the next.

b. Calculate the gross profit for each month and comment.

7-2. During a month, the following purchases of a certain brand of liquor were made:

January 8	5 cases @ $72.40 per case
January 15	5 cases @ $72.80 per case
January 22	4 cases @ $70.25 per case
January 29	6 cases @ $71.12 per case

At the beginning of January, there were sixty-three bottles on hand at a value of $6.10 each. Note that each case purchased contains twelve bottles. During the month, the following quantities were requisitioned by the bar:

Week ending January 7	58 bottles
Week ending January 14	56 bottles
Week ending January 21	51 bottles
Week ending January 28	53 bottles

Using the first-in/first-out costing method, and rounding figures to the nearest cent, calculate:

a. the total dollar cost that would have appeared on requisitions for each of the four weeks.

b. the inventory value of this brand in the storeroom at the beginning of January, assuming that no bottles were issued on January 28, but that twelve bottles were issued on the twenty-ninth and ten on the thirtieth.

7-3. After beverages are received by the receiver, they are transferred to the storekeeper who records the quantities received on the respective perpetual inventory cards. As items are requisitioned, the storekeeper records the issues on the related cards. At the end of each month, he lists, from the cards, the balance on hand for each type or brand, along with the cost price. The accounting office subsequently uses this inventory list as a check against the closing inventory figure of its beverage storeroom inventory reconciliation form. Discuss the weaknesses of this system. How would you change the system to improve control?

7-4. For a bar, for a weekly control period, you have the following information. Purchases: liquor $825.08, beer $309.18, and wine $585.80. Issues: liquor $909.48, beer $53.90, and wine $378.65. Opening inventory: liquor $2,032.48, beer $205.06, and wine $803.56. Actual inventory: liquor $1,937.44, beer $461.20, and wine $1,010.68. Reconcile the beverage storeroom inventory, and state whether or not you would be satisfied with the results.

7-5. A hotel has a weekly cycle for control of its bar storeroom inventory. On July 1, the opening inventory was liquor $4,822.95, beer $1,233.18, and wine $787.50. For the period July 1–6 purchases were: liquor $1,016.80, beer $412.10, and wine $349.02. On July 7, a purchase was received broken down as follows: liquor $328.02, beer $31.12, and wine $303.99. For the first six days of the same week, issues were: liquor $862.12, beer $361.04, and wine $703.88. On July 7, additional requisitions were processed: liquor $296.42, beer $121.15, and wine $187.46. The actual closing inventory on July 7 was: liquor $5,027.70, beer $1,190.55 and wine $531.87. Prepare the storeroom inventory reconciliation by category and in total for that week. Would you be satisfied with the results?

7-6. A hotel's cocktail bar had an opening total beverage inventory on June 1 of $2,008.10, and, on June 30, total inventory was $1,908.46. June beverage revenue totalled $8,214.40, and the bar that month operated at a cost of sales of 30.4 percent.

   a. Calculate the bar's inventory turnover rate for June.
   b. Would you consider this acceptable under normal circumstances? Explain.

7-7. A restaurant owner cannot afford the services of a storekeeper. He has made the chef responsible for receiving and storage of food. The dining room manager receives and stores alcoholic beverages, as well as issuing daily requirements to the dining room's service bar and managing the dining room operation. The dining room is generally quite busy. Food revenue is quite satisfactory, but beverage revenue compared to food revenue seems lower than industry figures indicate it should be for that type of dining room. However, the beverage cost percent seems to be in line with industry figures. The owner cannot be at the dining room during all the meal periods since he has to visit other restaurants he owns. His office is at one of the other restaurants and it is there that he does his paper work. Explain to the owner what you think might be the cause of the apparent shortage of beverage revenue. What would you suggest he do (without hiring extra labor) to correct the situation?

Beverage Cost Control: The Bar

⑧

Objectives

After studying this chapter, the reader should be able to do the following:

- List at least four ways in which theft or fraud can occur in a bar.
- Discuss the use of requisitions as the sole basis for beverage cost control.
- Discuss necessary practices for effective cost control, such as the use of standard recipes, measuring devices, and the value of a spillage allowance.
- Briefly discuss the standard cost control method, and, given appropriate information, solve problems using this method.
- Briefly discuss the standard revenue control method and, given appropriate information, solve problems using this method.
- Explain and use the weighted average method for calculating standard revenue per bottle.
- Briefly discuss the quantity control method, and, given appropriate information, solve problems using this method.
- Discuss banquet liquor control, and solve problems relating to this.
- Discuss the pros and cons of using automatic dispensing equipment for alcoholic beverages, and list the questions that should be asked before investing in this type of equipment.

METHODS OF THEFT OR FRAUD

Even though control of the beverage storeroom is relatively easy using the procedures outlined in the previous chapter, the same can not be said of bar cost control. This is particularly true where the bartender is also responsible for handling cash from sales. Some of the methods of theft or fraud that can be used by dishonest bar personnel include:

Loss from underpoured drinks

1. Underpouring drinks by, let us say, one-eighth the normal measure, failing to record the sale of each eighth drink, and pocketing the cash. Using a personal measuring device that is slightly smaller than the one normally used by the establishment is one way for the bartender to hide this dishonest practice.

2. Bringing in personally purchased bottles, selling the contents, not recording the revenue, and pocketing the cash.

3. Diluting liquor and pocketing the cash from the additional sales.

Substituting full-bottle sales for individual drinks

4. Failing to record the revenue from individual drinks until they add up to the normal number of drinks from a full bottle, then recording the sale as a full-bottle sale (since this would normally have a lower selling price than the total of the individual drinks), and pocketing the difference in cash.

5. Selling drinks, recording them as spilled or complimentary, and pocketing the cash.

6. Substituting a low quality liquor for a high quality requested by the customer, and pocketing the difference in selling prices.

7. Overpouring drinks (and underpouring others to compensate) to influence a larger tip.

Overcharging on tabs

8. Overcharging the number of drinks served to a group of people who are running up a tab, or sales check, to be paid later.

9. If automatic drink measuring devices are in use, obtaining the contents for, let us say, five drinks and spreading this content into six glasses, pocketing the cash from the sixth drink.

Watch for "counters"

This is only a partial list of many of the common methods of fraud. Management supervision and an awareness of possible dishonest practices can be a preventive measure. In particular, one should watch for collections of matches, toothpicks, or similar items that a bartender has in his working station; he may be using them as counters to record how much to remove in cash at the end of the shift. In addition to management supervision, some system of accounting control should be instituted.

CONTROL METHODS

This chapter concentrates primarily on control of liquor, rather than beer and wine. The reason is that, in the typical bar, liquor revenue accounts for the majority of sales, and losses or fraud are more likely to occur in this category than in beer or wine. However, the control methods to be described for liquor can be applied, often in a simplified form, to control of beer and wine.

Liquor sales generally highest

Requisitions

Some establishments use the daily requisitions, costed and totaled, as a basis for calculating a daily beverage cost. The total requisition figure is divided by total revenue and multiplied by 100. The resulting cost percentage could vary considerably from day to day, or period to period, unless the total requisition amount were adjusted for part bottles of liquor still in inventory at the bar. Even if this were done, we still only have an actual cost percent, with no knowledge of how it compares with what it should be or with the standard cost percent. This standard can fluctuate daily, depending on the sales mix. Methods that allow us to calculate standard figures for comparison with actual results will be discussed later in this chapter.

Requisition costs unadjusted for bar inventory

Standard Recipes

Regardless of the accounting control method or methods used in a bar, standard recipes must first be established for each type of drink. This is relatively straightforward for the basic types of liquor served, since the recipe is simply a standard portion of liquor (measured by some type of pouring device) to which may be added ice and water or some type of soft drink or mineral water. Where ice is called for, the type (such as shaved or cubed) should be included in the recipe. In the case of cocktails, the recipes will be more extensive, since they must include the quantity of each of two or more ingredients and, where necessary, the garnish to be included, such as a cherry, olive, or orange slice. These food ingredients are normally considered part of beverage cost of sales. In cocktail recipes, the type and quantity of ice to be used and the mixing method are quite important, since they dictate to a degree the quality of the end product and the quantity of liquid that will result when the drink is poured. The size and type of glass for each different type of drink should be included with each recipe since drink appearance is important. A two-ounce martini would not look right in a 5-ounce highball glass.

What to include on standard recipe

Importance of familiarity with recipes

Written copies of all recipes should be kept at the bar. It is important that all bartenders be familiar with all recipes, since consistent quantity and quality of drink are important for customer satisfaction. Finally, with standard recipes, the cost of each drink can be readily calculated. Only by calculating this cost can selling prices that will yield an appropriate cost percent or gross profit be determined. A typical drink recipe is illustrated in exhibit 8.1.

Measuring Devices

Shot glasses and jiggers

In no case where cost control is desired should any type of freehand pouring be allowed. To aid bartenders in measuring drink quantities, two basic types of measuring device are normally used: shot glasses and jiggers. The shot glass is generally used for the basic highball drink that the establishment serves, for example, one ounce or one and one-half ounces, or the equivalent in metric measure. The jigger is usually of stainless steel and measures smaller quantities of ingredients (such as one-quarter or one-third ounce, or the equivalent in metric) for cocktails. Some establishments also use mechanical or electronic pouring devices. Many of the electronic pouring and measuring devices can be linked to registers that automatically record each pour as the sale of a drink to aid in revenue control.

Establishing Drink Selling Prices

Consider gross profit in pricing drinks

Normally, drink selling prices are established to yield an overall desired beverage cost percent, in the same way as for food-menu prices. The reader is referred to the last section in chapter 5, where this topic is discussed, since many of the same basic principles apply. In addition, the reader is cautioned to keep in mind that an operation's gross profit is often a better measure of profitability than is the cost percent. This aspect of cost control, relative to food, was covered in chapter 6 and could be applied equally as well to a beverage situation.

Separating Full-Bottle Sales

Full bottles generally have lower mark-up

In some situations, for example room service in a hotel, customers may buy full bottles of liquor from the bar. Similarly, in some jurisdictions, customers are allowed to purchase full bottles for home or off-premise consumption. The price to the customer of the full bottle would normally be considerably less than the price of an equivalent number of drinks purchased individually. In some cases, it would be best to separate the

EXHIBIT 8.1. Drink Recipe

BRANDY ALEXANDER   Recipe no._____25_____

Ingredient	Quantity	Cost	Cost	Cost
House brandy	¾ oz.	$0.15		
Cream de cacao, dark	¾ oz.	0.18		
Cream	3 oz.	0.07		
Total cost		$0.40		
Selling price		$2.00		
Cost percent		20.0%		

Method

Shake all ingredients with small-cubed ice. Pour through strainer
into 5½ oz. champagne glass. Sprinkle with nutmeg.

revenue (and the cost) of such full-bottle sales, since otherwise the cost
percent, and gross profit, of individual drinks would be influenced
downward and not give correct information for proper analysis.

Since the drink lists in many bars can be very extensive, it might be
advantageous to provide bartenders with a price list such as that illustrated in exhibit 8.2.

EXHIBIT 8.2. Liquor Price List for Bartender

Bar_____ Effective date_____

Item	Drink size	Cost Drink	Cost Bottle	Selling price Drink	Selling price Bottle	Cost percent Drink	Cost percent Bottle

Interbar Transfer

Separate individual bar costs and revenues

In establishments with several bars, it is sometimes necessary to transfer beverages from one bar to another. In such cases, an interbar transfer form should be completed so that each bar's costs and revenues can still be analyzed individually. Such a form is illustrated in exhibit 8.3.

EXHIBIT 8.3. Interbar Transfer Form

From _____ Bar				
To _____ Bar		Date _____		
Item	Size	Quantity	Unit cost	Total cost

Ordered by _____   Filled by _____

Spillage Allowance

Some establishments permit a spillage allowance. This allowance acknowledges that it is not practical to expect that the liquor from a bottle can be accounted for down to the last drop. Also, drinks may be wrongly mixed and have to be thrown away, and some overpouring may occur. To compensate, a spillage allowance for each full bottle of liquor used is sometimes permitted. For example, if there were twenty-five standard drinks in a bottle, a spillage allowance of one drink per bottle may be established, and the revenue from only twenty-four is to be accounted for. In this case, revenue would be one twenty-fifth or 4 percent less than would be the case if all twenty-five drinks were accounted for. If a generous spillage allowance is made known to bartenders, they may be tempted to take advantage of it for personal gain. Whether or not a spillage allowance is permitted must be determined according to the policy of each individual establishment.

Effect of spillage allowance on results

STANDARD COST CONTROL

The standard cost control method compares the standard cost for a bar for a period of time with the actual cost for that same period. Where an establishment has more than one bar, the cost information should be kept separate for each bar. The comparison of costs can be in either dollars or percentages. The method assumes that recipes have been properly followed. The actual count of each type of drink sold during the period is multiplied by its recipe or standard cost and by its selling price. The quantity of drinks sold can be tallied up from sales checks or automatically tallied up by the sales or cash register. Exhibit 8.4 illustrates how the total standard cost and the total standard cost percentage are calculated. The actual cost figure for the same period can be calculated by taking the inventory at the bar at the beginning of the period, adding to it the total cost of all beverage storeroom requisitions completed for that bar during the period, and then deducting the value of the inventory in the bar at the end of the period. This figure must be adjusted for any interbar transfers, and also for transfers in from other departments (for example, fresh cream or eggs requisitioned from the kitchen) or transfers out (liquor transferred to the kitchen for cooking).

Use dollars or percentages

Calculation of actual cost

With the standard cost control method, the difference between the two percentages should normally be no greater than one half of one percent. Note that in our case it is 0.4 percent. Any variance greater than one half of one percent should be investigated. Normally, the actual cost would be higher than the standard cost since the standard cost is based on perfect bartending (unless an allowance for errors is built into the recipe costs).

Amount of difference allowed

An advantage of the standard sales control method is that it also allows comparison of the total standard revenue with actual revenue. Total standard revenue is based on the actual count of drinks sold, and, as long as all drinks sold were properly recorded without any pricing or other errors, the two figures should be in agreement. Any large differences between the two figures should be investigated. Also note that, with this method, if any bottles were sold as full bottles for less revenue than would otherwise be the case if that bottle had been sold as individual drinks, then both the cost and revenue figures for those full-bottle sales should be adjusted for in the comparison of standard and actual costs, and standard and actual revenue.

Comparison of standard and actual revenue

Finally, note that, with this control method, for each period (whether it is a day, a week, or a month), we will find that the standard cost percent will change. The reason is that, for each period, we use actual sales quantities, and, unless the sales mix stayed the same for every period (this would be highly unlikely in practice), each period's sales mix will affect the standard cost percent.

Standard cost changes each period

STANDARD REVENUE CONTROL

The standard revenue control method converts the quantity of liquor used, according to inventory records, into standard revenue to be compared

EXHIBIT 8.4. Standard Cost Control Form

Period ____ March 9–16 ____

Drink	Drink cost	Drink selling price	Quantity sold	Total standard cost	Total standard revenue
Scotch, house	$0.32	$1.50	1,430	$ 457.60	$2,145.00
Gin, house	0.25	1.40	1,211	302.75	1,695.40
Rum, house	0.30	1.45	854	256.20	1,238.30
			Totals	$2,436.20	$9,875.40

Standard cost percent $\dfrac{\$2,436.20}{\$9,875.40} \times 100 = 24.7\%$

Actual cost percent $\dfrac{\$2,475.60}{\$9,875.40} \times 100 = 25.1\%$

Difference 0.4%

with actual revenue. The method is not concerned with individual quantities of each type of drink sold for any particular period (as was the case with the standard cost control method already discussed). Instead, it attempts in advance to assign a standard value, or amount of revenue, that each bottle by type of liquor should produce. It assumes that standard recipes and drink sizes are in effect.

Assigning standard revenue to each brand

In the simplest of situations, the standard revenue per bottle for a particular type of liquor can easily be calculated. For example, if 1¼-ounce gin drinks are served and 1-liter (34 U.S. ounces, to the nearest ounce) bottles are used, there are 27 drinks in a bottle of gin (34 divided by 1¼), assuming no spillage allowance. If gin drinks sell for $2.50, standard revenue for each bottle of gin would be:

Calculating standard revenue per bottle

$$27 \times \$1.50 = \$40.50$$

Unfortunately, except in certain specialized situations such as a banquet, the contents of the typical bottle of gin (and of other types of liquor) are not normally dispensed in the same quantities for all drinks served. For example, gin might be served in 1¼-ounce quantities in highballs, in 1¾-ounce quantities in martinis, and in some other quantity in other drinks that contain gin. To resolve this, we can use a weighted average to calculate the standard revenue.

Complications that arise

Weighted Average Method for Individual Bottles

To use the weighted average, we first take a test period in which we tally up all the various kinds of drinks sold that contain gin. Our sales or cash register might well be able to provide us with this information. The test period should be as long as possible (at least a week) to even out peaks and valleys and have a fair representation of the sales mix for drinks containing gin. Let us suppose our test period revealed the following for the five drinks in our bar that contain gin:

Use of test period sales quantities

Drink	Quantity sold
Highball	1,640
Martini	720
Drink #3	120
Drink #4	40
Drink #5	80

The next step is to multiple the quantity of each variety of drink sold by the amount of gin each contains.

Drink	Quantity sold	Gin quantity	Total gin
Highball	1,640	1 ¼ oz.	2,050 oz.
Martini	720	1 ¾ oz.	1,260 oz.
Drink #3	120	1 oz.	120 oz.
Drink #4	40	1 ½ oz.	60 oz.
Drink #5	80	1 ¼ oz.	100 oz.
			3, 590 oz.

Total amount of gin used is therefore 3,590 ounces; thus, if we are using 1-liter bottles, 105.6 bottles (3,590 ounces divided by 34 ounces) would be used.

Next, we must determine the revenue derived for that same period from drinks containing gin:

Drink	Quantity sold	Selling price	Total revenue
Highball	1,640	$1.50	$2,460.00
Martini	720	$2.00	1,440.00
Drink #3	120	$1.75	210.00
Drink #4	40	$1.80	72.00
Drink #5	80	$1.60	128.00
			$4,310.00

The final step is to divide total revenue by number of bottles sold to obtain the standard revenue for each 1-liter bottle of gin:

$$\frac{\$4,310}{105.6} = \$40.81$$

We now run into one more minor problem with the weighted average approach. The martini uses dry vermouth as well as gin, and, in our case, we assigned all of the selling price of $2.00 for the martini to the gin content. This would be acceptable if vermouth were only used in martinis, in which case the standard revenue for each bottle of vermouth used would be zero. However, if any vermouth is sold as an aperitif and/or is used in any other drinks, then we must carry out a weighted average test on the vermouth as we did for gin. With reference to the vermouth used in the martinis, we can assign it a value of zero when calculating our standard revenue for the vermouth bottle. Alternatively, we can give it an arbitrary value — let us say 20 cents for each martini — and adjust our calculation of the standard revenue for gin by changing the martini selling price assigned to gin from $2.00 to $1.80.

Similar calculations would have to be carried out for each type of liquor carried in inventory. Once these calculations have been made, the standard revenue control method is quite simple to use. For each type of liquor, we simply add to the inventory at the bar, at the beginning of the control period (a day, a week, ten days, a month, depending on management policy), the quantity of bottles requisitioned from stores during that period, and then deduct the closing inventory at the bar. Any interbar transfers must be adjusted for. This is illustrated in exhibit 8.5. Note that part bottles are measured in tenths. The quantities used of each type of liquor are multiplied by their standard revenue per bottle, and, finally, total standard revenue is compared with actual revenue. Any difference between the two figures should be no more than 1 percent of standard revenue. In other words, actual revenue should be no more than 1 percent above or 1 percent below standard revenue. In our case, 1 percent of standard revenue of $4,521.96 is $45.22. Our difference is only $21.56, which is quite acceptable. A variance must be expected because standard revenue-per-bottle figures are based on a historic sales mix for each type of liquor used during the test period, and it is highly unlikely in practice that the future actual sales mix for any of the types of liquor sold will be the same. From time to time, various types of liquor could be tested to see if the sales mix has changed considerably. If so, the standard revenue for that type of liquor should be adjusted. For all types of liquor, standard revenue per bottle should be adjusted with each change in season. Also, if individual drink prices are altered, then standard revenues must be recalculated.

Converting bar inventory usage into total standard revenue

Variances to be expected

Weighted Average Method for Full-Bottle Sales

Finally, as was the case with the standard cost method discussed earlier in this chapter, if any full bottles are sold at less than the standard revenue per bottle (and this would normally be the case in practice), then this must be adjusted for in our calculations. One method would be to exclude these bottles from the inventory calculations and deduct the full-bottle revenue from total actual revenue. Alternatively, we can simply adjust the total standard revenue figure to bring it into line with actual revenue, including

Alternative methods for full-bottle sales

EXHIBIT 8.5.   Standard Revenue Control Calculations

Date _____ April 2

Item	Size	Opening inventory	Added per requisitions	Interbar transfers	Total	Closing inventory	Used	Standard revenue per bottle	Total standard revenue
Gin, bar	Q	4.6	12.0		16.6	1.9	14.7	$38.21	$561.69
Vodka, bar	Q	6.1	18.0		24.1	4.2	19.9	40.32	802.37
Scotch, bar	F	2.9	6.0	+ 3.0	11.9	0.2	11.7	46.90	548.73

Total standard revenue	$4,521.96
Total actual revenue	4,500.40
Difference	$ 21.56 –

revenue from full-bottle sales. In other words, if standard revenue per bottle were thirty-five dollars and a full bottle of that liquor were sold at twenty dollars, we simply deduct fifteen dollars from total standard revenue for comparison with total actual revenue.

QUANTITY CONTROL

The quantity control method ignores both dollars of cost and dollars of revenue. It concentrates solely on quantities converted into ounces. It compares the ounces of each type of liquor used according to inventory records with the ounces used according to sales records.

The method can be simply illustrated using just one type of liquor — for example, rum. Suppose a bar served, in addition to rum and mixer, four other drinks containing rum. The following shows the quantity of rum served in each of these five drinks, the quantity of each sold on a certain day according to sales records, and the total amount of rum sold that day (Rum Quantity times Quantity Sold).

Method uses only quantities

Drink	Rum quantity	Quantity sold	Total rum sold
Rum and mixer	1½ oz.	168	252 oz.
Drink #2	1¼ oz.	104	130 oz.
Drink #3	1 oz.	53	53 oz.
Drink #4	1¾ oz.	64	112 oz.
Drink #5	1½ oz.	28	42 oz.
			589 oz.

Calculating total quantity sold in ounces

As can be seen, 589 ounces have been sold. Inventory records for that day show that the opening inventory of rum was 3.5 bottles, that 18 bottles were issued by requisition, that there were no interbar transfers, and that the closing inventory was 4.3 bottles. Assuming that 1-liter (34-ounce) bottles of rum are used, inventory records thus indicate that 585 ounces were used:

$$3.5 + 18.0 - 4.3 = 17.2 \times 34 = 585 \text{ oz.}$$

Calculating quantity used in ounces

The difference between the two figures is 4 ounces. This would normally be considered quite acceptable, particularly since part-bottles are estimated in tenths and a mistake in estimating by one-tenth represents 3.4 ounces in a 1-liter bottle. If management allowed a spillage amount in this

Adjustment for spillage allowance

bar, the inventory-usage figures would have to be adjusted accordingly. For example, if management allowed a 1-ounce spillage per bottle, the 17.2 bottles according to inventory would be multiplied by 33 instead of by 34. This method has been illustrated for only one type of liquor. Some people think that the method would be too time-consuming to extend on a daily basis to the entire inventory, but electronic equipment may resolve this dilemma. Alternatively, since 80 to 90 percent (or more) of all liquor sold in most bars is from the basic house brands of the half dozen most common liquors (bourbon, rye, rum, gin, scotch, and vodka), application of the method could be confined to those six brands, since that is where loss or fraud is most likely to occur. Perhaps the six types could be analyzed on a random rotational basis as a way to evaluate the bar's operation with

Random use of methods

even less expenditure of time. Finally, this method lends itself well to use in conjunction with either the standard cost or standard revenue methods in situations where those methods show a higher-than-normal variance for any particular period or on any particular day. In other words, the quantity control method can be used to isolate responsibility for the variance to a particular type of liquor.

BANQUET CONTROL

If the banquet department has its own liquor storage area, it can requisition needed supplies from the main storeroom and be controlled in the same way as any other bar using one or more of the methods already described. If the banquet department does not have a controlled, lockable storage area, it must requisition items needed for each particular function from the main bar, returning unused quantities to that bar at the end of the function. This

Use of special interbar transfer form

would be a double interbar transfer and a specially designed form can be used to control the transfers and the function's beverage cost. A form that would accomplish this is illustrated in exhibit 8.6 with provision for signatures of those responsible for issuing and returning bottles. The Bottle Cost column figures are taken from the perpetual inventory cards so that total cost information can be calculated. The Total Drinks column figures are a multiplication of the Bottles Used column figure and the Drinks per Bottle figure, rounded to the nearest whole number. In our case, we assumed a one-ounce drink size. Total Standard Revenue is a multiplication of Total Drinks and Drink Selling Price.

Comparing standard with actual revenue

The total number of drinks sold can be compared with the total number of tickets sold if it is a no-host bar situation. The total standard revenue should also agree with the cash collected from ticket sales. If it is a host-bar situation, then the total standard revenue figure will be the amount billed to the customer.

EXHIBIT 8.6. Banquet Liquor Control Form

Room _____ Banquet _____ Function _____ Date ____ April 2

Contractor's Association

Item	Size	Bottles Issued	Bottles Returned	Bottles Used	Bottle Cost	Total Cost	Drinks per Bottle	Total Drinks	Drink Selling Price	Total Standard Revenue
Bourbon	1 L	12.0	2.1	9.9	$6.00	$59.40	32	316	$1.50	$474.00
Scotch	0.75 L	5.0	2.0	3.0	$7.50	22.50	25	75	2.00	150.00
				Totals		$185.40		718		$841.00

Cost Percent $\dfrac{\$185.40}{\$841.00} \times 100 = 22.0\%$

Bottles issued by ____ G.A. Jones

Bottles issued to ____ R.J. Henton

Returned by ____ R.J. Henton

Returned to ____ J.B. Cant

Ticket Information

Ticket price	$1.50	$1.75	$2.00	$2.25
Closing number				
Opening number				
Tickets used				
Less: voided				
Tickets sold				
Drinks sold				
Differences				

BEVERAGE DISPENSING EQUIPMENT

There are many different types of automatic and electronic beverage-dispensing equipment available for both alcoholic and nonalcoholic beverages. These types vary from individual dispensing heads that attach to each bottle and require the bottle to be raised for pouring, to dispensing devices that are linked electronically to a sales register.

With the more expensive models, the dispenser will only operate if a sales check is inserted in the sales register prior to the appropriate sales keys' being depressed. Bottles as large as 1.75 liters (approximately ½ gallon) can be stored, inverted, in a remote storeroom that is kept under lock and key.

Remote storage location possible

Using these larger liquor bottles with liquor dispensing equipment should produce cost savings, since the cost per ounce is usually lower for the larger sizes. The same savings are not feasible with a manual pouring system, because the weight of the glass containers makes them too difficult to pour.

Savings available

With dispensing equipment, the storage location could be several hundred feet away or even on a different floor. One location can serve several different bars. Beverages are pumped through flexible plastic hoses. Sales can be recorded for each separate bar by brand, and even by bartender, on individual counters. For bars operating in resort properties, various types of mobile, independent, self-contained, and motorized controlled bars are available.

Mobile models available

Advantages

Among the other advantages of liquor-dispensing devices are the following:

Machine advantages

- Bartender errors from spillage and over- or underpouring are reduced or eliminated.
- Losses from liquor theft may be reduced, particularly if the bar inventory is remote from the bar and only accessible to management.
- Drink preparation may be faster, and fewer bartenders may be needed.
- Bartender training may be lessened, and employee turnover problems may thus be reduced.
- Less manual dexterity is required by bartenders.
- Back-bar space is freed up.
- Sales control is improved, particularly if a drink cannot be served without passing through the system. If this situation

can be achieved, a critical control problem has been overcome. In such a situation, management does not need to worry about bartenders' bringing in their own bottles, because the sales will be recorded and the establishment will be entitled to the revenue! Cash control thus becomes far more effective.

- Accurate inventory information is available, since records of drinks sold by category and inventory are constantly updated.
- Monitoring and pouring of draft beer can be incorporated into some systems.
- Pricing decisions (for example, exactly when does the happy hour begin?) are not made by employees. With many of the new systems, management can change the prices from a control panel in an office remote from the bar.

Although the more sophisticated and expensive electronic bar control models do provide both direct cost savings (such as accurate drink measuring and complete draining of all bottles) and labor cost savings—as well as such indirect benefits as ease of control, since each drink dispensed is individually recorded by a remote drink counter, resulting in reduced liquor losses—it is a mistake to presume that a dishonest bartender cannot find a way around the system.

Direct and indirect benefits

Management should never assume that equipment can provide absolute control and that other controls and management supervision are no longer required. Bars where this type of equipment is installed might well continue to rely on some of the traditional manual controls outlined in this chapter, using the inventory information provided by the dispensing equipment drink counters as an adjunct to these controls.

Disadvantages

One should also consider the disadvantages of automatic dispensing equipment, which include the following:

Possible disadvantages

- In some cases, this equipment can slow drink service.
- Not all drinks can be dispensed through the equipment. Some drinks must still be mixed manually.
- The atmosphere of the bar and customer attitudes may oppose using dispensing equipment; in particular, customers may complain that they can no longer see the bottle from which the product is being poured.
- There will undoubtedly be employee resistance to change at the time the equipment is installed.

- In the event of equipment malfunction, it may be necessary to return to manual dispensing until the equipment is repaired.
- The cost of repair must be considered and added to initial equipment costs.

Evaluate pros and cons

Therefore, one must evaluate both the pros and cons before making the final decision.

Evaluating Systems

In order to analyze and evaluate the value of installing an automated system, one should ask and receive answers to at least the following questions:

Questions to ask

1. What is the present liquor cost percent?
2. What liquor cost savings is the system likely to provide?
3. Can most of the drinks sold be routed through the system, or will many of them still have to be hand-poured or hand-mixed?
4. How are the physical facilities (storage and bar areas) likely to be affected?
5. To what extent is employee productivity going to be improved, and will this have any effect on management productivity and overall labor cost in the bar operation?
6. Does the system do more than the bar really needs?
7. How reliable is the manufacturer, particularly with reference to repairs and service in the event of equipment malfunction?
8. How reliable is the equipment? What has been its performance record in other establishments?

SUMMARY

Control of goods in the beverage storeroom is relatively easy. The same cannot be said about the beverages once they reach the bar since there are so many ways in which losses can occur.

Standard drink recipes detailing, amongst other things, exact quantities of beverages to be served form the basis of good bar control. Measuring devices, such as shot glasses and jiggers, should be used for measuring those quantities. With liquor control, it is preferable to separate the cost of and revenue from full-bottle sales. Interbar transfers should also be properly recorded so that each bar can be controlled as an individual unit. With any control method, if a spillage allowance is permitted, this too should be adjusted for in the control calculations.

The standard control method compares the standard cost for a bar for a particular period of time with the actual cost for that same period. The quantity of each type of drink sold is multiplied by its standard cost and by its selling price to arrive at total standard cost and total standard revenue so that the standard cost percent can be calculated. This percent can then be compared with the actual cost percent. Under normal circumstances, the difference between the two figures should be no greater than one half of 1 percent.

The standard revenue control method converts the quantity of liquor used, according to inventory records, into total standard revenue so that it can be compared with actual revenue. With this method, the standard revenue per bottle for each type or brand of liquor used must first be calculated. This generally requires the use of the weighted average approach since, from any individual bottle, the liquor will be used in different quantities in various drinks, each with possibly different markups. These bottle standard revenue figures must be recalculated from time to time as conditions warrant. With the standard revenue control method, actual revenue should be no more than 1 percent above or below standard revenue.

The quantity control method ignores both dollars of cost and dollars of revenue. It concentrates solely on quantities. It compares the quantity of each type of liquor used according to inventory records with the quantity used according to sales records. Although, as a control method, it can stand on its own, it is useful in conjunction with either the standard cost or standard revenue methods since it can isolate any unwarranted variances of a specific type or brand of liquor shown by these methods.

If a banquet department has its own storage area, it can be controlled with one or more of the methods outlined already. Alternatively, special control forms may be required depending on the circumstances.

In the last few years, many different types of mechanical and, more recently, electronic dispensing/control equipment have been made available to aid in bar control. Before any purchase of such equipment is considered, all the pros and cons should be fully analyzed and a cost/benefit analysis carried out.

DISCUSSION QUESTIONS

1. List four ways in which theft or fraud can occur in a bar.

2. Explain why the total cost of requisitions for liquor issued from the storeroom to the bar is not generally the real cost of liquor used on any particular day.

3. Why do you think the type of ice to be used in a drink should be part of that drink's standard recipe?

4. Describe two types of measuring devices for liquor.

5. Why should the cost of and the revenue from full-bottle sales be kept separate from regular cost and revenue?

6. What is spillage allowance? Explain whether or not you think a bar should be permitted this allowance.

7. Briefly explain the standard cost control method. What is the normal difference allowed?

8. Why is it frequently necessary to use the weighted average approach to establish the standard revenue for specific types or brands of liquor?

9. Briefly describe the standard revenue control method. What is the normal difference allowed?

10. Briefly explain the quantity control method.

11. How can the quantity control method be used in conjunction with the standard cost or standard revenue methods?

12. List five advantages and three disadvantages of using automatic dispensing equipment for alcoholic beverages.

13. What are five questions to be asked prior to making an investment in automatic dispensing equipment for alcoholic beverages?

PROBLEMS

8-1. A cocktail bar is being analyzed by the accounting office at the end of a particular week. Inventory at the beginning of the week was $5,000, requisitions during the week totalled $4,652, and inventory at the end of the week was $4,852. Only seven different drinks are sold in this bar. The standard cost, selling prices, and quantities sold during that week are:

Drink	Standard cost	Selling price	Quantity sold
1	$0.40	$2.00	2,106
2	0.50	2.20	600
3	0.60	2.40	520
4	0.40	2.00	1.612
5	0.40	2.00	5.288
6	0.70	3.00	534
7	0.70	3.00	666

Calculate the standard and actual cost percentages, and explain why you would or would not be satisfied with the results.

8-2. A cocktail lounge sells only a limited variety of types of drinks. The standard cost, selling prices, and quantities sold during the week ending March 14 are as follows:

Drink	Standard cost	Selling price	Quantity sold
Gin	$0.30	$1.25	1,360
Rye	0.32	1.30	1,112
Scotch	0.37	1.40	1,440
Bourbon	0.35	1.35	1,811
Rum	0.29	1.30	759
Manhattan	0.40	1.50	2,115
Martini	0.35	1.50	2,764

Actual beverage cost for the week ending March 14 was $4,025, and actual revenue $15,912.

a. Calculate the standard and actual cost percentages for the week. Round the total standard cost and total standard revenue amounts to the nearest dollar.

b. For the week ending March 21, because of a special purchase, the cost per drink for scotch dropped to $0.35. There was no change in the selling price. Quantities sold during that week were gin 1,315, rye 1,216, scotch 1,415, bourbon 1,925, rum 850, manhattan 2,317, martini 2,599. Actual beverage cost for the week ending March 21 was $4,237, and actual revenue $16,283. Recalculate the standard and actual cost percentages (again rounding total figures).

c. Explain why the percentage figures changed from one week to the next. Would you be satisfied with the results of each week? Explain.

8–3. A bar employs the standard revenue control method, and 1-liter (34-ounce) bottles of rye are used. From the following information, and using the weighted average method, calculate the standard revenue for a bottle of rye:

Drink	Quantity sold	Rye quantity	Selling price
Rye highball	1,000	1 oz.	$1.50
Manhattan	80	2 oz.	2.00
Rye Alexander	100	1¼ oz.	2.50
Rye Sour	40	1½ oz.	2.50
John Collins	200	1½ oz.	2.70

8–4. A hotel uses the standard revenue control method in one of its cocktail lounges that serves only a limited range of drinks. The standard revenue per bottle figures are:

Scotch	$37.00
Bourbon	33.50
Gin	33.50
Rum	36.00
Vermouth	18.00

The lounge results are being analyzed at the end of the day. Inventory information is as follows:

Item	Opening inventory	Added per requisitions	Interbar transfers	Closing inventory
Scotch	8.2	7.0	– 1.0	10.4
Bourbon	9.0	20.0		2.6
Gin	6.4	10.0		3.2
Rum	13.6	8.0		15.6
Vermouth	4.0	2.0		5.2

Actual revenue for that day was $1,640.80. Included in this figure is the revenue for a full-bottle sale of gin. The full-bottle price for gin is $22.50. Calculate total standard revenue and explain whether you would or would not be satisfied with the results.

8–5. Use the quantity control method to state whether or not you would be satisfied with the following analysis of bar rye usage in a lounge on a particular day. Opening inventory was 7.5 bottles, and closing inventory was 3.2 bottles; 10 full bottles of rye were issued from the storeroom to the bar on that day. Assume that the bottles are 750 milliliters (25 ounces). Drinks sold and the quantity of rye they contain are as follows:

Drink	Drinks sold	Rye quantity
Rye Highball	282	1 oz.
Manhattan	20	$1\frac{1}{2}$ oz.
Rye Alexander	16	$1\frac{1}{8}$ oz.
Rye Sour	16	$1\frac{1}{4}$ oz.

8–6. At some of the banquets held in a hotel, the bar is operated on a cash basis. All drinks are the same price. Banquet customers buy drink tickets from a cashier at the door. The customers then present the tickets to the bartender to obtain drinks. The bartender, who handles no cash, will not serve any drink without a ticket. As each ticket is presented, it is torn in half by the bartender to prevent its reuse. Torn tickets are subsequently discarded. At the end of the function, an inventory of remaining full- and part-bottles is taken and deducted from the opening inventory. This figure is then divided by the standard drink size to determine total drinks that should have been sold. The number of tickets not returned by the cashier indicates the amount of drinks that were actually sold. This figure is reconciled with the cashier's cash remittance. If the bartender's and cashier's drinks sold figures are not in satisfactory agreement, further checking is done by the accounting department.

In order to cut costs, the hotel is considering eliminating the cashier's position and the sale of tickets. The customers will simply pay the bartender directly for drinks. Discuss the weaknesses, from a control point of view, of the proposed simplified system.

8-7. A banquet liquor control form indicated the following about a function held on a particular day:

Item	Bottles issued	Bottles returned	Bottle cost
Vodka	8.0	3.4	$6.50
Bourbon	19.0	3.3	6.75
Rye	18.0	4.2	7.00
Rum	9.0	4.6	7.50
Scotch	6.0	0.9	8.50
Gin	5.0	2.0	7.25

All bottles are quart size (thirty-two ounces). All drinks contain one and one-half ounces. Drink price for all brands is $1.50, except scotch, which is $1.75. Calculate the liquor cost percent for this function.

Labor Cost Control: Employee Policies

Objectives

After studying this chapter, the reader should be able to do the following:

- Explain the terms *job description* and *task procedures*.
- Discuss the role of a personnel agency in finding employees.
- List the procedures for proper applicant interviewing, and explain the value of an interview evaluation form.
- Explain the term *employee orientation*.
- Discuss the value of job rotation.
- Explain how employee evaluations should be conducted, and describe the procedures to follow if disciplinary action is needed.
- Describe and explain the value of an individual employee record card.
- List three procedures to follow to help reduce employee turnover.

This chapter is the first of three on labor cost control. In most hospitality operations, one of the major costs needing tight control is labor. Most hospitality operations have some legal requirements that they must conform to with regard to employees, including minimum wage levels, the provision of statutory holidays, fair employment practices, the right of employees to bargaining collective and to unionize, maintenance of safety standards, and pay withholdings such as income tax and unemployment insurance.

Sample of policies

In addition, hospitality operators need to institute some sort of employee practices, or personnel policies, as a minimum first step towards controlling labor cost. The owner of even the smallest enterprise usually has some personnel policies. An owner who simply says "When I need a new employee, I'll hire the first person I can find who seems capable of doing the job, and I'll pay the minimum hourly rate" has established the following policies:

- When the decision to hire will be made
- The fact that no systematic advertising of job openings will be done
- The fact that the person to be hired must appear capable
- What the rate of pay will be

Job Descriptions

One of the initial steps in formulating personnel policies involves developing job descriptions for each type of job or employee position.

In a small operation, the job description may be as simple as specifying that an employee must welcome customers pleasantly and look after their needs. A prospective employee being interviewed for this job is simply told what the job entails.

Complexity of jobs

In a larger operation, however, each job has more complexities, and it may be difficult—particularly if several different types of jobs need to be filled—to remember the many functions that each separate job entails. For that reason, job descriptions are best put into writing, and when a prospective employee is to be hired he or she can be provided with a written copy of the job description.

The job description describes what the job entails, what steps must be performed, and when the steps must be performed. Job descriptions should not be too detailed, but they should include sufficient information to enable both the employee and the supervisor to be certain of what duties the job entails.

There are no standard job descriptions that fit every operation. Although some common elements exist in job descriptions for any particular job type, the descriptions for each individual business must be written for that business.

Job descriptions must be kept simple, must be easily understood, and should include the skills (such as an ability to get along with the public) that are required if the employee is to perform well in the job. **Include skills required**

Job descriptions will be discussed further in chapter 11.

Task Procedures

In many small businesses, positions or jobs require the employee to carry out a variety of different tasks during a shift or work period. Indeed, the smaller the business, the wider this variety is likely to be, since several jobs might be assigned to a single worker. In such cases, exactly how a particular task is to be performed should be detailed step by step. These task procedures should also be stated in writing.

Task procedures could of course be demonstrated and taught without first being written down, but new employees will probably feel more comfortable—particularly if they are being shown a number of different sets of procedures that their job entails—if the demonstrated steps can be supported in writing. **Procedures in writing**

Task procedures will be discussed further in chapter 11.

EMPLOYEE SELECTION

Once job skills have been defined through job descriptions and task procedures, the next step is to match appropriate employees with any positions available.

Finding Applicants

In smaller operations, advertising for employees can be done informally, through family connections or friends or by having present employees spread the word through their families and friends. This is certainly a cost-free method. Some businesses advertise open positions in local newspapers, to encourage as many prospective applicants as possible to apply, although this does cost money.

Sometimes it is useful to use personnel agencies (whose offices are generally found only in the larger cities) to seek out needed employees. If the personnel agency is provided with job descriptions of the positions that need to be filled, it can use its professional skills to match suitable candidates to the vacancies. This can be an expensive method of hiring, **Using personnel agencies**

Costs versus benefits

but it does provide a built-in screening service. Screening can be a time-consuming task that involves sifting through applications and then interviewing. The time saved by using a personnel agency must be weighed against the cost of this service.

Application Form

An application form should be used each time a person applies for a job. Even if a position is not open at the time someone asks about a job vacancy, it is a good idea to have the person complete an application form anyway. A few days or weeks from now, staff turnover may create a vacancy that someone with just those qualifications could fill.

Uses of forms

Application forms are useful for summarizing, in an orderly fashion, basic information about job applicants. The forms permit initial screening, without raising the necessity to interview each applicant. A typical application form is illustrated in exhibit 9.1.

Interviewing

Interviewing all candidates who have submitted an acceptable application form can take considerable time. Up to an hour might be spent with each one (thus the advantage of using a personnel agency, which, for a fee, will carry out this work). The time spent in interviewing is necessary, however, to ensure that the person who is finally offered the job has the best combination of both technical and human skills to fit into the business.

Interview in private

All interviews should be conducted in a private area or office. The interviewer should have the prospective employee's application form available and, during the discussion, should be familiar with it so that relevant questions can be posed to the applicant about previous education or experience. A prepared list of questions to ask all applicants is useful, since consistency of evaluation is important.

The interviewer should ask questions about the applicant's present job (assuming that he or she has one) and why he or she wishes to leave that job. It may also be desirable to find out what the applicant's career expectations are. In other words, is the applicant too ambitious for the kind of job available and for the offered wage or salary rate? If technical skills in specific areas are required, the interviewer should ensure that the applicant possesses the necessary competence in those areas.

Opportunity for Questions

The prospective employee should have an opportunity to ask questions. The interviewer should provide a job description and should be specific

---

EXHIBIT 9.1. Application for Employment

Position applied for _____ Date _____

How did you hear about this possible job opening? _____

_____

Are there any reasons you may be unable to carry out some of the

normal job duties in this position? _____

_____

If yes, explain _____

_____

Name _____

Address _____

Town _____ State _____ Code _____ Telephone _____

Social security # _____

What experience, training or education have you had that would

qualify you for this job? _____

_____

Why are you interested in this job? _____

_____

Are you available for work:

Saturdays _____ Nights 6 to 2 _____ Days 10 to 6 _____ Sundays _____

Are you now employed? _____ If yes, where? _____

_____

References (names of previous employers preferred):

   Name   Company Name/Address/Tel #   Dates employed

1. _____

2. _____

3. _____

Please sign below if you will consent to your present or previous
employer's release of information or discussion of previous performance with us.

Signature of applicant _____

about working hours, rates of pay, days off, and all other matters related to working conditions. If a prospective employee being hired is to report to a supervisor, rather than to the interviewer, have the applicant and the supervisor meet. Let the supervisor have input into the final selection of the candidate. If the supervisor is to continue to do a good job, there must be compatibility between the supervisor and any new employee hired.

Supervisor input

Taking Notes

During the interview, it is useful for the interviewer to take mental or written notes about both the applicant's and his or her own reactions. Written notes can be placed directly on the application form. Alternatively, the interviewer could use an interview evaluation form, such as that illustrated in exhibit 9.2.

In summary:

Interview requirements

- Have a plan or pattern for all interviews.
- Make sure the applicant is at ease.
- Be attentive and interested in what the applicant has to say, and do not interrupt.
- Give the applicant sufficient opportunity and time to respond to questions.
- Before closing the interview, invite the applicant to ask questions.
- If notes are not taken during the interview (since this can be distracting to the applicant), all resulting mental notes and impressions should be recorded immediately after the interview.

Interview as screening device

If an interview is well prepared and handled, it can be an excellent screening device. It can reinforce the information on the application form, and it can reveal things that are not apparent on the application form. Sometimes a second interview is useful for obtaining an even clearer impression and understanding of an applicant.

Closing the Interview

A good way to end interviews is to advise the applicants of how they will be informed if they are selected for the job and of approximately when that decision will be communicated.

EXHIBIT 9.2.   Interview Evaluation Form

Date _____ Position _____

Applicant name _____ Interviewer name _____

	High 5	4	3	2	Low 1
1. General appearance and neatness					
2. Conduct during interview (poise, manners, tact, pleasantness)					
3. Communication skills, ability to explain, self-expression					
4. Apparent desire, motivation, and initiative					
5. Skills and apparent competence for job, previous experience, leadership potential					
6. Overall rating					

References contacted and comments:

1. _____

2. _____

3. _____

Summary of strengths and weaknesses:

_____

_____

_____

Interviewer's comments and recommendation for hiring or not:

_____

_____

_____

References

If references are provided on the application form, with the applicant's permission, these references should be consulted by telephone. If they are not to be followed up, there is no purpose in asking for them on the application form in the first place.

Telephone references preferable

It is generally preferable to talk directly to previous employers and supervisors, and to any other individuals identified for reference purposes. Telephone reference comments are easy to record, and people giving information on the telephone are more likely to be candid than they would be if they were required to provide the reference in the form of a letter.

Information that can be requested of previous employers includes the following: applicant's job title, tasks performed, dates of employment, reason for leaving, quality of work, absenteeism and punctuality, personal characteristics, strengths, weaknesses, and overall effectiveness. It may also be worthwhile to ask if the previous employer would rehire the applicant, if given the chance; and if the employer would not, why not.

With the information and knowledge gleaned from the employment application forms, the interviews, and the reference checks, an employer is in a position to decide which applicant to choose.

Probationary Period

Length of period

It is a good idea to hire new employees on a probationary basis. The importance of the job or the skill level at which the person was hired will determine the appropriate length of the probationary period.

Finally, once the selection has been made, the application forms of the candidates not selected should be kept. A week or month later, a position might open for which one of the presently unsuccessful candidates would be entirely suitable.

EMPLOYEE ORIENTATION

Every person employed should be given an orientation. Many new employees are uncomfortable in a new job, and the orientation program serves as an introduction to the new job and to the business. This orientation should be given by the supervisor with whom the employee is to work. The orientation should include information about any or all of the following:

Information to include

- The operation's history (when it was started, who owns it, and whether it is part of a chain or franchise)

- The operation's objectives
- A copy of the organization chart (if the business is large enough to need one), showing where the employee fits in and to whom he or she reports
- A copy of the job description and task procedures
- Hours of operation
- When shifts are changed (frequency), how much advance notice of change is given, and who produces these shift schedules
- Vacation entitlement, how it is calculated, and who produces vacation schedules
- Statutory holidays
- Dress and/or uniform requirements, and if uniforms are required, who maintains them and how frequently they are to be changed
- Appearance and grooming requirements
- Policy on employee meals—their cost, when and where they are taken, and whether any items (such as coffee or soft drinks) are free
- Conduct expected when on duty (promptness, attendance, how and to whom absence or illness should be reported)
- Pay periods, pay days, deductions made, overtime rates, pay advances, and how work hours are determined (time clocks, and so on)
- Other benefits (sick leave entitlement, health and/or life insurance, dental plan, and educational assistance)
- Training—who does it, and how long it is
- Probationary period, if any
- Evaluation process (how it is handled, who is responsible for it, when it is done, and what happens to the results of it)
- Promotion procedures (how to apply, and the criteria considered)
- Grounds for dismissal, and dismissal procedures
- Quitting (termination) procedures
- Any special rules (such as safety, sanitation, smoking, bonding, or special policies for tipped employees)
- Policy on customer complaints, and how they are to be handled
- Introduction to fellow employees
- If warranted, a tour of the facilities to show restricted areas,

the staff entrance, time clocks, change rooms, parking areas, and so on

- An opportunity for the employee to ask questions during the orientation

Written handbook

This list is only a suggested one. It needs to be adapted for each separate business. Many operators collect orientation facts into a written manual or handbook that the employee is required to study at the start of employment.

EMPLOYEE TRAINING

The orientation is the beginning of an ongoing employee training process. This process includes such points as employees learning what the operation's standards are, how they can be met, what level of performance is expected of them as employees, how to do the correct performance procedures, and how to adapt to day-to-day situations as they arise.

It should not be the employees' responsibility (even though, in practice, that is often the case) to train themselves in all these matters. The employee needs to be taught through discussion and demonstration, followed by practice.

Advantages of training

In small operations, this is usually done on the job by the manager; in a larger operation, training duties are assumed by the employee's supervisor. Proper training can reduce employee stress and absenteeism, lower employee turnover, limit costs due to careless use of supplies and equipment, and improve sanitation and safety. In addition, it can increase employees' morale, cooperation, interest in the job, job knowledge, productivity, and chances for promotion—all of which are going to lead to more satisfied customers. In short, it fosters professionalism.

On-the-job Training

A certain amount of on-the-job training will probably be necessary. Even when an employee is hired to fill a position in which he or she has previous experience, each operation has different routines and procedures, and these need to be demonstrated or taught to new employees. In addition, new employees need to be shown the location of storage areas and supplies, switches, keys, and other items related to the job to be performed. As well, safety and emergency procedures need to be explained or demonstrated.

Job Rotation

Job rotation is another useful technique. Employees are trained at various jobs so that they can be rotated (where a union contract does not prohibit this) from job to job as different needs arise. Besides giving the employee a variety of challenges, it ensures that employees can help out in different jobs in an emergency, reduces employee boredom, and (eventually) ensures that promoted employees make better supervisors, since they are familiar with all the jobs under their supervision.

Advantages of job rotation

EMPLOYEE EVALUATION

The final step in personnel planning is employee evaluation. Again, in a very small operation, this may simply be handled through management observation. A competent owner/manager can quickly determine whether or not a new employee is fitting in and is able to do a good job following proper training. Incompetent employees may have to be released or, if open positions are available, moved to a job whose demands are not as great. Competent employees should be encouraged to continue to do a good job and should be challenged (with more responsibility) or promoted when possible.

Competent and incompetent employees

Formal Evaluation

In a business with more than a few employees, evaluations may be carried out once or twice a year in a formal way, with the evaluator under instructions to fill out an evaluation form for each employee. In such situations, the employee should be allowed to read the evaluation and even to sign the completed evaluation form to indicate acceptance of what it says. A sample evaluation form is illustrated in exhibit 9.3.

In evaluating, the supervisor should judge employees with reference to the whole job. For example, an employee should be evaluated on his or her performance with the customers, with other employees, and with the supervisor—not just on one of those three specific relationships.

What to evaluate

The evaluation must be carried out objectively, despite the fact that the process itself is subjective. In other words, personal bias for or against an employee should not be allowed to affect the assessment. In some organizations, the responsibilities included on a job description serve as the basis for what is to be included in an employee evaluation. Indeed, some authorities believe that the points to be evaluated should match those on the job description.

Even if the evaluation is not formalized on a document that the em-

EXHIBIT 9.3. Employee Evaluation Form

Employee name _____ Position _____

Date employed _____ Date of evaluation _____

	Excellent	Good	Average	Below average	Poor
Knowledge of job: Clear understanding of duties related to job and ability to do the job					
Dependability: Conscientious, punctual, reliable					
Courtesy: To guests, fellow employees, and supervisor					
Cooperation: Ability and willingness to work with supervisors and fellow employees					
Work quality: Thoroughness, neatness, accuracy and completeness					
Work quantity: Ability to handle assigned volume under normal pressures and conditions					
Personal qualities: Personality, sociability, integrity, leadership potential					

	Excellent	Good	Average	Below average	Poor
Appearance: Hygiene and neatness					

Employee name ——————— Position ———————

Date employed ——————— Date of evaluation ———

Overall performance: Satisfactory ( )   Unsatisfactory ( )

Supervisor's signature ———————————————

Employee's signature ———————————————

ployee can see and read, the results of the evaluation—both the good and the bad points—should be discussed with the employee. Communicating with employees concerning their performance is always preferable to not communicating at all.

Pay Raises

The evaluation process also necessitates considering pay raises at least once a year (unless these are negotiated with a union). In the absence of a union contract, the factors that influence the size of wage increase to give an employee are these:

- The operation's ability to pay higher wages   **Influencing factors**
- The demands of the job
- The pay rate for that job, compared to the pay rate for similar jobs in competitive operations
- The results of the employee's evaluation
- The general inflation rate
- The local supply of and demand for employees

Promotions

Whenever job vacancies arise, it is usually a good idea to seek replacements from within the ranks of present employees—particularly if this will create a promotion for a deserving employee. Employees who recognize that there are advancement opportunities within the business have an incentive to stay, and they generally perform their jobs better.

Although seniority is sometimes made the basis for promotion into a vacant position, that type of promotion should only occur if the person being advanced has the qualifications and capabilities to do the job, especially if the job carries a measure of responsibility and authority. This is where the employee evaluation form can be helpful.

Discipline

Rules and regulations

Every establishment must have employment rules and regulations that employees are to follow. Some of these rules and regulations will be restrictive; others will exist for safety reasons; and yet others may serve to protect the rights of employees.

Making sure that employees know and understand these rules is part of the orientation/training process. In some cases where rules are broken, employees should simply be reminded of the rule(s). In other cases, disciplinary action may be necessary.

Such action could take the form of a written memo to the employee concerned that explains the measures being taken in response to the breaking of the rule, identifies the specific incident that prompted the action, details any further action that might be taken if the rule is broken again, specifies a time frame after which a review of the situation will occur, and provides for the employee to acknowledge receipt of the warning or disciplinary action.

Three copies of memos

One copy of the memo should remain with the employee, a second copy should go to the employee's supervisor (if there is one), and a third copy (preferably with the employee's signature on it, acknowledging that he or she has been made aware of the situation) should be placed in the employee's file.

Termination

At times, employees must be disciplined in the severest way: by termination of employment. This should only occur as a last resort, since it should be a response to the most critical of situations, and since generally cause for dismissal must be shown. Cause can often be justified by the number of disciplinary action memos that have accumulated in the employee's file.

Level of required performance

One of the values in having clearly written job descriptions is that they can indicate, at the time the employee is hired, the level of job performance required. If the employee has failed to meet that performance level, and this fact can be supported by memos in the employee's file, then cause for termination can be documented.

If it is necessary to terminate an employee, the actual firing should be done in private on a one-to-one basis by the employee's supervisor or, in a small operation, by the manager. The employee should be given the reason(s) for termination. A good way to round out the termination process is to emphasize the employee's strong points and perhaps to suggest alternatives for that person's future.

EMPLOYEE RECORDS

Every operation must maintain records about its present employees. The records might simply be a file folder containing the application form of each employee currently on the payroll, a notation on each form of the employee's current wage or salary, and any other information that needs to be recorded (such as disciplinary warnings).

What to include

Even a small establishment has staff turnover and may hire additional employees on a seasonal basis. In such cases, it is not easy for anyone to store all the facts about present and past employees mentally. Therefore, a separate employee record card or sheet should be maintained for each employee hired. Such a card is shown in exhibit 9.4. This card can be used to record the date when the employee was hired, the position filled, and the initial rate of pay. Subsequent changes in the status of the employee can then be recorded as they occur, alongside the date of the change. Changes in status include such things as a move to another job within the operation, a change in wage or salary, and the date when employment was terminated; each change recorded should be accompanied by the reason for the change, summarized in the "Comment" column.

Employee record cards are useful for providing up-to-date information about current employees, and also for preserving information about former employees who are being reemployed or are being reference-

Uses of record cards

EXHIBIT 9.4.   Employee Record Card

Employee name _____ Date employed _____

Initial position _____

Starting wage/salary _____

Date	Change status to	New wage/salary	Comments

checked by other prospective employers. Also placed in each employee's file should be the interview evaluation form (exhibit 9.2), if one was used, and the evaluation forms (exhibit 9.3), if a formal evaluation process is used. Any other correspondence or notes about the employee should also be placed in the employee file. In this way, all relevant information about each employee is maintained in a single centralized location.

Alphabetic files

It is a good idea to arrange the files in alphabetical order. The files for current employees should be kept together, and new files should be inserted as new employees are hired. As employees leave, their files should be pulled from the current employee group and placed, again in alphabetical order, with the files of all other former employees.

As a general rule, the files of past employees are kept for a minimum of two years and a maximum of five. The actual holding period is a matter for each owner/operator to decide. When the files are no longer to be kept, all the information in them should be destroyed.

Since employee files contain confidential information, access to any file should be restricted to a responsible person who is authorized to keep the employee files up to date, and to the employee concerned.

EMPLOYEE TURNOVER

Because of the high cost of employee turnover, an attempt must be made to reduce turnover in order to cut this cost. One way to reduce turnover, particularly during a new employee's first weeks on the job, is to observe the following four guidelines:

Guidelines to observe

1. Be honest about the job. Make sure that applicants understand both the good and the bad aspects of the job.
2. Make sure that applicants are not overqualified for the job. Overqualified individuals are likely to become unhappy and leave, since they are not challenged in the job.
3. Monitor new employees' performance from the first day, and let each new employee have early feedback of preliminary assessments.
4. Watch for signs of trouble such as absenteeism or drinking on the job. If problems are evident, get to the issue quickly to see if the problem can be resolved to everyone's satisfaction.

SUMMARY

Labor is a major cost in any hospitality operation, and for this reason labor cost control is critical. Such control begins with establishing a set of employee or personnel policies.

One of the initial steps in formulating personnel policies is to develop job descriptions for each type of job or employee position. Job descriptions should be supported with detailed sets of task procedures where these are warranted.

Once job skills have been defined through job descriptions and task procedures, the next step is to match appropriate employees or applicants with any positions available.

An application form should be used each time a person applies for a job; this form is useful for summarizing, in an orderly fashion, basic information about a job applicant. The application form should be available to the interviewer when each prospective employee is interviewed and questioned. Following the interview process, an interview evaluation form should be completed for each applicant, for later reference.

When new employees are hired, it is a good idea to have them complete a probationary period before attaining permanent employee status. Every person employed should be given an orientation that includes full information about the business and the job; each new employee should also be provided with an employee manual, if there is one. The orientation should mark the beginning of an ongoing employee training process.

The final step in personnel planning is employee evaluation. This evaluation, supplemented by an evaluation form, serves as a basis for justifying pay raises, promotions, discipline, or termination.

All documentary records about employees, including the application form, the interview evaluation, subsequent evaluation forms, and memos or correspondence, should be placed in an individual employee file that should remain confidential.

DISCUSSION QUESTIONS

1. Explain what a job description is.
2. What are task procedures?
3. Discuss the role of a personnel agency in seeking good employees.
4. List the procedures for proper interviewing of applicants.
5. Describe an interview evaluation form.
6. Explain what is meant by the term *employee orientation*.
7. What is job rotation, and why is it a useful technique?
8. Explain how employee evaluations can be carried out.
9. Explain the procedure to follow if disciplinary action must be taken.
10. Of what value is an individual employee record card?

11. List three procedures to follow to help reduce new employee turnover.

PROBLEMS

9–1. Assume that you are the owner/operator of a fifty-room motel. Prepare job duty lists for (a) a desk clerk, and (b) a maintenance worker. Restrict your lists to what you think would be daily, routine tasks. Each list should include no more than ten items.

9–2. Obtain blank application forms from each of two local hospitality industry establishments. Write a one page evaluation of each form, comparing and contrasting their strengths and weaknesses. Cover such matters as the information the form requires from the applicant, the clarity of any questions asked, and the space allowed for applicant to respond.

9–3. In response to an advertisement that you place in a local newspaper, you receive the following application for a motel manager (see pages 237 and 238). Study the application carefully. List the questions that you would pose if you were interviewing this candidate and wanted to clarify any of the points covered in the application.

9–4. Obtain an employee manual from a local hospitality industry hotel. Assume that you were to become an employee of that establishment. Evaluate the manual's strengths and weaknesses in conveying information to you as a new employee.

9–5. As manager, you are in the process of formalizing employee orientations for a new 150-seat restaurant and are writing an employee manual or handbook. Make a list of all the points that you should include in your orientation. In preparation for writing the manual, make a list of all the policies, including rules and regulations, that you want to establish. Pay particular attention to "conduct when on duty" (for example, is smoking permitted on the job? are employees allowed to place personal telephone calls when on duty?) and whether employees are allowed to use the restaurant premises (dining room and cocktail lounge) when they are not on duty.

Application Form

Name	Last (please print)											First					
Name	C	O	R	D	E	R	O					J	O	H	N			
Mailing address	4	5	8		3	R	D		S	T	.	N	O	R	T	H		
City	M	I	D	T	O	W	N											
Zip code	9	2	2	3	5													

Phone-home: | 6 | 8 | 4 | - | 4 | 6 | 8 | 5 |

Social security number | 8 | 8 | 1 | 0 | 4 | 3 | 9 | 8 | 2 |

Education

Name and location of school or institution	Course program, major field	Credits, diploma, degree attained	Dates	
			Started	Completed
Secondary or high school Midtown H.S.	Grade 12	Graduation	1974	1978
Vocational or trade school				
Technological				
Junior college				
University				
University State University	Commerce		1979	1980
Post graduate or other				
Special courses	Course content, duration, etc.			Year

(continued on next page)

9–6. Obtain a blank employee evaluation form from a local hospitality establishment. Evaluate its usefulness in providing essential information to the establishment's manager and to the employee. How would you reword this evaluation form if you had the opportunity?

Employment Record

Present or last employer Central Motel	From 1987	To 1988	Salary $24,000
Address Telephone Garden City	Position title Manager		
Duties Management duties	Supervisor's name George Tobin		
	Supervisor's title owner		
	Reason for leaving No advancement opportunity		
Previous employer Downtown Hotel	From 1985	To 1987	Salary $18,000
Address Telephone Hardiston	Position title Front office manager		
Duties Worked desk shift and supervised	Supervisor's name Harry Gabini		
other employees	Supervisor's title Manager		
	Reason for leaving Moved to Garden City		
Previous employer Hospitality Inn	From 1984	To 1985	Salary $12,000
Address Telephone Tacoma	Position title Chief desk clerk		
Duties Front desk clerk	Supervisor's name Stan George		
	Reason for leaving Moved to Hardiston		

Date: ___10/16/88___   Signature: ___John Cordero___

Measurement of Labor Cost

10

Objectives

After studying this chapter, the reader should be able to do the following:

- Explain why the emphasis on labor cost control has changed in recent times.
- List and discuss some of the factors that can cause labor cost percent to vary from one type of establishment to another.
- List the fringe benefits that are included in labor cost.
- Define the role of the operations analyst.
- Discuss some of the factors that can affect employee productivity.
- Discuss ideas for increasing employee productivity.
- Solve problems relating to labor cost and employee productivity including the use of productivity equations.

Recent causes of higher labor costs

The problem of labor cost control is not new. The need to minimize this cost in order to help maximize net income has always existed in the hospitality industry. But in more recent times the trend toward a shorter work week, longer vacations, a higher minimum wage, unionization, and many other related factors have caused the industry to concentrate on improving the effectiveness of manpower management in order to have better control. What has changed over the years is the relative emphasis placed on labor cost control.

Employee/guest room ratios

For example, in earlier times, it was not uncommon to have major hotels operate with a ratio of as many as 3 employees per guest room (total number of equivalent full-time employees in all departments divided by total guest rooms). Satisfactory profits were achieved and a high level of service was given guests. However, as operating costs in all areas have increased with the passage of time, and therefore have been controlled and minimized, more and more attention has been paid to a reduction in the level of service that a high employee/guest-room ratio provides. It is now not uncommon for major properties in North America to have an

Reduction in levels of service

employee/guest-room ratio as low as 0.5 per room. This reduction in ratio has not meant that such hotels can no longer be considered first class, but rather that guests have become accustomed to expect fewer frills in service. The alternative would have been to pay ever higher and higher prices. It should also be noted that, in some areas of the world (for example in the Far East), there are hotels still operating with extremely high employee/guest-room ratios. This is primarily due to the lower wages that the employees in these countries are paid relative to the prices charged to the guests.

In the same way that, with the passage of time, hotels have, generally speaking, reduced the level of service to combat the increasing wage-to-revenue ratio, so, too, have motels, restaurants, clubs, and other similar branches of the hospitality industry trended in the same direction.

LABOR COST RATIOS

Since the hospitality industry is so diverse, it is impossible to be specific in establishing guidelines within which the labor cost as a percentage of revenue should fall for any particular operation. The same applies, of course, to food and beverage cost percentages discussed in earlier chapters.

For example, in the case of hotels and larger motels with food and beverage facilities, the labor cost will generally be between 30 percent and 40 percent of overall revenue. However, it could well be lower than 30 percent in the rooms department and be above 40 percent in the food operation. In owner-operated smaller motels which provide no facilities other than rooms and where the owner works for the business, the labor cost might range from 10 to 30 percent of room revenue. In restaurants, whether individually owned or part of a chain, the range of possible ratios can be extremely wide. For example, a self-serve or drive-in fast-food operation could have a labor cost as low as 10 percent of revenue. A luxury restaurant operation might have a labor cost as high as 60 percent of revenue. The restaurant industry average generally falls into the 25 to 35 percent range.

Diversity of labor cost ratios

Causes of Differences in Labor Cost

Many factors can cause major differences in the labor cost percentage from one hospitality industry enterprise to another. Some of these are:

The physical plant.   The layout may dictate more or fewer employees on duty at any time. An efficiently planned layout will reduce the number of employees required. The age of the property can also be a factor. Older establishments are usually less efficient by today's standards and also frequently require more labor for janitorial and maintenance work.

Older establishments are usually less labor efficient

Location.   A well located operation will usually enjoy a higher level of business (and thus a reduced labor cost percent) than a similar operation less well located. For example, a motel on a major highway will, all other things being equal, enjoy a higher occupancy level on average than a competitive motel located close by but not on a major highway. Similarly, a restaurant catering to the business-luncheon trade and located in the centre of the business district will probably have a higher seat-turnover, and thus higher revenue and lower labor cost percent, than a similar restaurant located on the fringe of the business area.

Good location may mean lower labor cost

Market demands.   The particular clientele that an operation caters to can be affected by the demands of the market, and thus change the labor cost ratio. For example, a resort hotel catering to the middle-income-bracket customer might find its revenue dropping drastically and its labor cost percentage increasing as a proportion of revenue, in recessionary times or when unseasonal weather continues for a long period of time. Weather can also affect certain types of operation on a daily basis. For example, a drive-in restaurant catering primarily to ice-cream-related menu items can have a high fluctuation in daily revenue, and thus labor cost percentage, on cold, wet days.

Uncontrollable external factors

Government legislation.   Operations affected by government legislation (for example, a minimum hourly rate that must be paid) may be at a disadvantage over those operations not so covered.

Unionized employees generally earn more

Unions.   Establishments whose employees are coverd by a union contract will generally have a higher labor cost relative to revenue than would establishments whose employees are not covered by union contract. Unions generally obtain higher levels of pay and more fringe benefits (which are a part of total labor cost) for their members.

Use of equipment.   Establishments that can use and afford certain items of equipment may be able to reduce the number of employees and thus the labor cost. More automated dishwashing machines, electronic liquor-dispensing equipment, computerized front-office and accounting machines are all improvements that generally mean fewer employees are required.

Restaurant menus.   In restaurants, whether independent, part of a chain, or part of a motel or hotel, the menu items offered can have an effect on the labor cost. The menu is often dictated by the type of market one is catering to, but the number of individual items offered, the amount of kitchen preparation time required, the style of service needed for certain menu items, and the availability and use of preprepared or convenience foods, are typical of the factors that can affect the labor cost. Consider, for exam-

Convenience foods, effect on labor cost

ple, the last item mentioned: convenience foods. A hotel that designs its menus to make use primarily of prebutchered and preportioned meats would probably no longer require an in-house butcher. The purchase price of the food would probably be higher (since the supplier is now doing the butchering), but the hotel's labor cost as a percentage of revenue would decline, and it will probably find its combined food and labor cost percentage has also been reduced. The reason for this is that convenience foods have a labor cost "shelf" life. A butcher employed on a permanent basis would normally be paid a full day's pay regardless of volume of business. His wage cost is an expense for that day. Convenience foods, on the other hand, with a built-in labor cost, do not become an expense until the product is actually sold. The deferring of the labor cost expense in this way is a form of labor cost reduction. Unfortunately, most of the labor cost in the

Labor cost insensitivity to demand

hospitality industry is insensitive to demand for services. Most of it is fixed, regardless of volume of demand. For example, a hotel or motel must have a desk clerk on duty for each eight-hour shift whether the operation is 30 percent occupied or 70 percent.

Labor Cost Percentage

So far in our discussions, for the sake of simplicity, we have used labor cost as a percentage of revenue as a measure of the cost of labor. This measure is simple to calculate; as is also the case with food and beverage cost percentages, however, this simplicity hides some dangers. In fact, if not properly interpreted, the labor cost percentage can be quite misleading and can cause erroneous decision-making. Why this is so will be illustrated in chapter 11, when various methods of measuring labor cost and employee productivity will be discussed. It suffices to say, at this point, that the main objective of labor cost control is to try to obtain the maximum efficiency or productivity from employees while maintaining the quality standards of the establishment. These standards must be established by each individual establishment so that meaningful labor cost objectives can be set. The establishment of standards will also be covered in chapter 11.

Productivity standards

Other Methods

Other methods of analyzing labor cost provide alternatives to looking exclusively at labor cost percent. Three of these are the following:

1. *Sales per man-hour by department or subdepartment compared to a standard.* For example, if sales were $1,000 and 50 hours of labor were expended to generate those sales, sales per man-hour would be $1,000 ÷ 50 = $20. This $20 could then be compared to whatever the standard is for this situation. With this measure, it is important to watch trends over time. The main disadvantage of this method is that sales depend on relatively unpredictable guest counts (room occupancies, seat turnovers) and price changes, and even on the sales mix (which type of rooms will customers choose? what menu items will they consume?). If prices are changed by management, the standard must be changed.

Watch for trends

A further problem with this method relates to deciding what payroll hours to use. For example, should the analyst use only variable wage employee hours, or only fixed (that is salaried) hours, or both? For a salaried employee, what is the number of standard hours per day—8, 10, or some other number? In using this measure, it is therefore best to analyze labor in departments where salaried hours can be excluded, rather than in a department such as the front office where a minimum number of clerks must be on duty during each 8-hour shift regardless of volume. This tool is most useful as a short-run measure of productivity in areas such as the dining room or cocktail lounge, where dollars of sales per server hour worked can easily be calculated.

Use as short-run measure

2. *Dollar labor cost per guest served.* For example, if 500 guests are served in a dining room and the labor cost to serve those guests is $400, the labor cost per guest served is $400 ÷ 500 = $0.80. This measure is useful as long as wage rates are not changed. A wage rate increase, however, will increase the labor cost per guest unless it is compensated for by reducing the number of hours worked and paid for. It would be feasible to improve

**Risk with
this ratio**

the ratio (that is, to decrease labor cost per guest) if the number of hours worked can be decreased to more than compensate for a wage rate increase. Even with an increasing labor cost per guest, however, this ratio can hide a productivity improvement. Consider the following situation:

$$100 \text{ hours worked} \times \$4 \text{ per hour} = \$400 \text{ cost}$$

If 400 guests are served, labor cost per guest is as follows:

$$\$400/400 = \$1.00$$

Suppose that there is a 15 percent wage increase and a 10 percent reduction in hours worked, with no change in the number of guests served. The result would be the following change in cost:

$$90 \text{ hours worked} \times \$4.60 \text{ per hour} = \$414 \text{ cost}$$

If 400 guests are served, labor cost per guest is as follows:

$$\$414/400 = \$1.035$$

**Increase in
productivity**

In the preceding example, the wage increase (despite a reduction in hours worked) has caused an increase in the labor cost per guest served from $1.00 to $1.035. Nevertheless, there has been an increase in productivity, as will become apparent when we apply the next method.

3. *Guest count per man-hour.* Based on the figures from the preceding example, the guest count per man-hour in the first situation is as follows:

$$400 \text{ guests} \div 100 \text{ hours worked} = 4 \text{ guests per man-hour}$$

And in the second situation, the ratio comes out as follows:

$$400 \text{ guests} \div 90 \text{ hours worked} = 4.4 \text{ guests per man-hour}$$

This shows that there has been an increase in productivity. However, the productivity increase is not high enough to compensate for the increase in hourly wage from $4.00 to $4.60, as was shown by the labor cost per guest figure calculated earlier.

Nevertheless, the guest count per man-hour has the advantage of being unaffected by wage and price changes, and for this reason it may be the best measure of productivity over time, if properly interpreted. It also recognizes that sales result from guests, and not from reducing the number of employees or their wage rates. Hence, if more guests can be served with no increase in hours paid or rates of pay, there will automatically be a productivity gain.

Sales result from guests

This type of labor analysis is not applicable in all departments. For example, in a banquet department, the number of guests served per hour of labor may be far less significant than the banquet guests' spending. If the banquet sales department can sell a banquet for $11, rather than for $10 (a 10 percent revenue increase), this may be far more important than raising the guests-served productivity 10 percent (from 4 to 4.4 per employee hour worked).

A similar situation prevails in a cocktail lounge, where average check could be $5 or $15 per guest without any change in hours worked or paid for, or in total revenue. For example, during an hour each of three customers can occupy the same seat for 20 minutes, each spending $5. Average check is $5, and total revenue is $15. It has taken one hour of labor to serve three guests. Alternatively, one customer could occupy the same seat for the entire hour and spend $15. Average check is $15, and so too is total revenue, but in this case one hour of labor has been expended to serve only one guest. To compare guest count per hour worked in this type of situation is quite meaningless, since the same total revenue and the same amount of labor are involved, despite the big differences in average check and in the labor cost per guest served.

Meaningless comparison

What is Included in Labor Cost?

The cost of labor is the base rate plus additional benefits, which equals total cost. The base rate is the fixed salary that a person receives, stated on a weekly, monthly, or annual basis. For hourly paid employees, it would be the number of hours worked for a period of time multiplied by the hourly rate for the job. If overtime is involved, then the overtime rate would be used for the overtime hours. Generally, salaried employees do not receive overtime for extra hours worked. Usually, they would receive time off or some other form of compensation.

Hourly versus salaried employees

Included in the fringe benefits to be added to the base pay would be such items as vacation pay, workers' compensation, social security, unemployment compensation, group and/or medical insurance, dental insurance, cost of free meals, and sick leave. The cost of fringe benefits can be readily calculated in most cases and is often surprisingly high, frequently as high as 20 to 30 percent of the base pay. Because the amount of fringe benefits can vary considerably from establishment to establish-

Cost of fringe benefits

ment, it is often difficult to compare total labor cost figures for two otherwise similar operations. Therefore, on hospitality industry income statements, the base pay amount and the employee benefit amounts are generally shown as two separate expenses. However, when an establishment is setting labor cost objectives, it should clearly know what the employee benefit amount or level is and include it in cost calculations.

Who Controls the Cost of Labor?

Organization charts and labor cost

The question of who controls the labor cost in an organization really depends on the size of the operation and on its organization. For example, exhibits 10.1 and 10.2 show possible organization charts for a small motel and for a coffee shop, respectively—both owner-operated. It is quite likely that, in smaller hospitality enterprises of this type, no formal organization chart would be developed on paper (as is normal in larger organizations). Nonetheless, the "organization" is still there and is recognized by employees.

In such small, owner-operated establishments, control of the cost of labor would be in the hands of the owner/manager. Very little, if any, for-

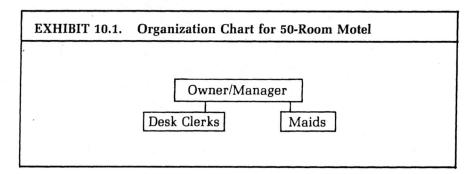

EXHIBIT 10.1.   Organization Chart for 50-Room Motel

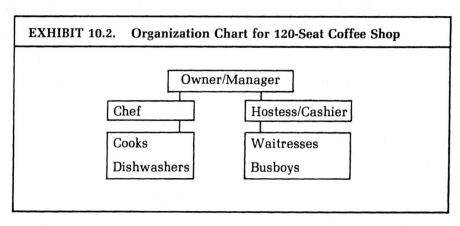

EXHIBIT 10.2.   Organization Chart for 120-Seat Coffee Shop

mal control would be practiced. Staff scheduling might even be carried out without any documentation. The only benefits paid to employees would probably be the ones required by statute, and the only labor cost control forms or records kept would be those relating to payroll payments.

Informal controls

As establishments grow larger, control of the operation by one person is no longer feasible, and much of the day-to-day administrative responsibility is turned over by the general manager to assistant managers, department heads, or supervisors. In larger-sized operations, formal organization charts are essential and are invariably documented and circulated to all those concerned so that the organization of the firm is understood.

Delegation of control

Typical organization charts for various kinds of larger hospitality industry enterprises are illustrated in exhibits 10.3, 10.4, and 10.5. Typically, as establishments become larger, their charts become more complex and their lines of communication more difficult to maintain. In these enterprises, the departmental managers or supervisors are heavily involved with (among other things) labor cost control, which includes such matters as labor cost budgeting, hiring and firing, staff scheduling, and recording hours actually worked by employees under their direct supervision. The objective is to achieve maximum utilization of manpower by planning, coordinating, and controlling personnel.

Very large establishments may have a personnel office that is responsible for such functions as recruiting, interviewing, and screening potential employees and looking after much of the paper work involved in manpower management. In addition, large organizations frequently employ labor cost specialists, or operations analysts.

Personnel department's functions

The operations analyst performs routine work such as keeping necessary records, calculating productivity figures, calculating labor cost statistics, and determining trends and deviations between forecast and actual data. He would participate in regular general meetings for preparing manpower forecasts and help departments with their individual forecasts. The prime objective of the job would be to initiate increased productivity and reduce labor cost by introducing new work methods and by analyzing existing plant design and layout to improve overall efficiency. The operations analyst might also be required to make recommendations to the general manager for changes in operating methods that will improve efficiency and thus productivity. Obviously a prerequisite to this position would be complete conversance with the establishment as well as with the local labor regulations and union contract.

Role of operations analyst

THE PROBLEM OF PRODUCTIVITY

One of the key words in measuring employee performance, and in labor cost control, is productivity. Traditionally, it is thought that, for many reasons, the productivity of employees in the hospitality industry, which is

Traditional low productivity

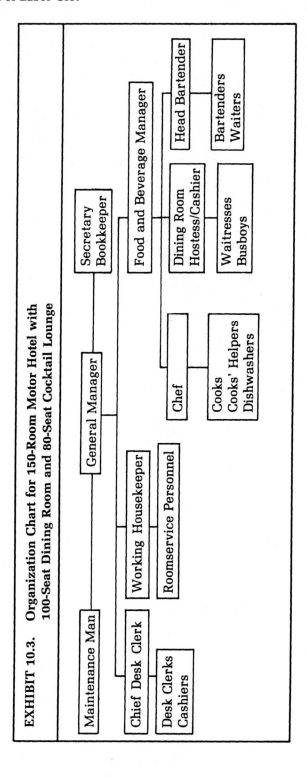

EXHIBIT 10.3. Organization Chart for 150-Room Motor Hotel with 100-Seat Dining Room and 80-Seat Cocktail Lounge

EXHIBIT 10.4. Organization Chart for Restaurant Complex

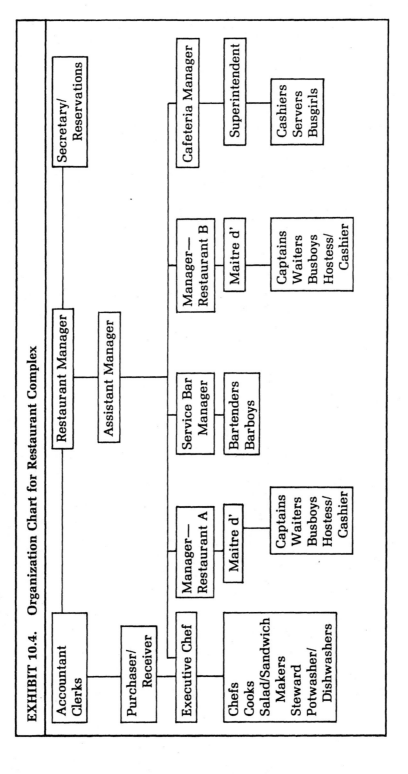

EXHIBIT 10.5. Organization Chart for a Very Large Hotel with Full Facilities

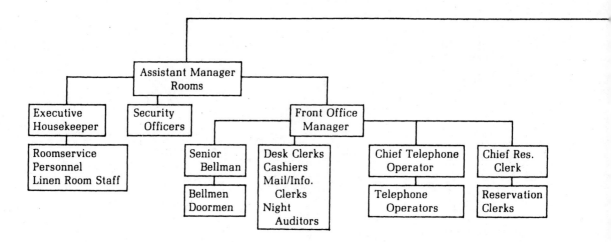

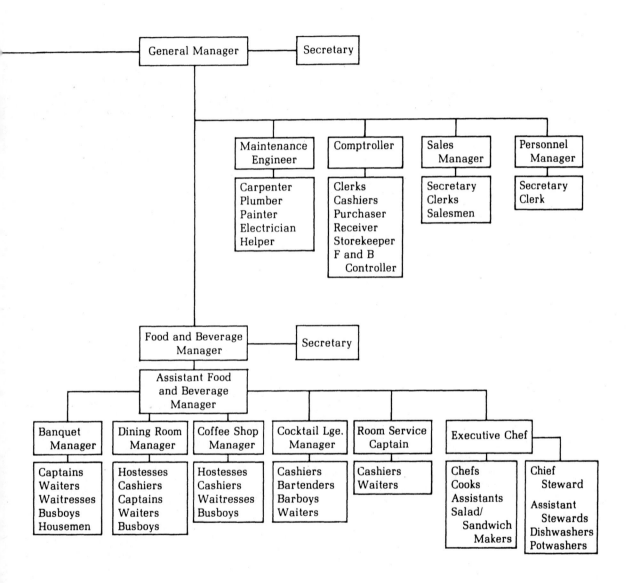

measured in different ways, has been very low compared with productivity in many other industries. Whether comparisons with other industries (such as manufacturing) are fair is open to question. Some of the many reasons why low productivity has prevailed are:

Fixed cost of certain employees

Fluctuating sales volume. The peaks and valleys of demand for the products and services offered by the typical hospitality enterprise, combined with an insensitivity of much of the labor cost to fluctuating and frequently unpredictable demand, can mean that at certain times nothing can be done about the productivity (or lack of it) of some employees. For example, 100 percent occupancy of guest rooms—rather than, say, 80 percent—does not require additional staffing at the front desk. The employees simply register the additional guests and become more productive. Unfortunately, the reverse is also true. As demand drops, it is difficult in many cases to decrease the labor cost. A 60 percent occupancy of rooms generally would not permit any reduction of employees at the front desk. They simply become less productive. In other words, the industry generally has a high fixed labor cost, so minor changes in volume of revenue can have a major effect on labor cost ratios and net income. Exhibit 10.6 illustrates this in the case of a restaurant. On a normal day, labor cost is 40 percent of revenue. On a good day, it drops to 37 percent; and on a poor day, it jumps to 45 percent. The reason for these swings is that, even if the variable portion of labor can be adjusted to revenue, the fixed portion cannot.

Labor cost percent affected by volume fluctuations

Limited ability to produce for inventory. Manufacturing industries that are subject to cyclical demand can continue to produce during low demand periods and hold the goods in inventory until demand again increases. Productivity is stabilized and the labor cost per unit of production can be held constant. This is not true of a hotel or restaurant. Since the industry is primarily a service one, it is impossible to store the labor cost. The only opportunity an establishment has to do this is to have food-production employees produce meals that can be frozen during low-demand periods. Alternatively, as mentioned earlier in this chapter, by using more convenience foods, the labor cost provided by suppliers and included in the price of the product can be stored. But a desk clerk's, a waiter's, or a maid's labor cost cannot be inventoried.

Difficulty of "storing" labor cost

Lack of labor saving equipment. Since the industry is highly labor intensive because of its service nature, it is difficult to replace employees with machines. Customers expect personal service. Where equipment can be introduced to reduce labor cost, then this should be seriously considered. For example, the use of certain types of beverage-dispensing equipment, discussed in Chapter 8, may mean that fewer bartenders are required.

Personal service expected

Poor layout of facilities. This is probably more true of older properties that were designed when the ratio of employees to customers was much

EXHIBIT 10.6. Effect of Volume on Labor Cost

	Normal Day		Poor Day		Good Day	
Revenue	$1,000	100%	$800	100%	$1,200	100%
Food cost	400	40	320	40	480	40
Gross profit	$ 600	60%	$480	60%	$ 720	60%
Labor cost:						
Fixed	$200		$200		$200	
Variable 20% × Revenue	200		160		240	
	400	40	360	45	440	37
Income before other expenses	$ 200	20%	$120	15%	$ 280	23%

Kitchen design and labor cost

higher than today. For example, many kitchens in older hotels were designed with sufficient equipment and space to produce food for extensive menus. Today's more limited menus save in some areas but may also mean that fewer kitchen employees now spend more time moving from one area to another, thus decreasing their productive time. However, many new facilities are still designed without enough consideration given to employee movement (and thus employee productivity).

Poor management and supervision. One of the most important tasks of top management in the reduction of labor cost is to hire and train the right kind of supervisors (department heads or managers). These managers must in turn be competent at training their employees to be efficient. Such managers should be hired on the basis of their administrative skills combined with technical skills—not just on the basis of their technical skills. A good technical employee may not be a good administrator. A good desk clerk may make a poor front-office manager. A superior waitress may make a poor dining room supervisor. The manager's or supervisor's skills encompass such abilities as selecting good employees, training employees to be more productive, enforcing standards, motivating employees, preparing staffing schedules, maintaining employee morale (to reduce employee turnover), and implementing procedures to control labor costs and other costs. A poor manager or supervisor will fail to extract the full potential from employees and thus will add to overall labor costs. This last point will be explored more fully in chapter 11.

Skills required

PRODUCTIVITY IMPROVEMENT IDEAS

Before moving on to that chapter, let us list some of the ways in which productivity may be improved. Not all of the ideas can be implemented in any individual establishment. Nor is the list necessarily exhaustive or in any particular order of importance. Some of the ideas mentioned may generate other ideas for an individual operation.

1. Preregistration of hotel guests so that time does not have to be spent at this task as each guest arrives.
2. Use of no-iron linens in a hotel that does its own laundering will save on laundry labor cost.
3. Use of disposables in a food operation may save on dishwashing costs.
4. Use of soft drink dispensing machines and self-serve ice machines saves on room-service labor cost.
5. Use of direct-dial telephones in guest rooms reduces

Use of "disposables"

switchboard labor cost; also, where it is legal, establishing room rates so that they cover the average number of local calls per occupied room can reduce guest-billing labor cost.

6. Consolidation of positions (such as receiving clerk and timekeeper or room clerk and front office cashier) where the work load does not justify two full-time positions.

   Consolidation of jobs

7. Elimination of positions that have become redundant because of technological change or for other reasons.

8. Use of an advance approval of overtime system, thus reducing that often unnecessarily high cost of labor. Exhibit 10.7 illustrates a form that could be used that obliges department heads or supervisors to be aware of the cost of each overtime situation and requires them to document reasons justifying it.

   Advance overtime approval

9. Holding over late banquet clean-up until the following morning rather than paying overtime.

10. Adjusting hours of restaurant operations to eliminate labor cost in very low demand periods.

11. Consolidating restaurant operations for meal or other periods when it is not profitable, from a labor cost point of view, to keep two or more restaurants open and competing for the same clientele.

12. Considering self-service in a restaurant rather than table service.

    Use of self-service

13. Using part-time bar employees to handle banquet bars rather than using regular employees on an overtime basis.

EXHIBIT 10.7. Overtime Authorization Form

Date_____April 5_____   Department_____Banquet_____

Employee name_____Jones_____

Position_____Houseman_____

Hours of overtime____2____ Rate of pay_____$6.00/hour_____

Total overtime cost____$12.00____

Reason: To set up meeting room for early breakfast on April 6

Authorized by_____J. L. Hinton_____
                                  Department head

14. Scheduling vacations in relation to work load or demand fluctuations, rather than have employees on vacation during peak periods necessitating hiring temporary employees.

15. Considering contracting for certain services such as janitorial work or maintenance so that full-time employees are not kept on the payroll during periods when there is insufficient work for them.

Improving layouts

16. Improved layout of equipment and/or work flow to consolidate work positions.

17. Rearranging restaurant seating so that employees can serve more customers.

18. Using room-service waiters to serve small banquets rather than hiring part-time banquet waiters who frequently have to be paid for a minimum of, let us say, four hours, when a banquet takes only two hours.

19. Using more convenience foods (this was discussed earlier in the chapter).

Part-time Employees

Part-time employees are often viewed as a solution to high labor costs. However, these employees can create problems if their use is not carefully planned and implemented. Properly determining what is known as the "employee mix" between full- and part-time employees is a matter requiring experience and judgment.

Employee mix

One of the problems that arises is the hidden cost of a part-time employee. Although the total cost per day for a part-time person is obviously less than that for a full-time employee, more individual employees will be needed than if only full-time employees were used. This entails a higher training cost for the extra people. There is also likely to be a higher turnover cost, which in turn increases the training cost for replacement employees. Other hidden costs relate to the dubious reliability of part-time employees. For example, since they may not have the same commitment to the establishment that full-time employees have, and since they may have full-time jobs elsewhere, absenteeism can occur because the full-time job takes precedence. That full-time job may even be a commitment as a homemaker! If the part-timers are students, their school work (or even school vacations) can take precedence.

Hidden costs

Part-time employees can, however, be an asset. For example, if a dining room has only a single turnover of seats at lunchtime and two turnovers at dinnertime, the full complement of employees required for the four-hour evening meal period cannot be gainfully scheduled (and thus given a full eight hours work for the day) for the four-hour luncheon period. A sensible solution to this problem would be to hire the extra dinner-time employees needed from among applicants who only want to work part-time (in the evening).

Fast-food restaurants, which frequently have several peaks and valleys of volume during a day, often hire students (who are only seeking part-time work) to work in their operations, scheduling most of them to work during the peak-volume periods. One of the advantages that fast-food operations have is that they can use mainly part-time employees, each of whom is given only a limited number of hours work per week. All of these part-timers are on call, as required. Because of their large pool of potential employees, these establishments can overcome the absenteeism problem. When employees prove themselves to be reliable, they can be given more hours of work and preferable shifts as a reward. Employees who are not reliable are simply dropped from the pool.

Fast-food restaurants

Overtime

Overtime pay is sometimes inevitable—for example, in an emergency when service must be continued beyond normal hours because of an unanticipated demand, or when there is no time to call in part-time people to cope with an unexpected demand situation. Overtime work is often seen as a cause of a higher labor cost, but it can be used strategically as a tool to reduce labor cost.

Use as strategic tool

For example, if an extra employee is needed for two hours of work but, if called in, must legally or by union agreement be paid for a minimum of four hours, it would be more profitable (less costly) to pay a full-time employee who has already worked a full shift to perform the extra two hours at time-and-a-half pay—which in this case amounts to the equivalent of three hours. The net saving is thus one hour of labor cost. It is also likely that the full-time employee is more skilled and better trained than the part-time employee who is called in only when the perceived need to avoid overtime arises.

Overtime becomes an unnecessary cost when it is the result of poor planning, and this will become obvious when a department head or manager is constantly okaying excessive overtime pay.

Incentive Schemes

Some companies have successfully introduced incentive schemes to increase productivity. These include such practices as paying bonuses for low absenteeism and/or a good record of punctuality, and extra pay for high productivity (for example, serving more customers than an established standard, or cleaning more rooms than a normal quota — although, in such cases, the possible reduction in quality of service and room cleanliness

Higher productivity versus lower quality

must be considered). Some major companies have also introduced profit-sharing schemes to reduce employee turnover and retain experienced employees for longer periods. Such schemes generally increase the share of profits with length of service.

Increasing Demand

Market analysis and strategy

The point was made earlier in this chapter concerning the high fixed labor cost of the hospitality industry. Rather than concentrate solely on a reduction of labor cost to conform to anticipated demand, an alternative might be to increase the demand during the slack period. This is a matter of analyzing the market and establishing marketing strategies that will increase demand. An optimum situation, though it may be difficult to achieve in practice, would be to have the establishment always operating at peak demand. In this way, productivity of all employees can be maximized.

Participative Management

Employees as an asset or resource

Participative management was developed in Europe. The concept is that employees are considered to be an asset or resource of the company rather than solely a cost. They are, therefore, invited to participate in the decision-making process and have their own ideas discussed in such matters as purchasing and budgeting, as well as in day-to-day operations. The department supervisor's or manager's task is to organize the employees input and ensure good communication. Since the employees participate in any savings resulting from their ideas, attempts to increase productivity would be of prime concern to them.

Training Programs

Cost recovery of training programs

Training and/or educational programs can frequently lead to improved productivity. Such programs are often perceived by management as costs that cannot be recovered, or that, since the cost recovery cannot be measured, one can never be sure that the programs are profitable. This may be true in certain cases. For example, it is not easy to measure the productivity of a supervisor or department head. In other cases, it is relatively easy to measure the number of guests that can be handled per hour by an efficient front office cashier, or the number of guests served per employee in a foodservice operation. In such cases, a simple equation can be used to measure the profitability of the training program investment. The equation to measure the productivity increase required to pay for the program is:

$$\frac{\text{Program cost per employee}}{\text{Annual hours worked by employee} \times \text{Rate of pay per hour}}$$

Productivity
increase equation

If a training program to improve the efficiency of a coffee shop waitress costs $200, and the coffee shop waitress works thirty-five hours per week for fifty weeks per year at an hourly rate of pay of $4, the increased productivity required would be

$$\frac{\$200}{35 \times 50 \times \$4} = \frac{\$200}{\$7,000} = 0.0286 \text{ or } 2.9\%$$

Calculation of
productivity
increase required

This would mean that about 3 percent more customers per hour or per shift would have to be served by that waitress to pay for the program. If the productivity of all employees undergoing the program can be increased beyond 3 percent, then not only will the program pay for itself, but a reduction of number of employees required, and thus reduced labor cost, should result.

Equipment Replacement and Productivity

The same type of evaluation made with reference to employee training can be applied to calculate the increase in employee productivity required to make replacement of old equipment with new equipment profitable. The equation would only have to be used in situations where the annual operating cost of the new equipment exceeds the annual operating cost of the old equipment. If annual costs are identical, no increased productivity is needed to pay for the equipment. If operating costs of the new equipment are lower, it goes without saying that the new equipment should be purchased since it will lower total costs even if there is no change in worker productivity. Operating costs include such items as energy, supplies, repairs and maintenance, insurance, interest on money borrowed for the new equipment, and depreciation.

Limited use of
equation

The equation, where new equipment costs are higher, is:

$$\frac{\text{New equipment annual operating cost} - \text{Old equipment annual operating cost}}{\text{Annual wage cost of employee(s) using equipment}}$$

Equipment
replacement
equation

For example, if the present operating costs of dishwashing equipment are $1,500 a year and operating costs of a new, faster dishwasher were $2,500, and if total annual labor cost of dishwashers were $20,000 a year, the in-

Calculation of productivity increase required

crease in productivity (or reduction of dishwasher-labor cost) to pay for the equipment would need to be:

$$\frac{\$2,500 - \$1,500}{\$20,000} \quad \text{or} \quad \frac{\$1,000}{\$20,000} = 0.05 \text{ or } 5\%$$

Adjustments for only partial use of equipment

In some situations, employees using equipment do not use it full time. For example, a front-office posting machine operated by front office cashiers would not have 100 percent usage since cashiers' responsibilities include other tasks not requiring the use of the machine. In that case, the denominator of the equation (annual labor cost) must be multiplied by the estimated percentage of time spent operating the equipment. This will tend to reduce the denominator, and, therefore, increase the productivity increase (or reduction in labor cost) required. This is so because the new equipment will not affect the productivity level of the other tasks performed that do not require using the equipment. If the productivity level of other tasks is affected, then the percentage multiplier used in the denominator of the equation should be altered accordingly.

SUMMARY

The problem of labor cost control is not new. However, because of such factors as the trend to a shorter work week, longer vacations, increasing minimum wage, and unionization, the relative importance placed on labor cost control has changed in recent years. Labor cost as a percentage of revenue can vary widely from one facet of the industry to another. A number of factors can cause this to be so, including the layout of the physical plant, its location, market demands, government legislation, unions, greater or lesser use of labor saving equipment, and restaurant use of more or fewer convenience foods. When expressing labor cost as a percentage of revenue, one should be aware of possible misinterpretations that can arise. The reader will recall that this is also true of food and beverage cost percentages.

The following three alternative methods of measuring labor cost were also discussed in this chapter: sales per man-hour by department or subdepartment, in comparison to a standard; dollar labor cost per guest served; and guest count per man-hour of labor.

Total labor cost includes not only the so-called base rate or salary, but also fringe benefits such as vacation pay, workers' compensation, social security, unemployment compensation, group and/or medical insurance, dental insurance, the cost of free meals, and sick leave. These fringe benefits may add as much as 30 percent to the base pay or salary.

Controlling labor cost depends to a large extent on the property and its organization, as indicated by its organization chart. Generally, as with food and beverage costs, responsibility in this area lies with the department head involved.

The major measure in effective labor cost control is an evaluation of employee productivity. Compared to many other industries, productivity in the hospitality business is considered to be relatively low because of such factors as fluctuating volume of sales, a limited ability to produce for inventory during slack times, a lack of labor-saving equipment, poor layout of facilities and poor management and supervision. Many ideas can be implemented to improve productivity, including introducing incentive schemes, increasing the demand for goods and services offered, and using participative management. Another way to improve productivity might be to pay for training programs for employees. The equation to measure the productivity increase required to pay for the program is:

$$\frac{\text{Program cost per employee}}{\text{Annual hours worked by employee} \times \text{Rate of pay per hour}}$$

Finally, productivity can frequently be increased by purchasing more efficient equipment, even if the operating costs of the new equipment are higher than before. In such cases, the increased productivity required to make the new equipment pay for itself can be calculated as follows:

$$\frac{\begin{matrix}\text{New equipment annual} \\ \text{operating cost}\end{matrix} - \begin{matrix}\text{Old equipment annual} \\ \text{operating cost}\end{matrix}}{\text{Annual wage cost of employee(s) using equipment}}$$

DISCUSSION QUESTIONS

1. List three factors that, in more recent times, have led to a greater emphasis being placed on labor cost control.

2. Discuss how the location of a particular hotel or restaurant can have an effect on its labor cost.

3. Give an illustration of how market demands can affect labor cost.

4. Explain how the use of more convenience foods can affect labor cost. What other cost(s) can affect this?

5. List five fringe benefits that would normally be part of total labor cost.

6. Discuss the role of the operations analyst in a large hotel.

7. Discuss how fluctuating demand can affect the productivity of bartenders in a cocktail lounge.

8. In what manner can good management and supervision increase employee productivity?

9. List three ideas of your own (excluding any listed in the chapter) that you think could increase employee productivity in the housekeeping department of a hotel.

10. What is participative management?

11. Give the equation for measuring the productivity increase required to pay for an employee's training program.

12. An equation can be used to determine from a cost and productivity point of view if new equipment should be purchased to replace old equipment. If the employees involved do not use the equipment full time, what effect does this have on the equation and on the productivity increase required?

PROBLEMS

10–1. A hotel with three operating departments had the following revenue and labor cost figures for a particular week:

	Revenue	Labor cost
Rooms	$35,400	$ 7,800
Food	42,600	12,700
Beverage	38,900	11,600

a. Calculate the labor cost percentage for each department separately and for the three departments combined.

b. Assume the revenue in the rooms department had been 10 percent higher that week and 10 percent lower in both the food and beverage departments, with no change in any of the labor cost amounts. Recalculate the labor cost percentages and comment about the changes that have occurred.

10–2. A chain restaurant company has three operations. For a particular month, you have the following information about each of them:

	Unit A	Unit B	Unit C
Revenue	$72,000	$90,000	$44,000
Customers served	60,000	70,000	40,000
Labor cost	$24,480	$31,850	$14,740

Calculate the average check, the labor cost percent, and the labor cost per customer for each unit, and discuss the results in terms of labor cost and productivity.

10–3. In a sixty-room motel, occupancy is normally at 70 percent and average room rate $25. At this level of occupancy, the salaries of the fixed cost employees (manager, front office personnel, and others) is $420 per day. Variable wage cost (for housekeeping employees) is directly related to the number of rooms used. For each room used, one-half hour of variable wages must be paid at an hourly rate of $5.

a. Calculate the income before other expenses, on both a dollar and a percentage basis (as illustrated in exhibit 10.6).
b. Recalculate the figures for both a 60 percent and an 80 percent occupancy, and, from these results, comment about the effect the fixed labor cost of this motel has on its income with fluctuating levels of occupancy.

10–4. For a specific group of employees in a restaurant, you have the following information for two successive weeks:

	Week 1	Week 2
Revenue	$9,780	$8,590
Guests served	4,670	3,775
Wages	$1,868	$1,510
Hours worked	744	580

For each week, calculate the labor cost per hour worked, the cost per 100 guests served, and the revenue per hour worked. Discuss each of these as a measure of the productivity of the employees for each of the two weeks. What other information might you like to have about this group of employees before making decisions about their productivity?

10–5. A hotel is contemplating employing another person in its marketing department. If he is employed, the sales calls made to office buildings in the hotel's area would generate an additional eighty rooms occupied per month with an average room rate of $30. Fifty percent of these rooms would be double occupied. The additional room guests will generate additional food revenue. It is anticipated 80 percent of the additional guests will eat breakfast at an average check of $2.75, 20 percent will eat lunch at an average check of $4.35, and 40 percent will eat dinner at an average check of $6.95. The additional food revenue will also create extra beverage revenue. This beverage revenue is estimated at 20 percent of lunch food revenue and 35 percent of dinner food revenue. The additional revenue will cause direct (variable) costs to rise in proportion to the increased revenue as follows: rooms 25 percent, food 65 percent, and beverage 50 percent. The new marketing department employee would be paid a salary of $1,500 a month. Fringe benefits will amount to 25 percent. Should the new sales employee be hired? (Round figures to the nearest dollar.)

10–6. A week-long training program for the six employees in a particular department will cost $1,500. Each of the employees in that department works a 37½ hour week and has three weeks' vacation per year. Rate of pay is $3.40 per hour. Other fringe benefits are 15 percent.

a. Calculate the increased productivity required to pay for the training program. What would this be in terms of extra customers to be served assuming each of the employees handles, on average, forty customers during a daily shift?

b. Recalculate part (a) assuming the training program cost was $1,800 and the employees worked a thirty-five-hour week.

10–7. A hotel is contemplating replacing an old item of equipment with a new one. The operating costs of the old equipment are $1,850 per year. The new equipment will cost $12,050, but a trade-in will be allowed on the old equipment amounting to $3,000. The new equipment is estimated to have a five-year life with no trade-in. Money will have to be borrowed to buy the new equipment. Interest rate is 10 percent. Other operating costs have been estimated at $375 per year for the new equipment. The equipment is operated twenty-four hours a day by three employees each working an eight-hour shift. Hourly rate of pay is $4 plus fringe benefits of 18 percent. Use a 365-day year.

a. Calculate the increased productivity required to pay for the new equipment.
b. Recalculate the productivity increase required assuming the new equipment had a $2,500 trade-in at the end of its life, and that it is only used 80 percent of the time by the employees involved.

Labor Cost Standards

11

Objectives

After studying this chapter, the reader should be able to do the following:

- State in what way labor cost differs from food and beverage cost.
- Define and describe *job analysis*.
- Define, describe, and prepare job descriptions and task procedures.
- Categorize employees as fixed, semi-fixed, or variable cost.
- Define and establish productivity standards for various types of employees.
- Describe and use a staffing guide.
- From given information, prepare volume forecasts.
- Prepare staffing schedules from given information.
- Calculate forecast payroll costs from given information, and list possible causes of variances between forecast and actual results.
- Define and discuss the cost of employee turnovers.

FIXED ELEMENT OF LABOR COST

Risk of reliance on percentages

In earlier chapters, both food cost percent and beverage cost percent were discussed as measures of effectiveness of the food and beverage control systems. In both cases, it was emphasized that there may be difficulties in relying solely on the percentage as a basis for evaluating actual operating results. The main problem is that one can have a high cost percent yielding a high gross profit or, alternatively, a low percent yielding a low gross profit.

Payroll labor cost percentage depends on five factors:

Five variables

1. The number of guests accommodated or served. This number is normally unpredictable, other than in the case of banquet guests, where a guaranteed number has been contracted for.

2. The average room rate or average check. This is relatively predictable, based on past performance.

3. The number of employees called in on duty. This can usually be predicted and controlled on the basis of volume forecasts.

4. The hours worked by employees who are not on a fixed salary. This is a known factor (other than when unforeseen emergencies such as those requiring overtime hours arise.

5. The hourly wage rate. This is normally a known and predictable figure.

Shifting variables

All of these variables are continually shifting with respect to each other. Some of them (such as the number of guests) shift randomly from day to day; others (such as wage rate increases) are relatively constant but shift over time. Therefore, the labor cost as a percent of sales should only be used as a planning and operating guideline. It should not be used as a real measure of payroll cost and employee productivity.

Labor cost percent can decrease if prices are increased (for example, during a time of inflation) while productivity goes down (for example, as fewer guests are served). This problem is not even apparent when labor cost percent is used as a measure of labor cost control.

Fixed element of labor cost

An analysis of labor cost that relies entirely on labor cost percent has an additional pitfall. This problem, which was mentioned in chapter 10 and illustrated in exhibit 10.6, relates to the fixed nature of a certain proportion of labor cost. This characteristic differentiates labor cost from food and beverage cost, which, almost without exception, are proportionate to revenue. The effect of this fixed element may be hidden over time, when labor cost peaks and valleys offset each other and tend to smooth out what might otherwise be a volatile cost percent.

If fixed salaries are excluded from a labor cost before it is calculated as a percentage of sales, however, the measure may have some validity—particularly where fixed salaries are low in comparison to variable wages and where the business can adapt variable wages quickly to suit fluctuating sales volume.

On the other hand, labor cost based on a standard of manpower predetermined on the basis of forecast volume of business overcomes the cost percent problems. Such manpower standards are based on the productivity of employees. This chapter discusses how to establish manpower standards and how to use them in labor cost planning and control.

The system of labor cost control described in this chapter, although not the only approach to controlling labor, is used by many larger hospitality industry enterprises. Many smaller enterprises also use it, probably in a less formalized way. In fact, there is no reason why any enterprise could not use the major aspects of this system in order to reduce its labor cost.

Application of system in small operations

JOB ANALYSIS, JOB DESCRIPTION, AND TASK PROCEDURES

Before labor cost standards can be established and implemented, certain basic steps should be taken. These steps include job analysis, and preparation of job descriptions and task procedures.

Job Analysis

Job analysis simply takes each type of employee position and questions every aspect of it. The type of questions could include any or all of the following:

Typical job analysis questions

Why is the job being done?
Why by this category of employee?
Why at this location or locations?
Why at this time of day?
Can it be done during a slack rather than peak period?
Is each job step necessary?
Why are the job steps carried out in that sequence?
Is it necessary to have time lags between tasks?
Are supplies moved a minimum distance without backtracking?
Is there too much rehandling of supplies?
Are there defined stations for location of work supplies?
Are these stations well designed?
Do the station locations minimize employee movement?
Can any travel distances be shortened?
Is one employee using a better method that other employees could follow?

These are only some of the questions that might be posed. As a result of carrying out job analysis, inefficiencies will be observed and can be cor-

Purposes served by job analysis

rected. Steps may be eliminated or given to others. The time to perform the job may be shortened, or the position eliminated. It may be discovered that the job can be carried out by more efficient methods including the use of equipment to free up employee time. The main purpose of job analysis is to review each job position, preferably at least annually, to determine its contribution to net income and to try to increase that contribution. Job analysis also makes it easier to prepare job descriptions (to be discussed in the next section).

Inappropriateness of assembly line techniques

In the hospitality industry, it is difficult to apply many of the successful techniques, such as time and motion study, that are used in assembly-line situations to aid in job analysis. On assembly lines, items are mass-produced, can be produced for inventory regardless of hourly or daily or even weekly volume, and are generally of a nonperishable nature. Most of the tasks performed by employees in these situations are continuously repetitive in nature, and it is easy to determine for the various job categories how many times a certain task can be repeated in an hour or during a shift. Very few hospitality industry enterprises have situations like this, although some of the major fast-food chains have been able to take advantage of some assembly-line job analysis techniques, combined with accurate hourly forecasting of customer demand, to improve employee productivity. In the housekeeping department of a hotel, it is also possible to

Determination of most efficient methods

determine the most efficient method for cleaning guest rooms, including a calculation of the amount of time it should normally take to clean a room if employees are trained to follow the efficient method, and thus determine the number of rooms a maid can clean in a normal shift. A similar situation might exist with waiters and banquet service.

But, in most cases, the speed and frequency with which tasks must be performed is dictated by the customers. For example, it would be easy, through time and motion study, to determine how long it takes an efficient sandwich maker to make a particular type of sandwich. Let us assume the figure is sixty an hour. This knowledge is only valuable if 60 customers ar-

Variability of customer demand

rive each hour and order that type of sandwich, or if 480 customers order sandwiches during that employee's eight-hour shift. Few establishments that wish to prepare fresh sandwiches on customer demand would be in that situation. Further, the person responsible for making sandwiches would probably have other tasks to perform, such as making salads, preparing vegetables for the next meal, or helping other employees who are overly busy. These other tasks would be carried out during slack periods when no customers are ordering sandwiches. The random nature of customer demand therefore does not allow tasks to become constantly repetitive.

Responsibility of the department head

In such cases, the question of how productive an employee should be as a result of job analysis is often a matter of observation and judgment. This method of job analysis would generally be carried out by the employee's department head, since the department head would normally be responsible for control of the labor cost in her department, and is in the best position to know the various employees' capabilities.

Job Description

Subsequent to job analysis, a job description should be prepared for each category of employee. The description includes what the job entails, the steps that must be performed, and when the steps must be performed. Job descriptions should not be too detailed, but they should include sufficient information so that both employee and supervisor are sure what the job entails, and not what they think it entails. A typical job description for a banquet houseman might be as follows:

What to include in a job description

1. Reports to the banquet coordinator who is supervised by the banquet manager.

2. Is responsible for set-up of banquet rooms for various events such as banquets, weddings, cocktail receptions, fashion shows, and similar functions. The layout for each individual function will be provided by the banquet coordinator.

Example of a job description

3. Is responsible for the cleanliness of the various banquet rooms both before and after each function. This cleanliness includes both general tidiness and dusting, ensuring that ashtrays and mirrors are clean, and that carpets are vacuumed before each function.

4. At each month-end, all lamps and banquet furniture must be cleaned.

5. At the end of the first week in each month, all upholstery is to be spot-cleaned.

6. At the end of the second week in each month, all carpets must be shampooed.

7. Banquet plants must be watered when necessary.

8. The banquet storeroom must be kept clean and tidy at all times.

9. The position requires that the person have good health and be strong since frequent heavy lifting may be necessary.

10. Since the person will have frequent contact with the public, such factors as appearance, politeness and personality are important.

11. The person must be flexible in order to adapt to pressure situations and last-minute requests by guests.

Task Procedures

Put task procedures preferably in writing

In the hospitality industry, most positions or jobs require the employee to carry out a variety of different tasks. Each task requires the employee to follow certain procedures for efficiency and to reduce losses from not performing the task the right way. In some cases, these procedures can be demonstrated and taught to employees. In other cases, it would be preferable to put them into writing and ensure that all employees performing that set of procedures read and follow them. A typical set of procedures for a front desk clerk, one of whose tasks might be to handle guests' credit cards, might be as follows:

1. When a guest checks in, ask if payment will be by credit card or some other method.
2. If it is to be credit card, ask to see the card.
3. Verify that the card is one acceptable to this hotel (American Express, Diners, Carte Blanche, Master Charge, or Visa).
4. If acceptable, check date on card to make sure it has not expired.
5. Copy credit card number and name as it appears on the card in the space provided on the guest's folio (account).

Example of written set of task procedures

6. As you return the card, remind the guest to see the front office cashier before departing to verify the accuracy of the account and sign the credit card voucher for the charge.
7. Before filing folio with the cashier, check credit card number to make sure it is not on the credit card company's cancellation list.
8. Initial the credit card number on the folio to show that this has been done.
9. If the card number is on the cancellation list, advise the front office manager or credit manager.

On check-out:

10. Check the guest account to ensure the credit card number has been initialed.
11. If it has not been, check the cancellation list and advise the front office manager or credit manager if it is listed. Do not return the card to the guest.
12. If not listed, complete the appropriate credit card company voucher, using the correct imprinter.
13. Have the guest sign the voucher. Check the voucher signature against the credit card signature.
14. Return the credit card to the guest with a copy of the voucher.

LABOR PRODUCTIVITY STANDARDS

A preliminary step to the preparation of labor productivity standards would be to ensure that the establishment's quality standards are well understood. For example, the productivity of a maid measured in number of rooms cleaned in a normal shift can be easily increased by reducing the time spent cleaning each room. This would not be a good idea if it encroaches on the quality standards (level of room cleanliness) and results in customer complaints. Similar situations would prevail in care taken in food preparation and presentation, or level of waiter and waitress service.

Jobs in the hospitality industry can usually be categorized into three broad types: fixed cost employees, semifixed cost employees, and variable cost employees. **Three job categories**

Fixed Cost Employees: Fixed cost employees, sometimes referred to as nonproductive employees, are those employees whose positions are not contingent on volume of sales unless there is a major change in this volume. These employees are generally on a monthly or annual salary, regardless of number of hours actually worked. As long as job analysis of each position in this category shows that the employee is needed, no productivity standard would normally be established. The kinds of positions that fall into this category are the general manager, most assistant managers and department heads, and many of the back-of-the-house positions such as maintenance and engineering, marketing, and accounting office and secretarial employees. **No productivity standards for fixed cost employees**

Although fixed cost employee positions, as mentioned, are not generally affected by revenue, employees in these positions can sometimes be used in slack times to assume jobs, either part- or full-time, that would otherwise be carried out by employees in the semifixed or variable categories. While this does not affect the labor cost of fixed employees, it does reduce overall labor cost. **Use of fixed cost employees for other categories**

Semifixed Employees. This production-related group of employees would be those whose positions are dependent to some extent on the volume of business. This dependence could be on a daily basis, or, alternatively, the employee might work each day but the hours of work (subject to a minimum guaranteed number of hours) might fluctuate daily according to business volume. In order to have cost flexibility, these positions would normally have an hourly rate attached to them.

This category would include employees such as cashiers, kitchen preparation personnel, switchboard operators, and restaurant hostesses. For each of these various positions, productivity standards should be established. **Examples of semifixed employees**

Variable Cost Employees. This group of employees is also referred to as the direct production group. The positions are entirely contingent on

Examples of variable cost employees

customer demand, both as to number of employees required each day and number of hours to be worked by each employee. It should be noted that many hospitality operations are subject to union contracts or government regulations to ensure an employee is paid for a minimum number of hours (for example, four) if called in any particular day. This category would include certain types of food-preparation employees, waiters, waitresses, and maids, to name a few. The establishment of productivity standards is most critical for this group of employees, particularly in establishments where volume can fluctuate quite widely on a daily basis, and even by meal period in restaurants.

Establishing Productivity Standards

Although productivity standards could be established based on past performance, there is no guarantee that past results were optimal. For example, based on historical records, the number of guests to be served for each banquet waitress may be established at thirty. How can we be sure that is the most productive number? It is for this reason that job analysis is helpful in determining the best number of customers that the average, reasonably good banquet waitress can cope with. Each establishment must carry out

Variation of standards between establishments

its own analysis and determine its own standards. For any particular position, standards will vary from one establishment to another because of the layout of the property (for example, how close the kitchen is to the banquet room area), type of menu, type of clientele, and many other related factors. (In some establishments, the standards may be written into the union contract and thus are not subject to unilateral change by either party.)

Coordination with the department head

After each type of position has been appropriately studied and all necessary factors have been considered, final standards should be established for each department with the close coordination of the department head concerned. In establishing final standards, the quality standard desired must not be ignored.

Each standard consists of a number of units (rooms, covers, beverage sales) that an employee is expected to "produce" within a certain period. Periods for maids, cooks, bellmen, and barmen are usually for a normal shift. For restaurant personnel, a meal standard would be established

Standards related to periods of time

depending on the length of the operating period of each meal. A food waiter might be expected to serve twenty people during lunch in the dining room over a four-hour period, for example.

An allowance may be given to food waiters in dining rooms for beverage sales by converting the actual beverage sales figure into equivalent food covers. The conversion factor used depends on the type of drinks sold (cocktails, wine sales) and on the beverage price structure of each outlet. For example, in a formal dining room with a high percentage of wine sales and a high-priced beverage list, the factor that will equal one food cover might be ten dollars. In a coffee shop, it might be as low as four or five dollars, due to a lower price structure. For food preparation employees, the standard would be based on total number of covers or guests served in sales areas.

In strictly beverage outlets (bars and lounges), the production standard is generally a monetary unit, for both bartenders and barwaiters. The reason for this is that the normal customer in an eating area has a meal, with or without drinks, and the time he sits there and his average spending fall within a relatively narrow range. This may not be true in a cocktail bar where one customer may occupy a seat and have ten one-dollar drinks. His average check would be ten dollars. Alternatively, ten different customers may occupy that seat in turn and each have a one-dollar drink. The average check for each is one dollar. Thus, the number of customers served in a lounge is not as realistic a standard as is revenue.

Monetary unit as standard in beverage outlets

For employees such as bellmen, the standard might be expressed in number of movements: guest arrivals or departures, laundry calls, or messages delivered. For housekeeping personnel, the standards would be based on rooms occupied (rooms cleaned for maids, rooms inspected for floor supervisors). For front office personnel, standards could be based on guest movements (registrations and check outs).

Typical standards for representative jobs in a larger hotel operation might be:

Position	Standard	Period	
Roomservice Personnel	16 rooms	8 hours	**Examples of standards**
Bellmen	25 movements	8 hours	
Coffee Shop Waitress	20 covers	4 hours	
Dining Room Waiters	15 covers	4 hours	
Cooks	90–100 covers	8 hours	
Dishwashers	150–200 covers	8 hours	
Bartenders	$300	8 hours	
Floor Housekeeper	80 occupied rooms	8 hours	
Room Clerk	100 room arrivals	8 hours	

Once established, the standards should be reviewed from time to time and be revised if necessary. For example, the introduction of a new piece of equipment ,or a redesign of a restaurant could change the affected employees' productivity.

Revisions to standards

STAFFING GUIDES

Staffing guides based on volumes

After standards are established, staffing guides are developed, department by department. These staffing guides will indicate the staffing levels required for various levels of business volume. These staffing guides could be compiled in terms of monthly volume, but they are probably more useful if prepared on a weekly volume—or even on a daily volume basis, in situations where staff levels can be adjusted daily in accordance with anticipated volume. In developing the guides, management must consider both minimum and maximum volume levels. The minimum level identifies the minimum number of employees necessary to maintain a smooth operation. The maximum level is the point beyond which no additional staffing is allowed. For example, in a guest-room situation, it makes no sense to staff beyond a 100 percent occupancy level; similarly, in a banquet situation, it would be useless to staff beyond the level required to handle the largest number of guests that could be seated at any one time. Exhibits 11.1 and 11.2 show partial staffing guides for a coffee shop (weekly staffing) and a housekeeping department (daily staffing), respectively.

Maximum staffing levels

Staffing guides only an aid

Just as productivity standards must be revised as conditions warrant, so, too, should the staffing guides. Remember, however, that staffing guides are an aid in labor cost analysis—not a substitute for it. They should be used for such purposes as discussing schedules with the responsible department heads; they should not be taken as a rigid guide for absolute implementation. Properly handled, they can provide a useful basis for negotiation with the relevant department heads when staffing schedule revisions are required.

EXHIBIT 11.1.   Coffee Shop Staffing Guide

Volume per week in covers	Category A Hostess Hours per week	Category B Waitress Hours per week	Category C Bus help Hours per week	Total Hours per week
Up to 1,260	120	224	112	456 min.
1,261–1,485	120	240	112	472
1,486–1,710	120	320	112	512
5,311–5,535	160	960	240	1,360 max.

EXHIBIT 11.2	Housekeeping Staffing Guide			
Occupied rooms	Number of floor supervisors	Number of day maids	Number of night maids	Total employees
420	3	28	7	38
405	3	27	7	37
390	3	26	7	36
375	3	25	7	35
360	3	24	6	33

FORECASTING

The next step in labor cost control is forecasting work-load units (guest rooms occupied, covers served, dollars of revenue) for each department. These forecasts are developed from records of past events, adjusted for current factors. Although for budgeting purposes many establishments forecast in months, for staffing these budgeted figures should be broken down on a weekly basis prior to each week of actual operations. In this way, the figures can be adjusted to reflect current conditions and recent trends that can affect volume of business. In a hotel, the weekly rooms occupancy forecast serves not only as the basis for staffing in the rooms department, but also as a basis for staffing food and beverage outlets that derive much of their business from the occupancy of guest rooms. A rooms occupancy forecast is illustrated in exhibit 11.3.

Initial staffing based on weekly forecasts

Food and beverage volume, even if dependent on rooms occupancy, varies by area (coffee shop or dining room) and by meal period, and non-guest-room customers must be included in the forecast. Since restaurants not located in hotels depend entirely on walk-in business, that is all they need consider in their forecasts. A sample restaurant volume forecast is illustrated in exhibit 11.4. Even though these illustrated forecasts cover weekly periods, the figures should be revised daily if possible, and the related staffing guides should then be used for staff scheduling. In a large hotel, it is necessary to have good communication between departments in preparing forecasts, because of the business one department derives from another.

Daily revisions to forecasts and staffing

EXHIBIT 11.3   Room Occupancy Forecast

	Period April 8–14	Sunday 8	Monday 9	Tuesday 10	Wednesday 11	Thursday 12	Friday 13	Saturday 14
Previous night's occupied rooms		311	336	332	369	394	324	329
Today's arrivals		107	98	121	120	70	65	112
Today's departures		82	102	84	95	140	60	84
Today's occupied rooms		336	332	369	394	324	329	357
Occupancy		75%	74%	82%	88%	72%	73%	79%
Previous night's guest count		401	439	430	490	521	408	410
Today's arrivals		168	152	194	190	112	100	178
Today's departures		130	161	134	159	225	98	130
Tonight's guest count		439	430	490	521	408	410	458

EXHIBIT 11.4   Restaurant Volume Forecast

Department	Period June 9–15							
	Sunday 9	Monday 10	Tuesday 11	Wednesday 12	Thursday 13	Friday 14	Saturday 15	Totals
Coffee Shop								
Breakfast	150	210	285	280	290	260	190	1,665
Lunch	200	280	300	310	310	330	250	1,980
Dinner	115	180	195	195	210	210	110	1,215
Dining Room								
Lunch	—	180	200	225	180	175	225	1,185
Dinner	350	175	175	210	210	240	275	1,635

An alternative to scheduling on the basis of guest counts is to forecast dollars of sales and then to schedule labor based on that. For example, if the standard is $20.00 of sales for each labor hour expended, and if sales are forecast at $1,000, then $1,000 ÷ $20.00 = 50 hours of labor should be scheduled. The disadvantage of this method is that it is sales-based rather than being guest-count-based. Still, it could be used in a beverage operation where the guest count is less meaningful than the figure for dollars of sales.

STAFF SCHEDULING

Stacked versus staggered schedules

There are two basic types of staff schedules: stacked or shift schedules, and staggered schedules. Stacked (or shift) schedules would be used in departments such as the front office of a hotel for employees such as clerks and cashiers. These employees normally work a full eight-hour shift regardless of volume of business. Those on the morning shift would all start at the same time and all leave at the end of their shift when the next group of shift employees start. However, in most departments of hotels and in food establishments, staggered schedules must be used. Even though staffing guides indicate the number of employees or man-hours that are to be used for each level of business or revenue, they do not indicate when those employees are to work. Generally, an analysis of number of customers served or dollars of revenue earned during each hour must be made. This analysis will indicate the low, the medium, and the high volume periods. Employees should be scheduled so that the maximum number are on duty during high-volume periods and the minimum number during low-volume periods, thus staggering the hours when employees are working.

A staggered schedule might appear as shown in exhibit 11.5. This type of schedule reduces idle time, provides for overlap of employees, recognizes variations during the day in level of sales, and can lead to reduction or elimination of overtime costs. In most cases, schedules for each department would be prepared in advance, week by week, and would show, each day for each employee, the scheduled times of arrival and departure. These times would be subject to daily review prior to each work day, for adjustment (where necessary) to a changed forecast. Days off would also appear on the schedule. A completed individual employee schedule is illustrated in exhibit 11.6.

Schedules prepared weekly

Once staff schedules have been completed, it may be useful to cost them out, calculating the cost percent to see whether it meets the establishment's overall labor cost percent goal (if it has one). If the cost percent does not meet this goal, rescheduling must be done where feasible within the established standards. Sometimes rescheduling is not feasible, because of the way the peaks and valleys of the business occur. If the overscheduling is permanent, a new labor cost percent plan will probably be required.

EXHIBIT 11.5   Staggered Schedule

EXHIBIT 11.6 Employee Schedule

		Dining Room		Week Commencing	April 8		
Employee	Sunday	Monday	Tuesday	Wednesday	Thursday	Friday	Saturday
C. Jones	9–5	9–5	9–5	9–5	9–5	off	off
J. Hathaway	off	off	8–4	8–4	8–4	8–4	8–4
S. Heil	7–3	7–3	7–3	7–3	7–3	off	off
P. Mintz	12–8	12–8	12–8	off	off	12–8	12–8
A. Smith	7–3	7–3	off	off	7–3	7–3	7–3
C. Cody	10–5	10–5	10–5	10–5	off	off	8–4

LABOR COST ANALYSIS

Since volume forecasting and labor scheduling is carried out on a daily basis, an analysis of actual labor cost with forecast or budgeted cost can also be made daily. This daily analysis is much easier than is the case with food or beverage because, with labor cost, we do not have the problem of inventories to contend with. The analysis compares, department by department, the actual man-hours or man-days used and to be paid for with the forecast man-hours or man-days for that day. In some larger operations, the comparision is even made on a meal period basis for the food department. In other establishments, where such daily variances are expected, the comparison is made only on a weekly, biweekly, or monthly basis. In such cases, it might well be that overstaffing and understaffing on individual days will even out and only minor variances will occur overall. Because the objective of the exercise is to discover all variances, then analysis should preferably be carried out on a daily basis. In this way, the causes of all variances can be determined and the entire process of forecasting, and thus controlling labor cost, can be made more effective.

No inventory problem in labor costing

Daily analysis preferable

Generally, variances can be caused by one or more of the following:

Possible causes of variances

1. Manpower guidelines that are inappropriate
2. Forecasts that are not accurate
3. Poor scheduling and excessive overtime
4. Volume fluctuations that were unpredictable

When making comparisons between forecast and actual hours, and when this comparison is made on a man-days basis, then the hours of part-time employees must be converted to equivalent man-days. If the standard man-day for a full-time employee were eight hours, then equivalent man-days would be calculated by dividing total part-time hours for all such employees by eight. The actual hours figures would be taken from payroll records (time cards or sign-in/sign-out sheets that have been approved by the department head).

Calculation of equivalent man-days

Comparisons between forecast and actual figures can also be made on a dollar basis. This requires converting hours forecast and hours actually worked to dollars. In the case of hourly paid employees, hours are simply multiplied by the related hourly rate of pay. In the case of salaried employees, the daily rate will vary depending on the number of days in a month. For example, an employee paid $1,500 a month is assumed to be responsible for his department even on his days off, and will have a daily rate of $50 during a thirty-day month and $48.39 during a thirty-one-day month. If a salaried person has a joint departmental responsibility, then his daily rate must be split, using some logical basis, between the two or more departments involved.

Daily cost of salaried employees

If desired, the labor cost analysis could include labor cost percentage figures. This simply involves dividing each department's labor cost dollars by its revenue and then multiplying by 100. But again do not rely too much on the percentage figures for analytical purposes. A sample daily labor cost analysis is illustrated in exhibit 11.7.

LABOR TURNOVER COST

One of the major, often hidden costs of labor is that of employee turnovers. A turnover is the loss and replacement of an employee. Turnovers occur for both voluntary and involuntary reasons. A voluntary turnover occurs when an employee leaves by choice. An involuntary one occurs when an employee has to be replaced because he or she is not suited for the job or for some other reason.

Direct and indirect turnover costs
Both direct and indirect costs are associated with each turnover. Direct costs include such items as advertising or recruiting, selecting, and orienting and training new employees. Indirect costs are more difficult to measure but are nevertheless there. For example, one cost is the low morale of other employees when good employees leave. This can also be translated into reduced customer satisfaction, compounded by the fact new employees may not initially provide the same quality of service. Double staffing, or overtime, may also be required while new employees are being trained. Also, an employee, knowing he is going to be leaving, might tend to reduce his level of service, adding to customer dissatisfaction and shifting the burden to other staff and, again, affecting staff morale.

Although total turnover costs are difficult to calculate accurately, it has been estimated that they could be as high as $500 per turnover. Since many hospitality enterprises have turnover rates as high as 200 or 300 percent a year, the total turnover cost can be enormous. In a 100 employee establishment, a 200 percent turnover means that 200 job separations occurred during the year. If each turnover costs $500, total annual turnover cost would be:

Total annual turnover cost

$$200 \times \$500 = \$100,000$$

One way to monitor this cost is to calculate the monthly turnover rate. The equation for this is:

Equation for labor turnover percent

$$\frac{\text{Number of separations during month}}{\text{Number of employees on payroll}} \times 100$$

EXHIBIT 11.7   Labor Cost Summary and Analysis

Date _____ April 11 _____

Department	Number of employees today		Labor cost today		Labor cost to date		Labor cost variance	
	Budget	Actual	Budget	Actual	Budget	Actual	Today	To date
Rooms								
Front office	10	10	$ 440	$ 440	$1,320	$1,320		
Housekeeping	42	43	1,280	1,310	3,840	3,900	$ + 30	$ + 60
Service	8	8	320	320	960	930		- 30
Switchboard	6	6	274	274	822	822		
Food								
Dining room	13	14	$ 456	$ 487	$1,368	$1,399	$ + 31	$ + 31
Coffee shop	7	6	245	217	735	707	- 28	- 28
Banquet	11	11	440	440	1,674	1,674		

Calculation of turnover percent

If the number of employees on the payroll has wide fluctuations during the month, then the denominator would be averaged by taking the lowest and highest number of employees and dividing by two. Suppose an establishment had 100 employees on the payroll and 15 separations occurred during a month. The turnover rate would be:

$$\frac{15}{100} \times 100 = 15\%$$

Annual turnover rates could be calculated in a similar way using annual figures.

Use of exit interviews to reduce turnover cost

Because of the high cost of employee turnover, any establishment would profit by trying to reduce the turnover rate. Some turnovers are uncontrollable (for example, death, disability, or retirement). The remaining turnovers are controllable to a greater or lesser degree. One way to reduce the turnover rate is to try to determine the causes for turnovers and then attempt to correct the underlying problems. An exit interview form is useful for gathering information. If an employee leaves without notice and with no opportunity for an exit interview, some relevant information may be obtainable from fellow employees. A word of caution: the reason employees give for leaving and the real reason may not be the same; it is essential to try to determine the real reason. An exit interview form is illustrated in exhibit 11.8, and a turnover analysis form appears in exhibit 11.9.

EXHIBIT 11.8   Exit Interview Form

Date___April 10___   Department _____Coffee shop_____

Employee name _____Darlene Robertson_____

Date employed _____April 6_____

Length of employment _____4 days_____

Employee's reason for leaving _____States she was not made aware_____
of shift hours

Supervisor's comment _____Was advised of shift hours when_____
employed but was unable to handle job pressure

Action taken _____None_____

Would supervisor reemploy? ___No_____

Supervisor's signature _____

EXHIBIT 11.9 Labor Turnover Analysis Form

DEPARTMENTS	VOLUNTARY					INVOLUNTARY				SERVICE				NUMBER OF SEPARATIONS		
	1. Personal	2. Opportunity	3. Dissatisfied	4. Unknown	TOTAL	5. Performance	6. Conduct	7. Staff reduction	TOTAL	a. Less than 30 days	b. 1–12 months	c. Over 1 year	TOTAL	Average number on payroll	This month	Year-to-date
Front Office																
Reservation																
Sales																
Service																
Housekeeping																
Telephone																

SUMMARY

As is also the case with food and beverage cost expressed as a percentage of revenue, it can be misleading to judge labor cost solely as a ratio to revenue. Labor cost also differs markedly from food and beverage cost in that it generally has a high fixed element that cannot be adjusted easily to fluctuating sales volumes. Forecasting revenue levels becomes very important in effective labor cost control so that the variable element, at least, can be correctly established.

The first step in labor cost control is job analysis, and preparation of job descriptions and task procedures. Job analysis takes each type of employee position and questions every aspect of it. The objective is to determine each job's contribution to net income and to try to increase that contribution. Subsequent to job analysis, written job descriptions should be prepared for each position. These descriptions describe what the job entails, the steps that must be performed, and when they must be performed. If jobs entail a number of different tasks, with each task requiring the employee to follow certain procedures to improve efficiency and reduce losses, then, for each task, a written set of procedures should be given to the employees involved.

The next step in labor cost control is the establishment of labor productivity standards for each type of employee or position. In setting standards, one must be aware of the category of employee one is dealing with. Generally, there are three major categories in most establishments: fixed, semifixed, and variable. Each standard consists of a number of units (rooms, covers, beverage sales) that the employee is expected to produce within a given period. Standards should be reviewed and revised whenever necessary.

The next step is to prepare staffing guides, department by department, for each category of employee or position within that department. The staffing guides are based on the previously established productivity standards.

The volume forecasting procedure is a most critical aspect of labor cost control. Forecasts are developed from past records and experiences adjusted for current conditions. Although these forecasts may initially be for a month ahead, generally they are finally refined down to one day ahead.

Subsequent to forecasting, and with reference to the staffing guides, staff schedules can then be prepared. There are two common types of schedules: stacked (or shift) and staggered. These schedules are generally prepared weekly, in advance, but should be subject to change each day if conditions or circumstances have changed.

The final step in the labor cost control cycle is an analysis of actual results with those forecast. The causes of variances between the figures should be determined wherever the variances are unacceptable. The objective is to try to overcome similar situations occurring in the future, thus improving the effectiveness of the labor cost control system.

Labor cost arising from employee turnover is a hidden cost that is generally quite high in most hospitality industry establishments. A useful technique is to calculate a periodic turnover rate. For example, the equation for monthly turnover would be:

$$\frac{\text{Number of separations during month}}{\text{Number of employees on payroll}} \times 100$$

Any reductions that can be made to this turnover rate will, of course, translate into reduced total labor cost.

DISCUSSION QUESTIONS

1. What differentiates labor cost from food or beverage cost insofar as the structure of the cost is concerned?

2. Describe *job analysis* and define its purpose.

3. Differentiate between job descriptions and task procedures.

4. List three positions, other than those mentioned in the chapter, that would fit into the category of fixed cost employees in a restaurant.

5. Differentiate between semifixed and variable cost employees.

6. Describe the term *productivity standard.*

7. What factors might require that productivity standards, once established, need revising?

8. In one or two sentences, describe a staffing guide.

9. Why is it important, in a hotel, that the food department be aware of the rooms department forecasts of rooms occupancy and/or room guest counts?

10. Differentiate between a stacked and a staggered schedule, and give an example, for a hotel, where each one might be used.

11. List three reasons why there might be a difference between forecast payroll hours and actual paid hours.

12. Give two examples of direct and two of indirect costs associated with employee turnovers.

PROBLEMS

11–1. In point form, prepare a job description for a job that you have held (preferably in the hospitality industry). Limit your points to a maximum of twelve.

11–2. Prepare the task procedures for one of the tasks included in this job description. Limit your procedures to no more than fifteen if possible.

11–3. For each of the following positions, state how you might establish a productivity standard. For example, in the case of a guest-room maid, the standard could be based on the number of rooms to be cleaned in a normal full-time shift.

a. A salad maker in a restaurant kitchen

b. A cashier in a hotel front office

c. A banquet waiter or waitress

d. A cashier in a cafeteria

e. A houseman in a hotel's guest-rooms department

f. A cocktail-lounge waiter or waitress

11–4. The restaurant of a resort hotel depends solely on its room guests for all its customers. There are 180 rooms in the resort. Rooms occupancy figures for next week are forecast to be:

Monday	80%
Tuesday	80
Wednesday	84
Thursday	84
Friday	90
Saturday	90
Sunday	85

Round the figures for number of rooms occupied to the nearest whole number. There are, on average, four people per occupied room per night. From past experience, management knows that 90 percent of the people occupying rooms eat breakfast in the restaurant, 70 percent eat lunch, and 80 percent eat dinner (some of the units have their own kitchens). Calculate the restaurant's forecast volume, in terms of number of covers, for each meal period for each day next week.

11–5. A hotel's rooms department has forecast the following for next week:

	Guest arrivals	Guest departures
Sunday	190	159
Monday	100	98
Tuesday	168	206
Wednesday	152	161
Thursday	194	134
Friday	112	225
Saturday	178	130

The Saturday night guest count for this week is 302. The hotel's restaurant is using this information to prepare its volume forecast for next week. On Saturday and Sunday, it knows from past experience, 75 percent of the previous night's guests eat breakfast in the restaurant, 50 percent eat lunch, and 60 percent eat dinner. For the other five days of the week, the figures are: breakfast 60 percent, lunch 20 percent, and dinner 40 percent. In all cases, round figures to the nearest whole number. In addition, the restaurant usually has the following count of walk-ins for each day of the week:

	Breakfast	Lunch	Dinner
Sunday	15	25	50
Monday	25	40	30
Tuesday	25	40	30
Wednesday	25	40	30
Thursday	25	50	40
Friday	25	60	55
Saturday	15	25	75

For each meal period for each day next week, prepare the restaurant's volume forecast in terms of numbers of covers to be served.

11–6. A hotel has the following forecast of rooms to be occupied for each day next week:

	Rooms occupied
Sunday	375
Monday	420

Tuesday	420
Wednesday	405
Thursday	390
Friday	375
Saturday	360

Use the housekeeping staffing guide illustrated in exhibit 11.2 to forecast the payroll cost for each day next week. The month is June. Floor supervisors receive a salary of $16,000 per year, but one is currently on a trainee salary of $12,000 per year. Day-maids' rate of pay is $4.25 per hour, and night-maids' rate of pay is $4.35. Fringe benefits for salaried employees are 22 percent, and for hourly paid employees, 16 percent. The standard shift for an hourly paid employee is 7½ hours.

11–7. The volume forecast of covers to be served in a restaurant on Monday is as follows, with guest counts rounded to the nearest ten:

6–7	a.m.	60
7–8		80
8–9		60
9–10		40
10–11		40
11–12		80
12–1	p.m.	80
1–2		20
2–3		20
3–4		20
4–5		40
5–6		60
6–7		60
7–8		100
8–9		80
9–10		20

The productivity standard for this restaurant is one waiter for each twenty covers. For Monday, prepare a schedule for waiters, using exhibit 11.5 as a guide. Assume that the standard shift for a waiter is eight hours. As far as is practical, each waiter working should have an eight-hour shift. Part-time waiters can be used, but the minimum shift cannot be less than four hours.

Control of Other Direct and Indirect Costs

12

Objectives

After studying this chapter, the reader should be able to do the following:

- List eight or more types of direct cost (other than food, beverage, and labor) for specific departments or establishments.
- Discuss various aspects of the direct cost control system outlined.
- Specify how a standard unit of usage could be established for individual items of cost, and calculate a standard unit from given information.
- Discuss certain aspects of zero-based budgeting (ZBB) such as the decision unit, the ranking process, measurement of work effectiveness, and ZBB's advantages and disadvantages.
- Suggest methods of measuring the effectiveness of individual decision units under ZBB.
- Define and use *variance analysis*.
- Define and use actual financial statements analysis methods such as comparative analysis, comparative common-size analysis, and average check, cost, and net income per guest analysis.

The preceding eight chapters have been concerned with the three major costs that all food and hotel operations have: food cost, beverage cost, and labor cost. This chapter is divided into three parts. Part one is about the control of other direct costs that are the responsibility of the operating department heads; included in this category would be various supplies, among other items. Part two covers control of the indirect or undistributed costs that most establishments have, including costs that are not normally controlled by the operating department heads, such as administrative and general expenses. Part three presents a discussion of variance analysis and actual financial statement analysis.

OTHER DIRECT COSTS

What comprises "other direct costs"?

Direct departmental costs include such items as china, glass, silverware, linens and uniforms, and various types of supplies. These supplies would include those for room guests (soap, matches, tissues, toilet paper, post cards, and similar items), cleaning supplies of all kinds, paper items (cocktail and paper napkins, paper placemats, coasters, aluminum foil, and doilies, to name only a few), and printing and stationery (letterheads, envelopes, message forms, and similar paper goods). In a drive-in restaurant, this category of direct costs would also include food containers such as hamburger bags and plastic cups.

Potential cost savings available

These items generally represent from 5 to 15 percent of total revenue in the typical hospitality operation. This is considerably less than any one of the three major costs but, nevertheless, through cost control of these items, sizeable savings can be made. Unfortunately, these potential cost savings often go unnoticed because of lack of control or lack of attention paid to cost increases in these items. Similar cost increases, on a percentage of revenue basis, would probably not go unheeded with food, beverages, or labor. But a $100 per day saving in these other direct costs still represents a total annual saving, or increase in net income, of $36,500. One of the main difficulties in attracting management's attention to these costs is that the relationship of these costs to revenues is assumed to be correct, and no analysis is ever carried out to determine the accuracy of that relationship.

Quantity Control Approach

For the sake of simplicity in this chapter, we shall refer to all the various other direct costs as supplies. The system of control to be outlined for these supplies will emphasize quantities that should be used, since quantities are eventually translated into dollars on income and expense statements. The system to be explained does not suggest control over every single different item of supplies, since many are used in insufficient quantity and have too low a value to warrant control system expenditures. In fact, in most establishments, it would probably be found that about 20 percent of the items represent 80 percent of the total dollar cost of all supply items. One should therefore concentrate on those that represent the greatest dollar value. The control system also assumes that the items to be monitored are put into lockable storerooms subsequent to purchase, and are controlled through a system of perpetual inventory cards and requisitions.

Impossibility of controlling every last item

After it has been determined which of the many different supplies will be controlled, a historic analysis of past consumption is made. This analysis should preferably cover a year's period to take care of peaks and valleys of usage. Consumption information can be taken from the perpetual inventory cards and should be listed monthly, item by item.

Historic analysis of past consumption

Consumption of each item is then related to some other logical standard unit. For example, the usage of guest soap could be related to the house count (number of guest/nights) during that month. Coffee-shop paper placemats could be related to coffee shop covers served during that month. Once tabulations have been made, an average monthly consumption figure related to the standard unit must be made for each supply item. For example, if the house count for a month in a hotel were 3,000, and if 600 post cards were used that month, the average monthly usage would be one postcard for each five guest/nights (3,000 divided by 600). In other cases, it may be logical to relate consumption to dollars of revenue rather than house count or number of covers. In some cases, the item in question cannot be related so obviously to a standard unit. For example, can the number of gallons of floor cleaning detergent in the kitchen be related to restaurant guests served? Probably not, since the kitchen floor would have to be cleaned regardless of the number of covers. In that case, the standard unit may just have to be left as a period of time—such as twenty gallons of cleaning fluid per month.

Relating consumption to a standard unit

If there are months when the average consumption of an individual item seems disproportionate to other months for that same item, the cause of the distortion should be determined and the usage figure for that month adjusted accordingly. Frequently, such distortions can be explained by the department head concerned.

Adjust for distortions

Once all usage figures have been thoroughly checked, an overall average monthly usage figure should be calculated, item by item. Exhibit 12.1 illustrates how this is done for a couple of hypothetical items. At this point, one might want to question how realistic the figures are. For example, an average of 2¼ guest letterheads per arrival seems reasonable. On the other hand, if coffee shop placemat figures indicated that two placemats were being used for each coffee shop cover, this might seem unreasonably high.

After these calculations have been made, they should be tabulated by

EXHIBIT 12.1.	Quantity Per Standard Unit Calculation	
	Item: Bar coasters	Item: Guest letterheads
January	1 for each $200 bar revenue	2 for each room arrival
February	1 for each $180 bar revenue	2¼ for each room arrival
March	1 for each $195 bar revenue	1¾ for each room arrival
Totals	12 for $2,280 of bar revenue	27 for 12 room arrivals
Average	$\dfrac{\$2,280}{12} = 1$ for each $190 of bar revenue	$\dfrac{27}{12} = 2¼$ for each arrival

Keep departments separate

department. It should be noted that, if the same item is used by two or more departments, the consumption calculations must be kept separate by department since the quantity used per standard unit can vary from one department to another. The departmental figures should be discussed with the department heads concerned so that they can have input. If necessary, after discussion, final amended figures should be prepared, department by department, for all supplies normally used. Copies of departmental lists must be provided to the departments. Copies of all lists must be filed with the appropriate storekeeper.

Relating Issues to Forecast

Forecasts as a basis for quantities requisitioned

The lists should be initially put into effect on a trial basis. The monthly budgets or forecasts prepared by the establishment become the basis for determining the quantities of supplies that should be used (requisitioned and issued from the storeroom) for each month. If departments have sufficient storage room of their own, they could requisition a month's supply to meet the forecast. For example, if the standard for placemats in the coffee shop is 1.2 for each cover, and the forecast is for 20,000 covers that month, the coffee shop will need 24,000 placemats (20,000 × 1.2) less any that it still has on hand from last month. If the coffee shop cannot store that quantity of placemats at a time, then it must requisition in smaller quantities as required. Needless to say, the storekeeper's responsibility is to monitor the requisitions against the standard lists and against the forecast for each department. Should he note that more of any item are requisitioned than the forecast and standard lists indicate, he should be instructed to make a note of this as a double-check on the month-end control.

Storekeeper's responsibility

Month-end Control

At each month's end, an analysis report should be prepared by the control office for each department. Each departmental report should indicate, for each item controlled, the forecast figures, the actual figures, and variances between the two in quantity, in percentage, and in dollars. In any calculation of actual usage figures, adjustment must be made for the inventory of each item on hand in the department. The calculation would be as follows: beginning-of-the-month inventory plus quantity requisitioned less end-of-the-month inventory equals quantity used. A completed departmental supplies analysis form is illustrated in exhibit 12.2.

Monthly control report required

Initially, the control system should be put into effect for a trial period of, let us say, three months. It should then be reviewed to see how it is working, to check if miscalculations have been made, and to see how closely quantities used per standard unit conform to previous calculations. Adjustments may again be necessary. Once final lists have been prepared, they can be put into effect on a more permanent basis. Subsequently, they would only need amending as it is perceived that conditions may have changed.

Reviewing usage standards

Just as the lists for one department may differ for the same item for a second department, so will usage lists differ, probably to an even greater degree, from one establishment to another even if they are part of the same chain and using the same product. Factors such as establishment layout, type of equipment used, and the demands of the clientele can all play a part in affecting consumption rates.

Psychological Control

Employees often do not consider supplies to be high cost items. On an individual basis, with some items, this may be true. Instituting the control system outlined for supplies may bring both direct and indirect benefits. Direct benefits would arise from the control system indicating an almost immediate reduction of the percent of supplies cost related to revenue. Over time, there may be a further indirect benefit from psychological control. As employees become aware through the control system of the cost of items, they may themselves become more cost conscious and begin paying more attention to overusage and other forms of wastage.

Direct and indirect cost benefits

EXHIBIT 12.2. Departmental Supplies Control Form

Department ___Coffee Shop___ Month ___April___

Item	Forecast quantity	Actual quantity	Quantity variance	Variance percent	Variance dollars	Comment
Paper napkins	37,800	40,200	+ 2,400	6.3%	$12.00	Rev. 5% over forecast
Coffee filters	500	620	+ 120	24.0%	$ 3.60	New quality used—not durable
Placemats	37,200	39,400	+ 2,200	5.9%	$66.00	Rev. 5% over forecast

ZERO-BASED BUDGETING

The preceding eight chapters and the first part of this chapter have concentrated on control of costs that are overseen (and controllable) by the operating department heads. These costs (food, beverage, labor, and supplies) are always fairly directly linked to revenue levels. Consequently, they are generally referred to as "direct costs."

However, there is one category of expenses in the hospitality industry that is not related as directly to revenue levels. These indirect expenses, more commonly referred to as undistributed expenses, include:

Indirect or undistributed expenses for ZBB

Administrative and general

Marketing

Guest entertainment

Property operation, maintenance, and energy costs

These undistributed costs are not normally charged to the operating departments, but are kept separate. There are also other fixed costs that an operation may have, such as property taxes, insurance, interest, and rent, that are also not charged to the operating departments. However, the level of these fixed costs is usually imposed from outside the operation. Since they are not subject to day-to-day control, or even to monthly or annual control, we shall not concern ourselves with them.

Undistributed expenses not covered by ZBB

Traditionally, the undistributed costs listed above have been budgeted for, and presumably "controlled," by what is termed *incremental budgeting*. With incremental budgeting, the assumption is made that the level of the last period's cost for any item of expense was correct. For the new period's budget or control period, one only needs to adjust last period's figure upward, or downward, to take care of current conditions. Management monitors only the changes to the budgeted amounts. Whether last period's total cost was justified is never at issue. The cost is just assumed to have been essential to the company's objectives. It is also too frequently assumed that, even with no form of management guidance, the department heads responsible for controlling the undistributed costs are practicing effective cost/benefit analysis, that they are keeping costs in line and preventing overspending. No doubt many of the expenses incurred in this category do meet these criteria. But it is also fairly safe to suggest that the reverse is also true in most establishments that use incremental budgeting.

Incremental budgeting versus ZBB

A relatively new technique that could usefully be used by hospitality industry enterprises to control these undistributed expenses is known as zero-based budgeting (ZBB). As its name implies, with ZBB, no expenses can be budgeted for or incurred unless they are justified in advance. Normally, most establishments would prepare budgets for undistributed expenses once a year. ZBB basically requires that each department head re-

Budgets reviewed from a zero base

justify, in advance, her entire annual budget from scratch, or from a zero base. ZBB has little value in direct cost budgeting because the use of the many already explained tried and tested techniques for these costs should ensure they are not out of line for any given revenue level. But ZBB, properly implemented for undistributed expenses, can not only control these indirect costs, but may lead to cost reduction from previous levels. The main reason for this is that it puts previously unjustified expenses on the same basis as requests for increases to the budget — increases that must also be justified.

Employee Resistance

In any establishment that practices budgeting for cost control, it would be safe to say that one of the major complaints from department heads concerns their investment in unproductive time (from their point of view) preparing and documenting budgets. Since ZBB, if fully implemented, can take even more time than normal incremental budgeting, it is obvious that, where it is to be used, those department heads and other employees involved must be prepared for it, and the general manager must be fully committed to it. He must create the right environment of understanding about ZBB. Without full commitment, proper communication, full explanation of how ZBB works, and how all the related documents are to be completed, it will probably do little to reduce or control costs.

Employee understanding and commitment

Decision Units

Size of decision units

One of the key elements in successful implementation of ZBB is the decision unit. The number of decision units will vary with the size of each establishment. For example, a small operation with only one employee in its marketing department would probably have only one decision unit for marketing expenses. A larger organization might have several decision units for marketing. These units might be labelled sales, advertising, merchandising, public relations, and research. A very large organization might further break down these units into decision units covering different activities. For example, advertising might be broken down into a print decision unit and a radio and television decision unit.

Each separate decision unit should contain no more than one or two employees and related costs. Each decision unit should be about the same size insofar as total cost for that unit is concerned. In this way, when all budget requests and justifications are finalized, the general manager can more easily evaluate each of them and rank each of them against all the other units that are, so to speak, competing for the same limited resource dollars.

Once decision units have been established, the next step is for each department head to prepare an analysis of each separate unit that is her responsibility. This analysis would be carried out each year prior to the start of the new budget period. A properly designed form should be used so that each department head will present the data in a standard format. For each decision unit the department head will document the following:

Analysis of individual decision units

1. *The unit's objective.* Each decision unit's objective must obviously relate to the establishment's overall objective or objectives. For example, the objective of a hotel marketing department's print-advertising decision unit might read as follows:

> To seek out the most appropriate magazines, journals, newspapers, and other periodicals that can be used for advertising in the most effective way at the lowest cost in order to increase the number of guests using the hotel's facilities.

Sample unit objective

2. *The unit's present activities.* This would include the number of employees, their positions, a description of how the work is presently carried out (the work flow), and the resources used. For example, a resource used by the print-advertising decision unit might be an external advertising agency. The total cost of present activities would be included in this section. Also included would be a statement of how the unit's activities are measured. For example, this might be the number of guests using the hotel's facilities versus column inches or cost of print advertising.

Measuring unit objective

3. *Justification for continuation of unit's activities.* In the case of our print-advertising unit, this might include a statement to the effect that it would be advantageous because the employee(s) involved are familiar with the marketing strategy of the hotel, with the various operating departments and their special features, and know what special attractions to promote in the advertisements. The explanation should also include a statement of the disadvantages that would accrue should the decision unit's activities be discontinued.

Reason for unit continuation

4. *A list of alternative ways of carrying out the activities.* In the example of the print-advertising decision unit, the alternatives might include taking over some of the work presently given to the advertising agency, having the agency take over more of the unit's activities, having more of the work centralized in the head office (assuming the hotel is one of a chain), doing more head office work at the local level, or combining the print decision unit's activities with those of the radio-and-television advertising unit. The list should not be overly long, but it should include as many alternatives as would be practical that differ from present activities.

Example of activity alternatives

Included with the list would be the advantages and disadvantages of each alternative, and, for each alternative, an estimate of the total annual cost.

No change from present is a possibility

5. Selection of alternative recommended.   The department head responsible must then recommend the alternative that he would select for each unit. One alternative would be staying with the present activities rather than making a change. The selection will be based on a consideration of the pros, cons, practicality, and cost of each alternative.

Establishing minimum necessary budget

6. Budget required.   The department head's final responsibility is to state the funding required for each decision unit for the next budget based on the alternative recommended. This request starts out with a base, or minimum level. This minimum level may be established at the level below which the unit's activities would no longer exist or be worthwhile. Alternatively, the level may be arbitrarily determined by the general manager as, let us say, 60 percent of the present budget. Whatever the minimum level established, each activity above that level is to be shown as an incremental cost. These incremental activities may or may not be subsequently approved.

Ranking Process

Once the decision unit activities have been documented as outlined, it is then the general manager's turn to begin the review process. In order to determine how much money will be spent, and in what areas or departments, the manager must rank all activities in order of importance to the organization. Once this order is established, the activities would be accepted up to the total predetermined budget for all activities.

Difficulty of ranking activities

The major difficulty in ranking is to determine the order of priority for all the operation's activities under review. In a small organization, this might not be too difficult, with the aid of a committee if necessary. Alternatively, each department head might be asked to rank all activities that come within her responsibility. This procedure can then continue through successive levels of mid-management until they reach the general manager. Another approach might be for the general manager to automatically approve, let us say, the first 50 or 60 percent of all activities ranked within each department. The next 10 or 20 percent might then be ranked by mid-management and also be automatically approved. Top management might subsequently only review all these rankings and then rank the remainder and decide how many of them will be funded along with funding for any proposed new programs not proposed or adopted at lower levels.

Incorporating ZBB into regular budget

The completed ranking process and approved expenditures constitute the new budgets for those areas or departments. This information can then be incorporated into the regular budget process that was discussed in chapter 2. Theoretically, as a result of ZBB, the activities of that part of the organization have been examined, evaluated, modified, discontinued, or continued as before. This should produce the most effective possible budget. At the least, it should produce a budget that one can have more confidence in than one produced solely on an incremental basis.

Advantages of ZBB

Some of the advantages of ZBB are that it—

1. Concentrates on the dollar cost of each department's activities and budget and not on broad percentage increases;
2. Can reallocate funds to the departments or areas providing the greatest benefit to the organization;
3. Provides a quality of information about the organization (because all activities are documented in detail) that would otherwise not be available;

ZBB pros

4. Involves all levels of management and supervision in the budgeting process and encourages these employees to become familiar with activities that might not normally be under their control;
5. Obliges managers to identify inefficient or obsolete functions within their areas of responsibility;
6. Can identify areas of overlap or duplication.

Disadvantages of ZBB

Some of the possible disadvantages of ZBB are that it—

1. Implies that the budgeting method presently in use is not adequate (This may or may not be true.);
2. Does require a great deal more time, effort, paperwork, and cost than traditional budgeting methods;

ZBB cons

3. May be unfair to some department heads who, even though they may be very cost effective in managing their departments, are not as capable as others in documentation and defence of their budgets. They might thus find themselves outranked by other, more vocal but less cost effective, department heads.

VARIANCE ANALYSIS

For any type of cost, as each period goes by (day, week, month, or quarter), forecast or budgeted figures should be compared to actual figures. This can be done by summarizing the figures on a report by department or by type

Variances require explanation

of cost. An illustration of one such report, summarizing labor cost data, is given in exhibit 11.7 of chapter 11. Significant variances on these reports would require explanation. Variance analysis is a useful technique for analyzing these differences. Since what happens to costs is frequently affected by what has happened to revenue, we shall begin by examining how variance analysis is useful for identifying causes of changes in revenue. Let us consider the following situation:

Banquet revenue, month of March			
Budget	Actual	Difference	
$50,000	$47,250	$2,750	unfavorable

The difference is unfavorable because our total revenue was less than anticipated. If we analyze the budget and actual figures, we might get the following additional information:

Budget versus actual breakdown

Budget 10,000 guests × $5.00 (average check) = $50,000
Actual 9,000 guests × $5.25 (average check) = $47,250
Variance (unfavorable) $ 2,750

This variance amount is actually composed of two separate figures— a price variance and a quantity (number of guests) variance. These are calculated as follows:

Price Variance   The price variance is $0.25 per customer more than budgeted. This is considered to be favorable.

Price variance calculation

9,000 guests × $0.25 = $2,250 favorable

Quantity Variance   The quantity variance is 1,000 guests, each of whom did not spend the $5.00 we had budgeted for. This would be unfavorable.

Quantity variance calculation

1,000 guests × $5.00 = $5,000 unfavorable

If we combine these results, our total variance is made up of:

Price variance	$2,250 favorable
Quantity variance	$5,000 unfavorable
Total variance	$2,750 unfavorable

We now have information that tells us the major reason for our difference between budget and actual is a reduction in revenue of $5,000 (due to fewer customers being served). This has been partly compensated for by $2,250 resulting from the average banquet customer having a more expensive meal. This tells us that our banquet sales department is probably doing an effective job in selling higher priced menus to banquet groups, but is possibly falling down in bringing in as many banquets or guests as anticipated.

Causes of variances

Costs can be usefully analyzed in the same way. Let us examine the following situation for a rooms department in a hotel:

Laundry expense, month of June

Budget	Actual	Difference	
$6,000	$6,510	$510	unfavorable

The difference is unfavorable because we spent more than we budgeted for. With the following additional information we can analyze this variance:

Budget 6,000 rooms sold @ $1.00 per room   = $6,000
Actual 6,200 rooms sold @ $1.05 per room   = $6,510
Variance (unfavorable) $ 510

Budget versus actual breakdown

The $510 total variance is made up of two items — a cost variance and a quantity variance.

Cost Variance   The cost variance is $0.05 over budget for each room sold. This is an unfavorable trend.

6,200 rooms × $0.05 = $310.00 unfavorable

Calculation of cost variance

Quantity Variance   The quantity variance is 200 rooms over budget, at a budgeted cost of $1.00 per room. From a cost point of view, this is considered to be unfavorable.

200 rooms × $1.00 = $200.00 unfavorable

Calculation of quantity variance

If we combine these results, our total variance is therefore made up of:

Cost variance	$310.00 unfavorable
Quantity variance	$200.00 unfavorable
Total variance	$510.00 unfavorable

Causes of variances

This tells us that, although our total variance was $510, or 8.5 percent over budget ($510 divided by $6,000 × 100), only $310 is of concern to us. The remaining $200 was inevitable. If we sell more rooms, as we did, we would obviously have to pay the extra $200 for laundry. Even though this is considered unfavorable as a cost increase, we would not worry about it since it would be more than offset by the extra revenue obtained from selling the extra rooms. Whether or not the other $310 overspending is serious would depend on the cause. The cause could be a supplier cost increase that we may or may not be able to do something about; or it could be that we actually sold more twin rooms than budgeted for, which would mean more sheets to be laundered and therefore cause our average laundry cost per room occupied to go up. In the latter case, the additional cost would be more than offset by the extra charge made for double occupancy of a room.

Let us have a look at another example:

> Coffee shop variable wages, month of May
> Budget 4,350 hours @ $4.00/hr. = $17,400
> Actual 4,100 hours @ $4.10/hr. = $16,810
> ───────
> Variance (favorable) $ 590

Breakdown of variances

Cost variance:

> 4,100 hours @ 10¢/hr. = $410 unfavorable

Quantity variance:

> 250 hours @ $4.00 = $1,000 favorable

Causes of variances

Note that the net variance is a $590 favorable amount. Variance analysis shows that there was a $1,000 saving on labor due to a reduced number of hours paid for (perhaps as a result of less business than budgeted for). However, the saving was reduced by $410 because the actual average hourly rate was higher than budgeted for. Was there an increase in the hourly rate paid or, because of poor scheduling, was there unanticipated overtime (which would tend to increase the average hourly rate paid)? This would need to be verified.

As can be seen, variance analysis can provide additional information that is of help in identifying causes of differences between actual and budgeted or forecast figures.

In some cases, however, it is not practical or realistic to analyze variances by relating them to number of guests, number of rooms, or number of hours paid for. This is particularly true of certain undistributed expenses, where the relationship between the expense and customer demand is not very direct. If ZBB is in effect for these costs, we should have a ready measurement method, since, for each decision unit, the department head is required to document how the unit's effectiveness is to be measured. In the maintenance department, for example, the effectiveness might be measured (as illustrated in exhibit 12.3) on the basis of a percentage of manpower utilization. Similar types of measurement can be used for each different decision unit. In the accounts payable unit, the work load might be measured by periodic calculation of total dollar discounts missed as a result of inefficiencies and delays in paying invoices. Accounts receivable might be measured by dollar amount and number of accounts outstanding for sixty-one days or more, indicating lack of effectiveness in following up on collections of those accounts.

Analysis of undistributed expense variances

The level of tolerance of variances must also be established. This tolerance should be expressed in both dollar and percentage terms. For example, 1 percent of $10,000 is $100, and 1 percent of $100 is only $1. It would not be very useful spending time investigating a 1 percent variance that only amounted to $1. However, one might be concerned about a 1 per-

Dollar versus percentage tolerances

EXHIBIT 12.3.   Manpower Utilization Analysis

Department_____Maintenance_____   Week April 15–21

Work description	Hours	Percent
Completing work orders	12	19.4%
Completing repair orders	10	16.1
Annual boiler overhaul	18	29.0
Routine maintenance	8	12.9
Various minor activities	14	22.6
Totals	62	100.0%

Total hours available   2 employees × 37½ hrs. = 75 hrs.

Manpower utilization $\dfrac{62}{75} \times 100 = 82.7\%$

Idle time $\dfrac{13}{75} \times 100 = 17.3\%$

cent variance that amounted to $100. Variance tolerances, expressed in both dollar and percentage terms, must be established for each area, and one would only investigate differences exceeding both tolerances.

Finally, one should not be concerned only with variances that show overspending. Underspending in an area or department can be as much a problem as overspending since the result of one department's underspending might mean that another department has not received funds that it could have used to advantage.

ACTUAL STATEMENT ANALYSIS

Detecting trends

In addition to variance analysis for comparison of forecast and actual figures, it is sometimes useful to compare income statement revenue and expense amounts for two or more actual periods to see what changes have occurred and to detect trends. Comparative statements, comparative common-size statements, and (for a food operation) average check, cost, and net income per guest analysis are some of the methods of comparison.

Comparative Statements

Calculation of percentage change

Exhibit 12.4 shows two annual income statements for a food department in a hotel. The statements include one column for the change in dollar amount from one year to the next, and another column expressing this change as a percentage increase from the first year to the second. For example, dining room revenue has gone up 10.1 percent, calculated as follows:

$$\frac{\$20,300}{\$201,600} \times 100 = 10.1\%$$

Determining reasons for changes

The other percentage change figures are calculated in a similar way. Note that, within each revenue area, except banquets, the revenue has increased, but total revenue has only gone up 2.1 percent. The reason for this relatively small increase in total revenue is that banquet revenue was down 7.7 percent over the year. If the reason can be determined (Is the sales department not doing an effective job? Is there a new, competitive operation close by? Are our prices too high?), it may indicate why certain costs have changed the way they have. Even with the total revenue increase, small as it is, net income has declined by $37,100 or 24.2 percent. This is a drastic change. With revenue up, all other things being equal, net income should also go up, not down.

Obviously, all other things are not equal, because analysis of costs

shows that the majority of them have increased at a greater rate than the
revenue increase. To select only one as an example, the laundry cost has
gone up by 18.7 percent. Are we using more linen than before? Has our
supplier increased his cost to us by this percent? Whatever the reason,
corrective action can be taken once the cause is known. Each expense can
be analyzed in its own way. In this particular illustration, assuming the increased costs were inevitable, perhaps the increased costs have not yet
been adjusted for in menu selling prices.

Taking necessary corrective action

Comparative Common-size Statements

Income statements can also be illustrated on a comparative, common-size
basis. This is illustrated in exhibit 12.5. Total revenue is given a value of 100
percent, and every other item on the statement is expressed as a fraction of
total revenue. For example, in year 0001, dining room revenue was 23.7 percent of total revenue, calculated as follows:

$$\frac{\$201,600}{\$851,600} \times 100 = 23.7\%$$

Calculation of item's percentage

The other departmental revenue figures are calculated in a similar way.
Expense items are also calculated in a similar way, using the total revenue
figure as the denominator. However, note that, if this were a combined
food and beverage operation, food cost should be calculated as a percentage of food revenue and beverage cost as a percentage of beverage
revenue, even if all other cost percentages are calculated using total
revenue.

One way of interpreting the common-size income statement information in year 0001 is to say that, out of every $1.00 of revenue, $0.379 was
for food, $0.326 for salaries and wages, $0.04 for employee benefits, and
$0.075 for all other operating costs, leaving only $0.18 for net income. In
year 0002, this net income decreased to $0.133 out of every $1.00 of
revenue. Comparative, common-size statements show which items, as a
proportion of revenue, have changed enough to require investigation.

Interpreting percentages

For example, one of the causes for the decline to $0.133 net income
from each dollar of revenue in year 0002 is that the amount spent on food
(net food cost) has risen from $0.379 to $0.393 out of each dollar of
revenue. This $0.014 increase may seem insignificant, but, if it had not oc-
curred, we would have made $12,167.00 more net income, calculated as
follows:

$$\$869,100 \times 1.4\% = \$12,167.00$$

EXHIBIT 12.4. Comparative Departmental Income Statement—Food Department

	For year ending December 31 0001	0002	Increase or decrease from year 0001 to 0002	
Revenue				
Dining room	$201,600	$221,900	+$20,300	+ 10.1%
Coffee shop	195,900	201,700	+ 5,800	+ 3.0
Banquets	261,200	241,100	− 20,100	− 7.7
Room service	81,700	82,600	+ 900	+ 1.1
Bar	111,200	121,800	+ 10,600	+ 9.5
Total revenue	$851,600	$869,100	+ $ 17,500	+ 2.1%
Cost of sales				
Cost of food used	$352,500	$373,700	+ $21,200	+ 6.0%
Less: employee meals	(30,100)	(32,500)	+(2,400)	+ 8.0
Net food cost	322,400	341,200	+ 18,800	+ 5.8%
Gross profit	$529,200	$527,900	− $ 1,300	− 2.5%

Departmental expenses				
Salaries and wages	$277,400	$304,500	+$27,100	+ 9.8%
Employee benefits	34,500	37,800	+ 3,300	+ 9.6
China, glassware	7,100	7,800	+ 700	+ 9.9
Cleaning supplies	6,400	6,800	+ 400	+ 6.3
Decorations	2,200	1,800	− 400	− 18.2
Guest supplies	6,500	7,000	+ 500	+ 7.7
Laundry	15,500	18,400	+ 2,900	+ 18.7
Licenses	3,400	3,500	+ 100	+ 2.9
Linen	3,700	4,200	+ 500	+ 13.5
Menus	2,000	2,500	+ 500	+ 25.0
Miscellaneous	800	1,100	+ 300	+ 37.5
Paper supplies	4,900	5,700	+ 800	+ 16.3
Printing, stationery	4,700	4,600	− 100	− 2.1
Silver	2,300	2,100	− 200	− 8.7
Uniforms	3,100	2,400	− 700	− 22.6
Utensils	1,700	1,800	+ 100	+ 5.9
Total expenses	376,200	412,000	+ 35,800	+ 9.5%
Departmental net income	$153,000	$115,900	−$37,100	− 24.2%

EXHIBIT 12.5. Comparative Common-size Income Statement—Food Department

	For year ending December 31 0001	For year ending December 31 0002	For year ending December 31 0001	For year ending December 31 0002
Revenue				
Dining room	$201,600	$221,900	23.7%	25.5%
Coffee shop	195,900	201,700	23.0	23.2
Banquets	261,200	241,100	30.7	27.7
Room service	81,700	82,600	9.6	9.5
Bar	111,200	121,800	13.0	14.1
Total revenue	$851,600	$869,100	100.0%	100.0%
Cost of sales				
Cost of food used	$352,500	$373,700	41.4%	43.0%
Less: employee meals	(30,100)	(32,500)	(3.5)	(3.7)
Net food cost	322,400	341,200	37.9	39.3
Gross profit	$529,200	$527,900	62.1%	60.7%
Departmental expenses				
Salaries and wages	$277,400	$304,500	32.6%	35.0%
Employee benefits	34,500	37,800	4.0	4.3
All other operating costs	64,300	69,700	7.5	8.1
Total expenses	376,200	412,000	44.1	47.4
Departmental net income	$153,000	$115,900	18.0%	13.3%

In the interest of brevity, various expenses have been added together in exhibit 12.5 under "all other operating costs." In year 0001, this figure accounts for 7.5 percent of revenue; and in year 0002, it accounts for 8.1 percent of revenue. This is a relatively small change and might normally go unnoticed. It may be small because large increases in some cases may have been offset by decreases in others. In practice, it would be preferable to detail each expense item in order to achieve full disclosure.

Full expense details are preferable

Average Check, Cost, and Net Income per Guest

Another method of statement analysis is to calculate and compare average revenue per guest, average cost per guest, and average net income per guest. Exhibit 12.6 is an illustration of this. The average check in each revenue area is calculated by dividing the number of guests in that area into the revenue for that area. For example, in the dining room, in year 0001, the average check is calculated as follows:

$$\frac{\$201{,}600}{35{,}130} = \$5.74$$

Calculation of average check

For the entire department, total average check is simply total revenue by total guests from all areas. Cost and net income figures are calculated by dividing each expense item and net income by total guests.

In our illustration, some of the facts that come to light are that the number of guests served in all revenue areas increased, except in banquets where there was a considerable decline. At the same time, in the banquet area the average spending per guest increased from $4.34 to $4.75. This is an increase of $0.41 per guest, or 9.5 percent ($0.41 divided by $4.34, then multiplied by 100). The combination of higher average check but reduced number of guests meant that our banquet revenue was $20,100 lower in year 0002 than in year 0001. Is this a desirable trend? Is our banquet marketing policy causing us to sell higher priced banquets but not allowing us to sell to as many customers? Has an increase in banquet selling prices driven away business? The answers to questions about changes in revenue figures can frequently indicate a cause for a change in cost figures.

Questions raised by average check changes

In terms of total average check in year 0002, we took in $0.04 more per guest ($3.99 less $3.95), but we spent $0.22 more per guest ($3.46 less $3.24); thus, our net income per guest declined $0.18 ($0.71 less $0.53). Obviously, our costs per guest have risen much faster than our revenue per guest. The individual items of expense, on a per guest basis, have all increased, some more than others. They need to be investigated to see if this trend can be reversed. Alternatively, selling prices may have to be in-

Average cost increases versus average check increases

EXHIBIT 12.6. Comparative Average Check, Cost and Profit Per Guest—Food Department

Department	Year ending December 31, 0001			Year ending December 31, 0002		
	Revenue	Guests	Average check	Revenue	Guests	Average check
Dining room	$201,600	35,130	$5.74	$221,900	36,210	$6.13
Coffee shop	195,900	71,200	2.75	201,700	78,200	2.58
Banquets	261,200	60,190	4.34	241,100	50,780	4.75
Room service	81,700	16,870	4.84	82,600	17,110	4.83
Bar	111,200	32,170	3.46	121,800	35,490	3.43
Totals	$851,600	215,560	$3.95	$869,100	217,790	$3.99

Operating costs	Costs	Guests	Average cost	Costs	Guests	Average cost
Net food cost	$322,400	215,560	$1.50	$341,200	217,790	$1.57
Salaries and wages	277,400	215,560	1.29	304,500	217,790	1.40
Employee benefits	34,500	215,560	0.16	37,800	217,790	0.17
Other operating costs	64,300	215,560	0.29	69,700	217,790	0.32
Totals	$698,600	215,560	$3.24	$753,200	217,790	$3.46

	Net income	Guests	Average net income	Net income	Guests	Average net income
Departmental net income	$153,000	215,560	$0.71	$115,900	217,790	$0.53

creased to compensate for increasing costs that cannot be controlled from inside the operation.

Even though three methods of actual statement analysis have been illustrated in this section, one would not normally use all three in practice. One would select the most appropriate to the circumstances. Also, comparison is not confined to annual periods, particularly if monthly financial statements are prepared. Nor is this type of analysis limited to food departments. Beverage and rooms departments can be similarly analyzed.

Select appropriate analysis technique

SUMMARY

Food, beverage, and labor are major costs that are the direct responsibility of the department head concerned for control purposes. However, there are many other types of direct cost that must also be controlled, such as china, glass, silverware, linen, uniforms, and various types of supplies. Generally, these other direct costs range from 5 to 15 percent of revenue. Since it is not practical to have absolute control over every last item of these other direct costs, one should concentrate on the items in this category that represent the highest dollar value.

From a combination of past usage figures and discussion with employees involved, one can produce standard unit of usage figures for each item to be controlled. This usage figure should be initially calculated on a monthly basis, and then the monthly figures can be used to calculate an overall average. Usage lists, once finalized, can be provided to the departments concerned and to the storekeeper. These lists, together with the monthly volume forecasts of business, form the basis for calculating the quantities of the various supply items, adjusted for inventory still on hand, to be requisitioned from the storeroom. At the end of each month, an analysis report can be prepared comparing forecast and actual quantities for each item, with explanations for any major differences.

Indirect costs are not as easy to control as the direct costs. Indirect costs, or undistributed expenses, include administrative and general, marketing, guest entertainment, property operation, maintenance, and energy costs. It is difficult to relate these costs to volume or revenue levels. Zero-based budgeting (ZBB) is a method of controlling them. With ZBB, each category of cost is broken down into decision units. Each decision unit is then analyzed using the following format:

1. The unit's objective
2. The unit's present activities
3. Justification for continuation of the unit's activities
4. A list of alternative ways of carrying out the activities

5. Selection of the alternative recommended

6. Budget required to carry out the alternative

This analysis would be prepared by the department head responsible for the cost prior to each budget year. Once all the decision units have been analyzed, they must be ranked in order of priority by management. Once the ranking is completed and the expenditures are approved to whatever level management decides is appropriate, this information then forms the annual budget for those indirect costs.

With any type of budgeting, whether for direct or indirect costs, variance analysis is a useful technique for analyzing actual with budget figure differences. For revenue figures, the analysis will break down differences into price and quantity variances, and, for expense figures, the breakdown will be into cost and quantity variances. Management must determine what level of variance will require further investigation.

Actual financial statements can also be analyzed against each other. The following three forms of such analysis were discussed:

1. Comparative analysis

2. Comparative common-size analysis

3. Average check, cost, and net income per guest analysis

DISCUSSION QUESTIONS

1. List eight direct costs (other than food, beverage, and labor) that you think it would be important to control in a coffee shop.

2. Give an example of a situation where the usage of the same supply item might differ considerably in each of two departments that uses that item.

3. Why does the text suggest that the control of certain supply items may act as a form of psychological control?

4. What are the indirect costs that can be controlled with ZBB?

5. Give an example of a decision unit in a hotel's accounting office, and write a one-sentence objective for that decision unit.

6. Briefly describe the ranking process under ZBB.

7. Give two advantages and two disadvantages of ZBB.

8. Define *variance analysis*.

9. With reference to question 5, state how the decision unit you

selected can have its effectiveness measured against actual results.

10. Briefly describe comparative financial statement analysis.

11. Briefly describe comparative, common-size financial statement analysis.

12. How is net income per guest calculated?

PROBLEMS

12–1. For each of the following items, state what you might use as the standard unit:

    a. Water glasses in a coffee shop

    b. Guest account forms in a front office

    c. Side plates in a dining room

    d. Individual guest soap-bars in the rooms department

    e. Dishwashing machine detergent in a restaurant's kitchen.

    f. Drink stir-sticks in a cocktail bar

12–2. You have the following information about the usage of a particular item whose standard unit is to be dollars of revenue:

	Used	Revenue
January	200	$40,000
February	210	$41,000
March	205	$41,000
April	315	$42,000
May	205	$41,000
June	208	$53,000
July	199	$41,000
August	203	$42,000
September	206	$43,000
October	204	$42,000
November	195	$38,000
December	190	$37,000

    a. For each month, calculate the standard revenue unit (to the nearest dollar) for each one of this item used.

    b. You will note that, in both April and June, the figures seem quite different from the remaining months.

Investigation shows that, in April, a case containing 100 of this item was water damaged and had to be discarded, and, in June, revenue included $11,000 from a large function at which none of this item was used. Adjust for these two unusual situations and then calculate the average monthly standard unit for this item to the nearest dollar.

c. For next month, revenue is forecast to be $41,000. There are presently thirteen of this item on hand. How many should be requisitioned from stores to carry the department through next month? A safety margin of ten items should be allowed for.

12–3. For each of the following decision units, state how the work effectiveness might be measured:

a. A hotel marketing-department salesperson required to call on metropolitan office buildings to market the hotel's banquet facilities

b. The credit manager in a hotel, one of whose tasks is to approve requests for credit by guests using the hotel's rooms

c. An accounting department employee whose responsibilities include collecting overdue accounts

d. A purchaser in the purchasing department of a chain restaurant operation

12–4. Calculate appropriate variances for each of the following situations:

a. Budgeted liquor sales at a banquet were 1,500 drinks @ $1.05 each on the average. Actual sales were 1,550 drinks at $0.95 on average.

b. Estimated banquet food sales for a month were 20,000 covers (guests) @ $3.60 each. Actual sales were 21,000 @ $3.75.

c. Budgeted banquet food cost for a week was 1,000 covers @ $3.00. Actual cost was $3.10 for 980 covers.

d. A coffee shop budgets 12,000 customers for a month with an average check of $5.45 and an average food cost of $2.05. Actual customers were 12,800, actual average check was $5.27, and actual food cost $2.01.

e. At a convention buffet, 450 customers were expected. One bar employee was hired for a four-hour period for each thirty guests. Budgeted wage rate was $3.75 per hour. Overtime was not anticipated but could occur. After the event, payroll records indicate that sixty-four hours were actually paid for, with a total labor cost of $245.60.

12–5. You have the following income statements, covering two successive months, for a hotel's food department:

	August		September	
Revenue				
Room service	$ 32,900		$ 27,100	
Dining room	161,800		134,900	
Tavern	20,800		18,000	
Coffee shop	115,400		107,200	
Banquets	142,900	$473,800	161,400	$448,600
Cost of sales		135,900		126,400
Gross profit		$337,900		$322,200
Operating costs				
Salaries and wages	$159,600		$163,200	
Employee benefits	27,100		24,400	
Linen and laundry	8,800		8,700	
China, glass, silver	16,100		15,200	
Supplies	14,700		14,500	
Other expenses	25,200	251,500	19,100	245,100
Net income		$ 86,400		$ 77,100

Present these statements in comparative form, and comment about any significant differences.

12–6. Present the information in problem 12–5 in the form of comparative, common-size statements, and comment about any significant differences.

12–7. With reference to problem 12–5, the following are the guest counts in each revenue area for each of the two months:

	August	September
Room service	2,721	2,214
Dining room	13,802	11,298
Tavern	2,412	1,841
Coffee shop	29,100	25,711
Banquets	20,019	20,476

Prepare figures for average check, cost, and net income per guest, and comment about any significant changes from August to September.

12–8. A company owns two restaurants in the same town. Operating results for the first three months of the current year are as follows:

	Restaurant A		Restaurant B	
Revenue		$154,300		$206,100
Cost of sales		60,200		78,900
Gross profit		$ 94,100		$127,200
Direct expenses				
Wages	$45,600		$70,400	
Supplies	12,700		16,800	
Other	4,500	62,800	6,100	93,300
		$ 31,300		$ 33,900
Indirect expenses				
Rent	$ 6,500		$ 9,000	
Insurance	2,000		3,000	
Other	3,200	11,700	3,600	15,600
Net income		$ 19,600		$ 18,300

The owners of the company are concerned that Restaurant B has higher revenue yet lower net income than Restaurant A. Use comparative, common-size analysis to prepare a brief report explaining the situation to the owners.

Information Systems and Control 13

Objectives

After studying this chapter, the reader should be able to do the following:

- Define and discuss the concept of a *management information system* (MIS).
- Explain how an MIS may be viewed differently, depending on the level of the employee in an organization.
- Identify the four levels in the decision-making pyramid.
- Discuss each of the four levels in the decision-making pyramid.
- List and discuss each of the four steps in the decision-making process.
- Solve problems requiring the use of the four decision-making steps.
- Define and discuss *management by exception*.

**Action
needed**

This book has frequently mentioned the word *control,* such as in the terms *food cost control, beverage cost control,* and *labor cost control.* Control is based on two requirements: information and action. There can be no control without information; and generally, the more information available, the better the control. However, there also cannot be control without action, when action is called for. For example, a manager can sit at a desk, surrounded by page after page of computer printouts that provide information about the operation—so much information, in fact, that the manager is unable to sort out the relevant from the trivial, and thus can make no decisions and take no action. In other cases, the manager may have the relevant information available but not be the sort of person capable of taking action; such a person may harbor the illusion of being in control simply because all the right statistics are available. Information is important, but decision making and action are more important.

Size of Information System

**Rational
decisions
required**

To have operational control of a business, a manager must make constant decisions. And to make rational decisions, the manager must possess essential information and a system that provides this information. Consider a teenager selling lemonade to passers-by outside her house in the summertime. Money from sales is put into a box on the table. At the end of the day, the youngster counts up the money received, records it in a diary, and decides, from the sales made, whether or not it has been a good day and worth the effort. In other words, the teenager uses an information system, based on sales, to decide whether or not to stay in business. Her information system is simple and unsophisticated, but it is suitable for that particular business. Obviously, as a business expands, the information system has to expand with it and become more complex.

**Example of
information
needed**

For example, consider a hotel that is contemplating offering its room guests, as a new marketing tactic, a "free" hair shampoo package in the bathroom. At first glance, this seems to be a relatively trivial matter. But what information is needed? First, the decision maker must have information about the type of guest that forms the hotel's market. Is the guest a vacationer or a businessperson? Is the guest male or female? If the hotel is an international one, is the nationality of the guest important? Is age relevant? What about average length of stay? Obviously guest registration cards must be designed to elicit these data, and someone must be delegated to sort through the cards and to summarize the data into meaningful information.

The manager also needs data from suppliers concerning types of shampoo available, types and sizes of packages, and information about costs and about the availability of any quantity purchase discounts. Finally, the manager must have information about the added costs of storing, distributing, and controlling the shampoo through the housekeeping process.

Information Already Exists

For many day-to-day decisions in most hospitality enterprises, much of the necessary information already exists. Some of it is required by law (for example, accounting records kept for tax-filing purposes). Other information exists as a by-product of normal business transactions (such as the drawing up of purchasing records and sales invoices). Further information exists as a result of transactions between departments (for example, in the form of requisitions given to the storeroom for needed supplies). But quite a lot of available information is not even formalized (such as the chef's knowledge about the best way to tackle each day's food production requirements).

Information from various sources

MANAGEMENT INFORMATION SYSTEM (MIS)

When the production of information is formalized, as is the case in larger businesses, it is usually termed a *management information system* (MIS). MIS can be defined as an integrated system for providing information to support the operating and decision-making functions in a business. The system may be manual, computerized, or a combination of the two.

   The appearance of a business's MIS varies, depending on the level of the viewer within the organizational hierarchy. A restaurant server sees the sales register (a part of the MIS) as a piece of equipment that makes up sales checks and provides duplicates for ordering food from the kitchen. The restaurant manager views the register as a machine that provides daily summaries (reports) showing sales in total, by category, and by server. The accountant sees it as one of a series of sources of information about the restaurant—other sources being similar registers in the coffee shop and bar—that provide information about total restaurant sales. If this were a chain restaurant, the chain's top management would view the accounting record of sales for the restaurant as a basis for comparison with the sales at other restaurants in the chain's overall MIS.

Different views of MIS

Four Levels

Four levels can be identified in the decision-making process, which can be viewed as a pyramid. These four are data production, data sorting, information production, and decision making. The figure below illustrates the pyramidal structure of the decision-making process.

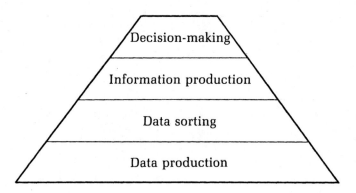

Level 1 – Data Production

What is to be retained?

At the base of the pyramid is the production of data. These data are often a by-product of regular business activity (cash register tapes, sales checks, guest registration cards). Management must establish what is to be stored (and for how long) and what is to be discarded immediately. For example, are dining room sales checks to be kept for a week, a month, a year, or five years?

Level 2 – Data Sorting

Classifying data

At the next higher level of the pyramid, data are sorted, converted, combined, or manipulated into more useful sets of data. In other words, the data must be classified so that specific items can be recalled or retrieved without the entire batch having to be processed. For example, labor cost information for each employee on duty each day can be stored by day and then by pay period; but does the system allow labor cost to be sorted by specific type of employee or by department, so that these data can be accessed without the need to go through all records for an entire month?

Level 3 – Information Production

Converting data to information

The converted sets of data produced at level 2 in turn provide the third level in the pyramid: the information level. Data gain the status of information when they acquire meaning. For example, raw payroll information has little meaning; but when it is converted (as shown in exhibit 11.7) into a form useful for analytical purposes, it is far more meaningful for decision making.

Normally the process of collecting and converting data to provide information is routine, and it often can be done mechanically or by computer. Doing such processing is not the manager's job; rather, the manager's task is to interpret the resulting information and to perform the actual decision making. Nevertheless, the manager must be involved in establishing the information-gathering system, to ensure that it will provide the information needed to make the right decisions.

Management involvement

As organizations get larger, the information system they rely on becomes more structured. For example, in a small restaurant, the one and only cook may know all the recipes by heart; but in a larger restaurant, recipes must be formalized so that all cooks can follow the same food preparation formulas and procedures, thus maintaining a standard food cost (and quality) for each menu item. The most desirable system to use depends on the specific organization of the business and on its needs. Consequently, as the organization changes over time, so will the information system: what is good today may not be appropriate in five years' time.

Computerized systems facilitate the linking and conversion of data from different areas of an operation into useful information. For example, a room service department manager could constantly access forecast front office guest room occupancies in order to staff the room service department more adequately and to control labor cost day by day.

Use of computers

Sometimes, comparing sets of data can provide useful information. For example, it may be of value to relate last month's labor cost to this month's, or this month's labor cost to the cost for the same month last year. At a very elementary level, such comparisons are not too helpful, since they do not take into account conditions that have changed between last month and this month, or between this month and the same month of last year. Moreover, if August last year had five Sundays, and this year it has only four, this can distort comparisons. Making comparisons on the basis of indices or percentages improves their reliability, as does comparing data to a standard (as is done in the standard food cost system described in chapter 6).

Further improvement in information occurs when variances between actual and standard figures are broken down into differences in quantity and differences in cost or price, as described in chapter 12. This breakdown indicates how much of the variance is due to poor planning (quantity variances) and how much to a failure to achieve standards (for example, cost and price variances in a food cost control system). At this point, the information system has reached the stage of providing valuable factual grounds on which to solve problems and make decisions.

Analyzing variables

Level 4 – Decision-Making

The information provided by the system is used to identify and help solve problems at the decision-making level of the pyramid. The better the decisions, the higher the sales and/or the lower the costs will be, resulting in more profit. The types of decisions to be made dictate the information to be collected; the information, in turn, indicates the data that are needed, thus regulating the entire data collection system.

Every manager is constantly faced with the necessity to make problem-solving decisions. These can be routine and simple—many of them requiring little action—or complex and crucial, requiring action that will have extensive ramifications. Most decisions require the use of information and (frequently) the use of judgment.

In problem solving, four decision-making steps can be identified:

1. Defining the problem.   The first step is to define the problem. If this is not done, proper analysis of information and identification of alternatives cannot proceed. If the problem remains undefined or is incorrectly defined, time and effort will be wasted and costs generally will increase. Problems are not always easy to define. Sometimes it is necessary to begin by defining the parameters of the problem—in other words, to decide what the problem really is, and not just what it seems to be on the surface. For example, consider the case of a chain restaurant that built a large new restaurant at a resort during a tourist boom. When a recession started, sales dropped considerably below the break-even point. In deciding to build, management had defined the problem as a matter of meeting an ever-growing demand by tourists for places to dine. But the definition of the problem should have included investigating the nature of the tourist boom and checking to see if there was a likelihood of a recession. As this example shows, a problem might be part of a surrounding problem—or be hidden by another one. Good managers recognize such situations and in response may have to set problem priorities.

Some problems are obvious (for example, the number of guest complaints about housekeeping standards) and may easily be solved. Other problems are equally obvious but not easily solved. In still other cases, problems may never be solved, since there is no pressure to solve them. For example, there may be complaints about housekeeping standards, but hotel room occupancy is continuously running at 100 percent and management inertia prevails.

In some situations, there is extreme pressure to solve a problem because of a deadline. For example, a batch of a particular menu item has been spoiled during preparation in the kitchen, and the manager knows that there will be serious customer dissatisfaction in the dining room if the item is not available when the restaurant opens. The solution is to put maximum effort into preparing a new batch of the item in time for the next meal. Any other problems are pushed aside.

The interest and experience of the manager may also dictate which problems are defined and solved. A manager whose background experience is entirely in food operations may pay attention only to problems that arise in that area, in order to ensure the smooth running of that depart-

Need for judgment

Deciding what the problem is

Obvious problems

ment, which he or she feels is the most important part of the business. If a manager has a more varied background, this concentration of effort is less likely to occur.

Before they can be solved, problems must be identified. If the manager is not aware of a problem, obviously no action can be taken. Such awareness can come through structured channels (for example, from accounting information or from formal meetings) or through unstructured channels (for example, the "grapevine," observation, intuition, or experience). The grapevine is often a very important part of problem identification channeling, particularly in a large organization. But it is equally important for the manager to know if information obtained by this means is reliable. Sometimes the formal, structured channels of information about problems (for example, the accounting records) are too slow to show that a problem exists, or only confirm what the unstructured information channels have already evidenced.

Structured and unstructured channels

Finally, a problem is often identified from discrete pieces of information that need to be put together to point to a problem. A good hospitality manager can often conceptualize problems this way, whereas another manager—even with the same unassembled pieces of information—might never be aware that there is a problem.

2. Listing alternative solutions. The second step in problem solving is to list alternative solutions. As mentioned earlier, the solution is often obvious. In other cases, however, the solutions are not apparent; and indeed there may be several solutions, some of which may conflict with others. Creativity is required in listing alternative solutions, but that creativity should not be subordinated to the decision maker's bias or prior experience.

Solutions not always apparent

3. Gathering necessary information. The third step in problem solving is to gather all necessary information about the problem and its alternative solutions. The information gathered must be relevant, since that increases knowledge, reduces uncertainty, and minimizes the risk of making the wrong decision. Much of the information may have already been produced at level three of the pyramid (information production). The information must also be presented in a format that is understood and must be received early enough to affect any decisions made. The decision-making process is often a matter of judgment based on the best information available.

Information must be relevant

Obviously, the more accurate the available information is, the more value it has for decision making in such matters as planning and cost control. Speed of information and the risk of incomplete information are also factors to be considered. It is sometimes better to work from a rough idea of the daily food cost, without taking inventory, than to delay in order to have a more accurate food cost 24 hours later after taking inventory. On the other hand, in a feasibility study for expanding the business, the risk is high enough to justify taking extra time in preparing the feasibility to lessen the risk of making the wrong decision. It is generally necessary for the manager, given the constraints of time and data availability, to have enough of the important information to be able to consider alternative solutions to problems. Obviously, however, the longer the time spent in collecting data and information, the greater the cost.

Use of accounting records

For many decisions, accounting records, forms, and reports are a major source of information. This type of information is verifiable, objective, and quantitative, and it can provide specific data about an activity, event, or problem. The three most important aspects of accounting information are that it be relevant and appropriate for the problem at hand, that it be current, and that it be accurate within the measurement standards imposed by the demands of potential problems.

It is important, however, to differentiate between an accounting system and a control system. An accounting system merely records information (often too late to identify problems), whereas a properly planned control system determines, for example, what the costs should be in a business (assuming everything goes as planned) and ensures the availability of records and reports that will rapidly indicate whether this is happening.

Objective performance measurement

Accounting information is particularly valuable for purposes of measuring actual performance against a goal—for example, measuring actual food cost against a standard food cost. The more objective the measure of performance is, the more likely a manager will be to succeed in reaching (or at least approaching) that standard. The value of accounting information is that it can provide a relatively objective basis for evaluating performance. Important in this measurement is the term *controllable cost* (defined in chapter 1). A manager's performance should not be measured in terms of costs that he or she cannot control.

4. Making the decision. The fourth step in the decision-making process is to make the decision. Even after the three previously outlined steps have been taken, decision making may still be difficult because important variables of the problem may affect one another. Compared to managers in many other businesses, hospitality managers face more difficulties in this area, since they are subjected to continuous pressures and deadlines that can be ongoing 24 hours a day, 7 days a week. This leaves the typical

Lack of time

manager little free time for thinking through problems and their solutions; yet that manager's effectiveness is still normally measured by the end result of the decision-making process.

The solution chosen can sometimes depend on the prospective outcomes of other potential solutions. For example, a hotel banquet manager has to choose between a group that wants to arrange for a high-school graduation dinner and dance and a group that wants to hold a formal symphony society reception and dinner; both groups wish to hold their functions on the same night, in the only space available. In this case, the banquet manager might select the symphony society function over the high-school "party" in order to avoid potential problems with party-going graduates who might drink too much and become difficult to control.

Sometimes problems continue to persist after an apparent problem-solving decision is made. For example, the disappointed graduates in the preceding example might hold their party in a nearby hotel, but at the end of their evening might decide to "invade" the symphony society function and disrupt it for revenge.

Persistent problems

Sometimes the decision maker needs appropriate communication skills in order to convince others (for example, other department heads who may be affected by a particular solution) that a certain decision, given the alternatives, is the best one.

In some situations, the information gathered can provide its own decision. The use of perpetual inventory cards as an aid to inventory control was described in chapter 3. These perpetual inventory cards can show, for each storeroom item, the minimum and maximum inventory levels permissible. If the minimum stock level for a specific product is 5 and the maximum is 15, and if inventory has dropped to 5, then 10 more of the item should be ordered, and therefore the decision is made to order 10 more for delivery within three days.

Information provides solution

In such a situation, however, no attempt is made to relate the purchase to current conditions. What if consumption of that product is no longer as high as it used to be? Perhaps the maximum inventory of 15 should be reduced to 10 and the reorder point to 2, until conditions change again. Making such decisions on the basis of manual information may be difficult, but computerized inventory systems can be programmed to provide comprehensive information on such matters as rate of consumption of inventory products, quantity discounts, and inventory holding costs. In an intelligently designed computerized system, the use of fixed reorder points for any item might be completely abandoned; instead, the computer will consider all relevant factors, item by item, and only print out a list of items to be ordered and the proper quantity of each.

Use of computers

OTHER CONSIDERATIONS

Several other decision-making factors that may be relevant in establishing a management information system remain to be discussed.

Management by Exception

One type of decision making is known as "management by exception." With management by exception, small deviations from the normal pattern that do not require management action are not drawn to its attention. For example, the standard food cost is established at 40 percent. As long as the food cost variance is only one percentage point above or below 40 percent (that is, in the 39 percent–41 percent range) it is considered acceptable. Only if food cost falls below 39 percent or rises above 41 percent is it drawn to management's attention, to see if any action is required.

Opportunity Cost

Comparing actual and possible results

A further refinement in decision making involves examining the assumptions that were made when earlier plans were formulated and then comparing not only actual and planned results, but also actual and possible results. The possible results represent opportunity costs. For example, suppose that a hotel could increase its sales by accommodating bus tour groups. If bus tour groups are not accommodated, or if only a limited number of them are accepted, the potential revenue from those not accommodated constitutes an opportunity cost; this opportunity cost representing lost revenue could be built into the information system for management to use in comparisons with actual results.

Responding to incompleteness

One difficulty with building opportunity costs into the information/decision-making system in the preceding example is that some bus tour groups that made requests for rooms and were turned down may have eventually canceled their reservations anyway—even if they had been accepted. But if effective decisions are to be made, a well-designed information system must be able to respond to some incompleteness of information and may possibly suggest where additional data might be collected to make the information more complete. Obviously, at this level of sophistication, information manipulation would be exceedingly complex without the aid of a computerized system.

Cost of Systems

Information is not free

Many managers are prevented from producing more sophisticated information—in particular with reference to implementing a computerized system—by the fact that the costs are often considered, but no price tag is put on the benefits. In fact, some managers consider that there should be no cost for information gathering, whether for having a daily food cost percentage available or for producing a manager's daily report. These are simply by-products of the accounting and/or control system, and to spend money to provide more and better information makes no sense. For many managers, the concept that information is not free creates a dilemma that is difficult to resolve.

An information system should be judged by how well it facilitates the achievement of a given goal or set of goals. The main criterion for judging

one system against another is cost-benefit. Systems cost money and benefit an organization by helping decision making. If two systems cost the
same amount, the one that provides more desirable operating information
for decisions is preferable. For example, this might be the decision-making
factor in judging which of two computerized accounting systems to install, when they both cost approximately the same amount.

Computerized Systems

When a computerized management information system is introduced into
a business, management frequently assumes that the new system will yield
labor savings and will eliminate jobs. The employees most at risk as a
result of this management attitude are front-office clerks, accounting
clerks, and cashiers. On many occasions, however, the new management
information system only serves to prop up a failing manual system, and it
ultimately increases (rather than reduces) labor costs. When this happens, there is no improvement in control—only the addition of more infor- **Moving from**
mation. **manual**

    This can happen when hotel guest accounting and night audit proce- **to machine**
dures are moved from the manual system (the hand transcript) into the **systems**
mechanical age, with the same number of employees required in most
cases. Similarly, more recently, computerized front-office systems have
been introduced, with little reduction in labor cost, since just as many
employees are still needed to deal face-to-face with guests at the front
desk. The advantage of the computer in such cases may be that it provides
savings in other areas (reduction in costs from accounting errors) or provides much more meaningful information than a manual system can (for
example, a continuously updated guest room status information system
for housekeeping use).

    Where a computerized information system is installed merely to re-
place a manual one, little has been gained. Why not use information produced by the computer to make decisions about maximizing the average
room rate, or about developing a more useful marketing strategy?

    Using a computer as an electronic clerk is only of value if more infor-
mation is produced for the same (or for lower) costs, and a computer clerk
often does not accomplish that. Indeed, computer-based systems should
be different from manual procedures so that they provide not only control
over past events but also control over future events. This improvement is **More valuable**
made by having the system provide more valuable information; and with **information**
a computerized system, information can be available that would be too
expensive to produce manually or would be impossible to produce because of lack of time.

    An example of this is food cost control based on standard recipes
(outlined in chapter 5). In chapter 5, this procedure was demonstrated us-

Understanding manual systems

ing a manual system. Only restaurants with very limited menus could possibly do this manually (at a great cost in labor that might dwarf its benefits); restaurants with extensive menus would not be able to do it at all. An understanding of how this can be done manually, however, provides a basis for understanding what to look for in a practical computerized system. A similar situation prevails in the case of trying to keep a guest history system up to date in a hotel front office on the basis of guest registration cards. In a large hotel, the work would be extremely voluminous. A computerized guest reservation/registration system, on the other hand, can cope with this task easily.

Management Challenge

Designing and integrating an information system into a hospitality enterprise are a challenge for any manager. The more appropriately it is designed to support cost control and decision making, the more effectively the enterprise will be able to compete in the marketplace and achieve its already established objectives.

Changing nature of decisions

As hotels and restaurants make greater use of computers, they will produce increasingly sophisticated information systems. As this improvement in technology has its impact on the industry and on the people who work in it, the computer systems in a particular business might well change the nature and type of decisions that managers have to make.

Good managers will have ready access to up-to-date, relevant information and will develop skills for using that information in decision making. Analysis and interpretation of information will be more important. Managers must move away from their role as information processors, towards a new role as decision makers.

SUMMARY

To have operational control of a business, a manager must constantly make decisions. In order to make rational decisions, the manager must have information and a system that provides it. Much of the necessary information for many day-to-day decisions already exists, because of legal requirements, as a result of normal business transactions, and through other channels.

When the production of information is formalized, it is usually referred to as a "management information system" (MIS). MIS can be defined as an integrated system for providing information to support the operating and decision-making functions in a business. The appearance of an MIS in a business depends on the level of the employee viewing it within the organization.

Four levels can be identified in the decision-making process: data production, data sorting, information production, and decision making. At the decision-making stage, four decision-making steps can be identified:

1. Define the problem.
2. List alternative solutions.
3. Gather necessary information.
4. Make the decision.

One type of decision making is known as management by exception, where only deviations outside an acceptable normal range are brought to management's attention for decision making.

The critical factor in deciding how well a management information system is operating is the matter of how well it facilitates the achievement of a given goal or set of goals. The main criterion for judging one system against another is cost-benefit.

Designing and integrating an information system into a hospitality enterprise are a challenge for today's manager. This is particularly true as hotels and restaurants make greater use of computers to maintain increasingly sophisticated information systems.

DISCUSSION QUESTIONS

1. Even without a formalized management information system (MIS), much useful information is available to management. Explain two ways in which this is so.
2. Define an MIS.
3. The appearance of an MIS to an employee in a business depends on the level of the employee within the organizational hierarchy. Explain why.
4. Differentiate data production from data sorting, and give an example of the difference.
5. Data production and data sorting are the first two steps in the decision-making pyramid. What is the third step? Explain what is involved in this third step.
6. It is not the manager's task to produce and sort informational data. Nevertheless, the manager should be involved in establishing the information-gathering system. Explain why.

7. The first step in decision making is to define the problem about which a decision is needed. Discuss the difficulties involved in defining a problem.

8. The interest and experience of the manager can dictate which problems are solved. Why should this be so? Discuss an example of this from your own experience.

9. If defining the problem is step one in the decision-making process, what is step two?

10. What primary criteria must be satisfied in order for information to be useful in the decision-making process?

11. Define *management by exception*, and give an example of a circumstance where it might be used.

12. Give an example (other than the one in the text) of how an opportunity cost can be part of the decision-making process.

PROBLEMS

13-1. The food and beverage director of a hotel has decided that five new entree items will be added to the dining room's menu for the coming tourist season. The introduction of these new menu items is going to affect a number of different hotel departments or areas and the functions performed in them. State what these functional areas are. Then list the questions that need to be answered by the management information system in each functional area before the new menu items are introduced.

13-2. As the manager of the maintenance department of a hotel, you are paid a basic salary, plus a bonus. The bonus is an extra $1,000 each time your expenses are under budget plus 2 percent of the amount you are able to save. For the past six budget periods, you obtain the following results (U stands for unfavorable, or over budget, and F for favorable, or under budget):

Period	Budget	Actual	Variance
1	$80,000	$82,000	$2,000 U
2	80,000	79,000	1,000 F
3	78,000	74,000	4,000 F
4	72,000	74,000	2,000 U

Period	Budget	Actual	Variance
5	72,000	73,000	1,000 U
6	72,500	72,000	500 F

    a. As a rational person, what would you do if you were the department manager running the maintenance department over again from period 1, given the preceding information?

    b. What would you recommend doing, if anything, to change this hotel's maintenance department's bonus system if you were the hotel's general manager?

13–3. Labor cost is often the highest cost, as a percentage of sales, in a hospitality enterprise. Most hotels and restaurants have well-established management information systems that provide data for payroll control, for the production of employee checks, and for satisfying legal requirements regarding payroll deductions and remittances.

    Few of these establishments, however, have information systems that provide anything beyond basic payroll requirements (such as hours worked, rate of pay, gross pay, pay deductions, and net pay). List eight classes of information that you think a good *personnel* (as opposed to payroll) system could supply management with, regarding an establishment's employees.

13–4. A manager's information requirements differ from one level to the next within an organization. Lower-level managers require information in very detailed form, while top-level managers require this information in summarized form. Explain why this is true, and give two examples from your own work experience that show how the nature of information changes as it moves up the organizational ranks.

13–5. Several department heads in a medium-sized hotel share the same two secretaries for typing and related office services. These secretaries have provided excellent and prompt typing and office services in the past. Following is a list of eleven events that pertain to the department heads and their secretaries. For each event, identify which of the four areas of the problem-solving process the item belongs in. The four areas are (1) defining the problem, (2) identifying alternatives, (3) gathering information, and (4) making the decision.

a. Two department heads have complained to the assistant manager that they now are having to wait longer than in the past to have work done.

b. The secretaries have priorities for doing work. Telephone calls are handled first; correspondence is next; internal memos are third; and other work comes last.

c. One department head complained that one of his memos contained several typing errors.

d. One department head suggests replacing the less efficient typist.

e. A typist reports that one department head (the hotel's chef) has pressured her to do private typing work for a recipe book that he is writing.

f. The office photocopying machine broke down last week and took three days to be fixed. This has happened several times recently.

g. The assistant manager says that the chef's book manuscript should be typed and be paid for privately.

h. The assistant manager is considering asking the general manager to hire a third secretary on a part-time basis.

i. One of the secretaries was recently away in hospital for a week, and a less efficient replacement was hired to fill in during that period.

j. Department heads are to be reminded of the secretaries' priorities.

k. A maintenance contract that guarantees same-day repair of the photocopier is to be arranged.

13–6. The bell service department of a large hotel normally has a bell captain and nine bellmen on duty on the day shift during the peak tourist months. During the past peak month, there have been unusually many guest complaints about the slow service received, creating a problem for the rooms department manager to resolve.

Following are descriptions of fifteen situations or events pertaining to the bell service department. For each separate item, identify which of the four areas of the problem-solving process the item belongs in. The four areas are (1) defining the problem, (2) identifying alternatives, (3) gathering information, and (4) making the decision.

a. Several guests have complained to the front-office manager that they are receiving service with a longer-than-usual wait or are receiving poor service.

b. The bell service department has priorities for jobs. Guest check-out baggage is handled first. Second is guest check-in baggage. Third is delivery of other items to guest rooms. Fourth is sale of airport limousine, bus tour, and theater tickets. Fifth is other requests for service.

c. One guest complained that his theater ticket was for the wrong night.

d. One guest suggested replacing the bell captain with a better organizer.

e. One guest complained that his request to have flowers purchased and then delivered to another guest's room never happened.

f. The paging system that allows the bell captain to signal to bellmen away from the service area has malfunctioned three times in the last month and has taken as long as 24 hours to repair.

g. One of the desk clerks suggests that the sale of theater and bus tour tickets be handled by a new person, who would operate strictly on a commission basis.

h. The rooms department manager will consider having a commission arrangement for next summer, since it is too late to do anything about it this year.

i. The bell captain suggests hiring one more bellman.

j. One bellman has been away sick for the past two weeks.

k. In the sick bellman's absence, he has been replaced by a temporary employee who is not familiar with the hotel and its operating procedures and whose work is marginal.

l. Guests who complain are advised of the bell service desk's order of priorities.

m. During the past month the hotel's occupancy has been 10 percentage points above normal for the month, creating extra demands by guests for service.

n. The rooms department manager has approved hiring one extra temporary bellman for as long as occupancy stays above normal.

o. A new paging system will be purchased, with a maintenance contract guaranteeing instant service.

13–7. A catering company has received a request from a private association to handle a 1,000-guest banquet at $12 per person, to be held two days from now on the association's premises (rather than in the catering company's own hall) some distance from the catering hall's kitchen. The menu will include a cold appetizer, an 8-oz entree steak with two vegetables, and a cold dessert. All steaks must be cooked well done. The catering company's manager must inform the association's secretary by 1 p.m. today whether or not the company will accept the business. On the following chart, show whether the critical characteristic of each informational item is relevance, timeliness, or accuracy. Place an X in the appropriate column if the characteristic is satisfied, and a 0 if it is not. The first item is given as an example.

Information item	Relevance	Timeliness	Accuracy
a. At 10 a.m., the manager is advised that enough prime rib of beef can be delivered to the kitchen by 9 a.m. tomorrow morning. (The most important characteristic, relevance, is not satisfied since the customer wants steak. The information is timely, but has nothing to do with the problem. The accuracy of the information cannot be determined from the facts.)	0		
b. A quote on the purchase cost of 1,000 8-oz steaks of the quality desired is received at 3:30 p.m.			
c. The chef says unsatisfactory-quality steaks can be purchased at a cost saving from another supplier.			
d. The manager is told that 4 extra cooks will have to be hired to produce the menu. Each will be paid for 4 hours, but the correct figure is 6 hours.			
e. The association making the request may be a poor credit risk.			
f. The association plans to charge its members $2 per person more than the price it will pay the catering company.			

Information item	Relevance	Timeliness	Accuracy
g. The cost quotation for renting trucks to move the prepared food to the hall is higher than estimated.			
h. The association's secretary advises that it is willing to pay the catering company half the total price tomorrow, and the balance in cash at the end of the meal.			
i. Steaks of an acceptable quality could have been purchased for $1 per pound less last week.			
j. The chef advises that he would never be able to handle this order if the steaks were wanted less than well done because of the transportation distance.			
k. The chef says that he should be able to figure out the food cost on this function by tomorrow.			

Computers and Cost Control

14

Objectives

After studying this chapter, the reader should be able to do the following:

- State the main advantage of a computer system over a manual system.
- Define computer terms such as *time-sharing* and *networking*.
- Differentiate between a microprocessor and a microcomputer.
- Differentiate between computer hardware and computer software, and list the main hardware items that make up a computer system.
- Discuss computer software languages and the ways in which software can be obtained.
- Differentiate between an integrated software system and an application-oriented software system.
- Discuss various types of application-oriented software such as word processing, a database manager, and a spreadsheet, state what each will do, and define an *integrated work station*.
- Define and differentiate between an ECR and a POS.
- Describe how a recipe- or ingredient-based food cost control system works.
- Describe how a front-office computerized guest room security system operates without the use of standard room door keys.

COMPUTERS IN HOTELS AND FOODSERVICE

In all the previous chapters in this book, manual systems of cost planning and control have been demonstrated. Today, though, many hotels and foodservice operations are using computers in this area of management.

Computers in society

In the three decades or so since computers first began to be commercially produced, they have become a major factor in our lives. We are all aware that they are used extensively in military and national security, in power generation, in transportation systems of all kinds, in manufacturing, and in banking. Despite this major role in society, computers have only slowly become a major force in the hospitality industry. Initially this was due to their very high cost and excessive space requirements. For that reason, only chain operations and exceptionally large independent operations used them.

Low-cost microcomputers

However, the introduction of the small and low-cost (but still very powerful) microcomputer, or personal computer, has made computers available to even small independent hospitality entrepreneurs, who account for most hospitality operations. Today's microcomputers are so low in price that an independent computer could be used cost-effectively by a single department within a larger operation—for example, to maintain storeroom inventory records.

Computers are not entirely new to the industry. For example, some hotels have been using computers in their reservation, guest history, registration, and guest accounting area for many years, as well as in back-office accounting. Similarly, many restaurants have been using computerized sales registers to record sales dollars, sales per server (for labor productivity analysis), and sales of individual menu items (for menu analysis) for a decade or more. More recently, computers have been put to valuable use to remove much of the drudgery inherent in manual cost control systems such as budgeting, inventory control, and recipe costing.

Speed and Accuracy

The main difference between a computerized system and a manual one is the computers' speed; computers are also invariably more accurate! It must be emphasized, however, that computerized systems cannot do anything that cannot be done manually. Computers can produce information

Decision making still required

a lot more rapidly, but they do not relieve management from its major responsibility for decision making once the information is produced.

Computers no longer have to be expensive, take up otherwise valuable space, or require a highly skilled technician to operate. No longer need they be operated by specialist computer departments, remote from day-to-day operations and decision making, producing voluminous reports long after the information they contain has become obsolete.

The new, low-cost computers may dictate a change in the way that hospitality managers behave on the job. It may be a matter of competitive survival for these managers to learn to use computer resources effectively and to harness the wealth of information they can provide.

TYPES OF COMPUTERS

In the early days, computers required specialist operators and dedicated, air-conditioned rooms. The computers were often remote from the departments that needed the information they could provide. Sometimes the main computer could be accessed by terminals of one type or another in individual departments, or in individual operations that were part of a chain. A large, centralized computer of this type is often referred to today as a "mainframe" computer.

Mainframe computer

Minicomputers

With the introduction of minicomputers, the situation changed. A minicomputer was smaller and cheaper than its mainframe predecessors. A branch of a chain organization, although still perhaps linked to the head office's mainframe, could now afford to have its own minicomputer on the premises. Moreover, a number of users could be connected through terminals to the microcomputer at the same time—an arrangement known as computer time-sharing. When a user accesses the minicomputer, the computer can quickly locate that user's information, receive and process instructions from the user to manipulate or add to that information, and then re-store it until the user next requests it. In order to do this for several users, the computer must perform a lot of housekeeping to ensure that information from different users is not mixed up, and to respond to each user in turn if several are using the computer at the same time.

Computer time-sharing

The result is that time-shared computers (either mainframe or minicomputer) run at only about 50 percent efficiency. As the computer gets busier (because more users are accessing it), it begins to slow down. Its response time is also irregular, and a user may not know—if the computer does not respond promptly—whether the machine is slowed down from heavy use or because the user has entered information that the computer does not understand and cannot process.

Low efficiency of time-sharing

A minicomputer may also require a complicated set of instructions and an expensive communication system, as well as extra levels of security, including passwords and protected security levels, to link it with all its users and to prevent unauthorized access to confidential information.

Finally, with a large, time-shared computer or a minicomputer with several users, every user is out of business when the computer breaks down, unless there is a backup computer linked to the first one.

Common information

Despite these shortcomings, mainframe and minicomputers are valuable in situations where common information must be shared by several users. This might be the case in a hotel where guest reservation, registration, and accounting information is to be accessed by front-office personnel, accounting office employees, and even, for some purposes, by employees in housekeeping and marketing.

Microcomputers

The heart of a microcomputer is the microprocessor, which is sometimes referred to as a microcomputer on a chip, but is actually only a processing and controlling subsystem on an electronic chip or on a very small part of the actual microcomputer. These computer chips are so small that 20,000 of them can fit into a regular-size briefcase. When the microprocessor chip was introduced, it dramatically changed the accessibility of computer power and substantially reduced the cost of this power. Now, a complete stand-alone microcomputer, or "personal computer," as it is sometimes called, can cost as little as a few thousand dollars and can easily fit on a manager's desk or on a table beside that desk. No specialist expertise is required to operate these computers. Indeed, it is no more necessary to know how a computer works in order to use it than it is to know how a car works in order to drive it.

Microprocessors

Although the terms *microprocessor* and *microcomputer* are sometimes used interchangeably, they do not mean the same thing. A microprocessor is the physical design and structure engraved on the chips that make a microcomputer function. Microcomputers derive their name from the fact that their systems are miniaturized. A microcomputer could therefore be simply described as a small computer—although that can be misleading, since today's microcomputers are as powerful as mainframe computers were twenty years ago.

Microcomputers today are so low in price, so independent, and so versatile that it is often better (and cheaper) to buy an extra machine for a special type of job than to create a special time-sharing program for several users. Indeed, independent microcomputers can be linked together to access information that users need from time to time (such as reservation information in a hotel). This linking together of several independent computers is known as "networking."

Networking

As the networking capability is further advanced, it may someday be possible for a hospitality enterprise to transmit its needs by microcomputer to a network of suppliers' computers—for example, for inventory ordering. Another future possibility is the electronic funds transfer, where point-of-sale terminals in a hotel or restaurant are connected directly to a terminal at a local bank, which in turn is networked to terminals at other banks. When a customer pays a bill by bank credit card or by check, the card or check can be verified by the local bank's terminal, which then transmits instructions to the customer's bank so that the funds are immediately transferred to the hotel's or restaurant's bank account. The results of this system will be time savings of one or more days (with a concomitant increase in interest income) and reduced losses from dishonored credit cards and NSF checks. **Use in banking**

HARDWARE VERSUS SOFTWARE

The hardware of a computer system is the actual physical equipment that responds to a predetermined set of instructions in a self-directed fashion. **Computer programs**

These instructions are developed by programmers. Once a program (or set of instructions) is put into the hardware, the computer can carry out those instructions without any operator intervention. Any intelligence that a computer has must be programmed into it, and any weaknesses in that intelligence are attributable to the program.

Each individual computer may be required to operate with many different programs for different jobs. Each program is copied into the computer when it is needed. When a new program is fed in (loaded), the previous program is replaced. When the machine is turned off, any program currently in the machine is erased from its memory. Because of the temporary status of each program in the computer, programs are known as software. Software is generally stored on tape or on disks; when it is loaded into the machine, it is not removed from the tape or disk, but only copied into the computer's electronic memory. Therefore, software storage tapes or disks hold the permanent record of the program. **Storing programs**

The problem for a hotel or restaurant in implementing a computer system involves finding good software. Software has to be written (contain instructions) in a program language, or set of codes, that the computer can understand. The computer then converts these instructions into a more efficient (but less intelligible) machine language of its own, before it actually carries out the instructions. There are more than 2,000 different computer languages available to programmers today, and many of these languages may have several dialects of their own. **Machine languages**

Sometimes the word *firmware* is used to describe a piece of software that is built into the computer. In other words, firmware is a piece of hardware that behaves like a piece of software. It generally comprises some circuits that always load certain instructions into the computer as soon as it is turned on. For example, firmware might contain security identification codes that require users to identify themselves properly in order to use the computer at all or in order to use some of its restricted applications. **Firmware**

Hardware Systems

Different types of hardware

Computer hardware systems often consist of a number of components, since a small microcomputer by itself cannot do much without the aid of some other hardware, or peripheral equipment. The main part of the computer, where all the work or manipulation is performed, is sometimes referred to as the "central processing unit" (CPU). To load the instructions, or program, into the CPU, another device is required. On microcomputers that operate from programs stored on disks, the input device is known as a disk drive. On some microcomputers, the disk drive (or drives, if there is more than one) may be built right into the CPU. There must also be another input device, to enable the user to interact with the CPU as work proceeds. This input device is a keyboard, and it closely resembles a typewriter keyboard. Again, the keyboard is sometimes built into the CPU rather than existing as a separate hardware device linked to the CPU. Yet another hardware device is the monitor or screen or cathode-ray tube (CRT) or video display unit (VDU), which displays the output of the computer session: prompts to the user from the CPU, data and instructions input from the keyboard by the user, and the end result of the work that is being done. On some microcomputers, this monitor may be an integral part of the CPU. Finally, for most output work, the system must be connected to a printer. The printer is invariably a separate piece of equipment, attached by cable to the CPU.

Hardware compatibility

Obviously, there must be a high degree of compatibility between these various pieces of hardware if all the parts are to work together. In addition to compatibility of hardware, the software used must have language compatibility with each of the pieces of hardware.

Software

Canned software

The question sometimes arises whether it is better to obtain software specifically written for an individual hotel's or restaurant's needs or to buy an already-written software package (known as "canned software"). Arranging to have software specifically written is far more expensive than buying a canned program. And because hotels and restaurants are generally small businesses, they do not normally have the resources necessary to carry out the systems analysis and program design work necessary to develop their own computer software. Furthermore, their software requirements in areas such as general accounting, budgeting, and payroll differ little from those of other businesses.

Buying software

There are three ways to buy software. First, a computer manufacturer will offer software it has developed to go with the computers it sells. Second, an independent software developer will sell programs modified to run on various computers. Third, a software developer may write specific programs to run only on specific computers.

Canned programs have usually been widely tested and sold, and as a result most errors (bugs) originally in them have been caught and corrected. In most cases, canned software can be seen in action through demonstrations before a decision to purchase is made. The costs to buy and install it and to train employees to use it can be determined in advance, and any compromises that are necessary between an operation's needs and the software's capabilities can be reached in advance.

Advantages of canned software

A successful, widely used canned software package thus offers proven performance for an economical price. In addition, specialized software packages are now available for the hospitality industry in such areas as food and beverage cost control.

Obviously, the benefits of using off-the-shelf software have to be considered against the disadvantages. A software package written for broad hospitality/foodservice requirements may not be as convenient or as fast as one that is custom-designed, but the tradeoff is that it is much cheaper and relatively bug-free.

Costs versus benefits

INTEGRATED SOFTWARE SYSTEMS

Analysis of the flow of information in a hotel or restaurant will reveal that some of the same information is used more than once. The name of a guest who registers in a hotel, for example, may be used in reservations, registration, guest history, housekeeping, and accounting. A food item in inventory may be used in receiving, storing, issuing, recipes, production, and sales control.

With a computer system, it is feasible, sensible, and advantageous to use software that is integrated. In integrated software systems, the objective is to record an item of data only once, and thereafter to use it in the same form in every possible way to provide information for planning and control purposes. If the item of data had to be entered into the computer each time it was wanted, extra time at the keyboard would be expended and errors could be made, demanding additional time and money to correct. If the entry need be made only once, error possibilities are reduced and the process is simplified.

Using integrated software

A hotel or restaurant can be viewed as a system for which a completely integrated package of computer software could control and plan every single operational aspect. However, a completely integrated software package to handle all operational aspects of a system would be extremely costly and complex. It would probably incur higher training costs because of its complexity, and it might also create severe maintenance and data security problems. Further, if one part of the system failed, it would create difficulties in all departments or areas of the business. For these reasons, a small property would find a completely integrated system difficult to justify financially.

Complexity of integrated systems

APPLICATION-ORIENTED SOFTWARE SYSTEMS

Dedicated systems

At the other extreme is a software system that is single-application-oriented. A computer system that is application-oriented (sometimes referred to as a "dedicated" or "stand-alone" system) is generally designed to handle one specific type of job and allows for much less integration. An example is a payroll system that is not integrated with labor cost budgeting, or a food inventory control system that is not integrated with purchasing and food costing.

Because of their relative simplicity, application-oriented software systems can be evaluated fairly easily to see if they will perform precisely the limited jobs they are intended to carry out. These systems are cheaper than integrated systems to buy and install, and they can be introduced into an operation over time as finances allow. An ideal situation would be to move from a piecemeal, stand-alone set of application systems to an integrated system over time—as long as each part can be made compatible with the others. In this type of in-house network, each computer system is able to operate on a stand-alone basis but can network with all others to allow transmission of certain data back and forth.

Networking some information

Obviously, the narrower an application-oriented system is, the easier it is to develop and the lower its cost will be. It will also be more efficient, since it controls fewer functions and may be more reliable. At the same time, the narrower an application system becomes, the less efficient it may be in terms of overall control. If a food inventory control system has to be supported by a separate food cost control system, then two packages of software are required, two different computer hardware systems may be needed, and two sets of user/operator systems have to be learned.

Initially, most microcomputer applications in the hospitality industry were stand-alone applications. But as the power and the memory capacity of these machines have improved over the past years, the software systems available have become less stand-alone and more integrated. Consequently, microcomputers now offer software capable of doing as much as or more than could be done on minicomputers a few years ago.

Deciding on applications

The manager's tasks are to decide which applications of a hotel or restaurant should be linked and which should be kept separate, and to seek software that is compatible with those objectives.

Three common stand-alone or application-oriented software packages are word processing packages, database managers, and spreadsheets.

Word Processing

The term *word processing* refers to a computer system that is programmed to manipulate words (text). Any small computer can be programmed for word processing. Surprisingly, many people do not think that machines used exclusively for word processing are true computers. But if a machine can be programmed to do full-service word processing, it can be programmed to do other things as well. (There are on the market some electronic typewriters with very little memory that can do some limited forms of word processing but are not true word processors or computers.)

It is wrong to think that computers purchased primarily to do word processing will reduce office labor costs. Studies have shown that this does not happen. But purchasing a low-cost computer to use primarily for word processing is a good way to introduce computers into a business. They can be very useful where a large amount of correspondence is handled, such as in a hotel front-office reservation area (where a standard format of letter can be used) or in a catering company (where a standard banquet contract is used and only certain information—such as the number of expected guests, the menu selected, and the price of the meal— needs to be inserted).

No reduction in labor costs

The main purpose of a word processor is to facilitate text creation and editing, and the ease with which this can be done is a major factor in selecting word-processing software. One of the major advantages of word-processing equipment over regular typewriters is that documents can be printed more attractively. With some models of printer, for example, type styles can easily be switched back and forth. More sophisticated word-processing software can include spelling checkers, with a built-in dictionary of as many as 30,000 words. If a word is typed that is not in the dictionary it will be highlighted by the spelling checker. If it is a technical word not found in the regular dictionary, it can be added to a supplementary dictionary so that it will not be highlighted the next time it appears.

Changing typestyles

Database Manager

A database is any collection of records or data—for example, addresses of regular customers, a food or beverage inventory listing, personnel records, or a file of recipes. A database manager is simply a software package that allows quick access and ready manipulation of the records that are in a particular database. In other words, it is much like a filing system in a regular office. A database manager that offers easy sorting and selection procedures is invaluable.

Database as filing system

It is often useful to work with an integrated software package that includes both word processing and a database manager. For example, it may be desirable for a hotel to send out a standard form letter to all the travel agents it does business with regularly, advising them of a change in room rates or commission rates. The computer can be programmed to take each travel agent's address in turn, type it on the hotel's letterhead, type in the letter, and then move to the next address and letter on a new page, repeating the procedure until all addresses have been processed. All of this can be done without any operater intervention, once the process has begun.

Spreadsheet

Using for budgets

Spreadsheet software basically consists of a large electronic sheet with rows down the side and columns across the top. Most managers have struggled with budgets, using pencils and column pads and have become frustrated when they wished to see what would happen, for example, if the food cost ratio to sales were altered over a 12-month annual budget. The number of changes that would have to be made to food cost, gross profit, and net profit in this case would amount to 36 changes of numbers, considerable erasing and correcting, and a risk that one or more errors would result. An electronic spreadsheet, once programmed, allows a manager to answer "what if" questions, error-free, in seconds and prints out the results. Indeed, multiple "what if" changes can be made simultaneously at rapid speed.

Forecasting menu item demand

Spreadsheets lend themselves to budgeting and to such matters as forecasting. For example, a sophisticated spreadsheet might store in its memory a record of all the various menu items a restaurant offers, including how many of each are sold (on average) by meal period and by day of the week for each specific month. The spreadsheet could then forecast for the current month, based on past performance, how many portions of each menu item need to be produced by the kitchen for each meal period on each day of the current month. Spreadsheets are also convenient for employee scheduling, to improve labor cost control.

Integrated Work Stations

As far as planning and control are concerned, the three application software packages just described (word processing packages, database managers, and spreadsheets) are closely related and are major types of software packages for small computers. A computer ought to be able to pass data from its database manager to a spreadsheet, and then pass the results to a word processor for addition of text and final printing of a report (including graphics, where these would be valuable).

Indeed, single software packages are available for many microcomputers today that include all three of these software systems on one disk. These are known as integrated work stations.

ACCOUNTING PACKAGES

General accounting is another area that lends itself well to an integrated package. Most businesses with a manual system of accounting use an integrated approach for their general ledger, sales, accounts receivable, purchases, accounts payable, payroll, and inventory control. In hotels, front-office reservations, registrations, and guest accounting can also be integrated into this system. There are today many software packages available for computerizing this work. In some situations, it may not be feasible or practical to integrate each of these subsystems on the hotel's main computer. For example, it may be desirable to split off food inventory control so that a separate specialized software package with additional (and useful) features can be brought in to handle this area.

Many packages available

Similarly, it may not be practical for a hotel or restaurant to computerize its payroll, given that the expense of maintaining computerized payroll software is comparatively high. Each time the laws (and attendant percentages) governing employment change (minimum wage rates, tax deduction rates, unemployment insurance rates, and so on), the software must be rewritten to reflect those changes. For this reason, many establishments contract out their payroll to computer service companies that specialize in this kind of work. However, some in-house systems can be equipped with magnetic strip readers. The magnetic strips are affixed to employee ID cards; then, as each employee arrives at or leaves work, he or she inserts the ID card into the reader. In this way, employees can be clocked in and out of work for purposes of obtaining employee hours worked data (to be given to the service bureau).

Contracting out payroll

ECR AND POS SYSTEMS

For locations where sales are recorded—particularly in food and beverage areas—two kinds of systems are available: an electronic cash register (ECR), and a point-of-sale (POS) system. Basically, the ECR is a stand-alone electronic register; in contrast, a POS system links several ECRs to a separate, often remote computer, and the POS system's sales registers are primarily keyboards rather than separate machines. Unfortunately, the terms ECR and POS are often used interchangeably. Technically speaking, however, a POS system is much more sophisticated than a stand-alone ECR—although even an ECR can provide a great deal more information on cost of sales than could its predecessors (mechanical sales registers).

ECRs versus POS systems

Electronic Cash Registers (ECRs)

ECRs have allowed management to dispense with cashiers in most establishments, since the servers can act as their own cashiers, and since the machine records (among other things) sales by server so that each knows how much cash to turn in at the end of each shift.

Most ECRs today (even though there are many different models avail-

Prompting steps

able from many different manufacturers) have some sort of video display, often just a strip window within which a limited number of characters can be shown; but increasingly larger-view units are appearing on the market so that, for example, the entire bill for a group of people at a table can be seen on the screen. More sophisticated models have keys that light up to prompt the operator about what to do next, or show messages on the screen that specify subsequent steps to take or that explain mistakes.

These ECRs have automatic pricing (so that pricing errors can be eliminated), change control features (in some cases even linked to automatic change dispensers to reduce losses from change-making errors), and automatic tax calculation (for jurisdictions where food and/or beverage sales are taxable).

Computerized ECRs can summarize sales not only by server (broken down into cash and charge details), but also by various categories such as appetizers, entrees, and desserts. In chain operations, this sales information might be networked to the head-office computer for further, more detailed processing.

Some ECRs can be programmed to print out the most popular combinations of appetizer, entree, and dessert that customers choose. This is useful information for menu and sales mix planning.

Inventory control

Some ECRs can also provide inventory control for items that can be quantified easily, such as steaks. In order to be used for complete inventory control, the ECR would have to be programmed to remember the recipe of each dish, and that sort of inventory control might better be left to a separate computer control system. Alternatively, the ECR might be linked to another computer and might send sales information to this computer so that the food cost control work can be done there.

Some ECRs contain built-in time clocks, allowing servers to clock in and out of work on the machine by using a magnetic-stripped employee ID card; this procedure then forms the basis of information for staff planning and for the payroll system. At the end of each shift or day, summary reports of employee hours worked—both by employee and in total—can be taken from the terminal. Concurrently, information can be accumulated in the ECR for each weekly or biweekly payroll period. The clock can also

Patterns of sales

be used to track patterns of sales by time of day or to record times of guest arrivals and departures in the restaurant. This could be valuable for staff scheduling, for labor cost planning, and for kitchen food production planning.

Other ECRs have scales attached to them for automatic price calculation of items (such as salads) that are sold by weight.

With most ECR systems, sales checks need not be preprinted with sequential numbers. Blank standard sales checks can be purchased (at a lower cost, without numbering) and the ECR machine will print a consecutive number on each when the check is begun. If the same check is used for a reorder, the employee must instruct the machine that a previous check number is being used. If the server does not use the previous number when adding items to an active sales check, the machine will simply assign the check a new number. If a dishonest server tried collecting the full amount of the check from the customer and only turning in the amount of money from the reorder, the first number would show up as a missing check and the discrepancy would be spotted.

Integrated Point-of-Sale (POS) Systems

Generally a point-of-sale (POS) system is a series of individual sales terminals linked to a remote central processing unit (CPU) located, for example, in the manager's office. Food and beverage POS systems may be used as stand-alone systems, but they are more commonly linked to other POS terminals in other sales locations. They can also be linked to other equipment, such as to a printer in the kitchen that tells the kitchen what has been recorded in the register and needs to be prepared in the kitchen, without requiring the server (who has rung up the item on the register) to walk to the kitchen. The kitchen might also be able to send messages back to the front register to prompt servers when it is time to pick up prepared food orders. Hotel POS systems in food and beverage outlets may be linked to the front-office accounting system so that hotel guests charging food and beverage items in the restaurant or bar can have the amounts added to their front-office accounts automatically.

Linking POS systems

In other words, a POS system has much more power and capability than a single ECR and can produce a much broader range of management reports, by sales outlet and in total for an entire operation. The system has a larger visual display (CRT) and generally is totally programmable and easily modifiable within the business to accommodate changes in pricing and many other items. It can be linked to a chain operation's head office, where data from individual outlets can be analyzed by the mainframe computer, results can be compared from unit to unit, and data can be consolidated by region and for the chain as a whole. In some systems, analysis reports for each individual unit can be sent back to the unit, through a process known as "downloading." Where it is in place, downloading could also be used to provide each unit's computer with new menu pricing and recipe costing information. A POS system can also accommodate a large number of peripheral devices (including remote ones) such as printers, and its cost/benefit advantage increases as the size of the business grows larger.

Management reports

Downloading

The major disadvantage of a POS system is that, if the CPU fails, each POS terminal in the entire system fails (since terminals cannot operate independently of the CPU), unless the system is backed up on floppy or hard storage disks, or unless the individual terminals can be upgraded to operate in at least a limited way with some memory capability and to produce some reports independent of the CPU.

FOOD CONTROL SYSTEMS

Complexity of recipe costing

In chapter 5, a method of food cost control based on accurate costing of standard recipes was illustrated as a manual procedure. Unfortunately, because of the constant flux of food costs, a restaurant with an extensive menu would find the task of keeping recipe costs up to date by manual means prohibitively time-consuming. Even a restaurant with a limited menu would find the job very time-consuming and thus hardly worth the effort. Even though calculations of standard food cost can be simplified to avoid constantly having to recost recipes (for example, by using a market cost index, as explained in chapter 6), the simplifications introduce inaccuracies that can quickly make a comparison of the actual food cost with a standard food cost virtually meaningless.

Recipes as a Basis for Control

Use of uniform product code

Computers can take all the drudgery out of this work, by using a software database system that operates from a computerized file of recipes and their ingredients. As new purchases are made, the inventory (ingredient) quantity and cost information is entered into the computer from the invoices. Terminals can also be equipped with a wand reader at the receiving area. The hand-held wand is designed to read each item's uniform product code (UPC). The UPC, a series of black bars on a white background, is found today on most packaged goods. The wand reads this code in the same way that a supermarket register reads it at the checkout stand. In a hotel or restaurant, the wand reader would automatically enter product information (quantity, size, price) into the computer. If an item does not have a UPC code, the relevant information for it has to be entered into the computer manually.

Flagging recipes

As new ingredient information is entered, the computer automatically updates all total recipe costs (using current portion costs or a weighted average, depending on management's preferences) for any recipes containing these ingredients. A report can be printed out showing what recipes are affected and what the new food cost is in dollars and percentages for each recipe; it may even flag the recipe to call to management's attention the need to change the menu selling price.

Food Production Control

Each day before production commences, the chef or department head merely enters into the computer the name of each recipe item and the number of portions to be produced that day. The computer then prints out the standard cost for all of those recipe items (individually and in total), prints out the recipes and the ingredient lists for the required numbers of portions, and prints a requisition listing the ingredients and specifying the quantities required from the storeroom. If more than a required quantity must be requisitioned for a particular day (for example a #10 can of an item, when only half a can is required for production), the computer makes a note of this excess and takes it into account when future requisitions are prepared.

**Printing
requisitions**

Inventory Control

As requisitions are printed out, the computer also adjusts the storeroom inventory count for period-end stock-taking and provides a value for items requisitioned but not yet used in production (for example, the half #10 can mentioned earlier). From time to time, a normal storeroom inventory reconciliation must be carried out, comparing the physical count of items actually in stock with the computer listing of what should be there, according to production usage.

**Inventory
reconciliation**

Taking a physical (or actual) inventory is also easier to do with a computer. There are programs available that will print an inventory form, complete with current item costs, leaving only the count quantity to be inserted manually. After the count is performed, the figures can be entered into the computer, and a final printout can be made showing extensions (item count times price) for all items and the total inventory value.

**Adjusting
purchases
to volume**

The computer can also adjust the volume of storeroom inventory required, in accordance with the level of business. Thus, instead of leaving it to management to establish a fixed minimum and maximum level of stock for each storeroom item, the computer can adjust the reorder level and the order quantity to the actual demand (which changes over time or by season) for that item. Each day, the computer then prints out a list of items that need to be ordered, the quantities needed, and the economic order quantity (if this is built into the system). In cases where particular suppliers are under contract to provide specific storeroom items at contracted prices, the actual purchase orders can be prepared for those suppliers. Even if purchase orders are not used, a printed list can be prepared for the receiver so that delivered items and their quantities can be checked against the list.

Management Reports

Finally, management reports can be prepared to show such things as planning errors (overproduction of menu items because of poor forecasting). A completely comprehensive food cost control system would have built

Other management reports

into it (through linkage to POS registers) the actual sales histories of various menu items, in combination with other menu items, and would provide the kitchen with daily food production requirements to minimize such things as overproduction planning errors.

Other management reports might show operational errors (wastage because standard recipes were not followed) and costing errors (loss of potential revenue in comparison to actual revenue because selling prices have not kept up with rising food costs). Other possible reports might relate to dead stock (ingredients that have remained unissued from stores for a certain specified period) that is tying up money in inventory, and to pricing trends for major purchase items (to assist in forward menu price planning).

FRONT-OFFICE SYSTEMS

The main objective of a front-office system for a hotel or motel is to maximize revenue or sales. For this reason, most front-office computer systems are oriented to revenue control (rather than to cost control). In addition, they are generally based on the reservation, registration, and guest accounting needs of the property, although they can also be linked to food and beverage POS system terminals.

Control of telephone costs

Still, front-office computer systems can provide cost control in certain areas. For example, they can be linked to the telephone system to monitor (and add to the guest accounts) charges for both local and long-distance calls, so the hotel does not end up paying for telephone costs as a result of failing to charge them to guest accounts.

The front-office system can also provide other departments (such as housekeeping and food and beverage areas) with constantly updated information relating to rooms occupancy and guest counts, thereby ensuring that adequate staffing can be arranged and that departments will not be overstaffed.

Security Control

More recently, front-office systems have been able to help control security costs. A computer can be programmed to allow certain keys to open doors during limited periods each day. This might mean that housekeeping staff can gain access to rooms only during the room makeup period. The system can also issue guests "keys" that are simply plastic cards (about the size of a credit card) and have data encoded on them on magnetic strips, or in the form of a series of punched holes (see exhibit 14.1). The guest room door will have on it a device that reads the card and allows the door to be opened only if it is the proper "key."

Plastic room "keys"

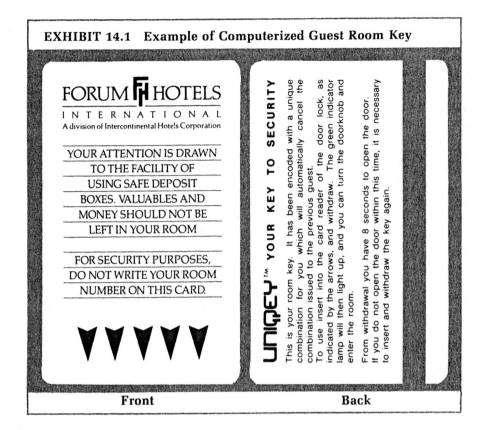

EXHIBIT 14.1   Example of Computerized Guest Room Key

FORUM FH HOTELS
INTERNATIONAL
A division of Intercontinental Hotels Corporation

YOUR ATTENTION IS DRAWN
TO THE FACILITY OF
USING SAFE DEPOSIT
BOXES. VALUABLES AND
MONEY SHOULD NOT BE
LEFT IN YOUR ROOM

FOR SECURITY PURPOSES,
DO NOT WRITE YOUR ROOM
NUMBER ON THIS CARD.

UNIQEY™ YOUR KEY TO SECURITY

This is your room key. It has been encoded with a unique combination for you which will automatically cancel the combination issued to the previous guest.
To use insert into the card reader of the door lock, as indicated by the arrows, and withdraw. The green indicator lamp will then light up, and you can turn the doorknob and enter the room.

From withdrawal you have 8 seconds to open the door. If you do not open the door within this time, it is necessary to insert and withdraw the key again.

Front   **Back**

When a guest registers, the computer issues a new guest "key" (in the form of a card) that bears a unique code for that guest and for that specific room. At the same time, the computer erases the old code for that room in the device on the guest room door (so that a departed guest cannot reuse the old card) and creates a new code corresponding to the arriving guest's card. Departing guests do not even have to turn in their "keys" on leaving; these can simply be discarded. In cases of emergency, the card reader device can be overridden by a conventional key used by authorized hotel personnel. The plastic key cards can also be used as internal credit/ID cards that guests can use to charge food or beverages consumed in the hotel's dining room/bar areas to their room accounts.

Emergency situations

Small hotels and motels can install computerized equipment at the front office that can be operated by an arriving guest. The computer will accept certain credit cards, automatically charging the amount for that room to the credit card, issuing a "paid" invoice, and issuing a plastic key coded to let the guest open the door of the assigned room. No longer is an all-night employee required to register late-arriving guests or to check out early-departing ones!

SUMMARY

In the years since computers were first commercially produced, they have come to exercise a major influence in our lives. The introduction of the small and low-cost microcomputer has made computer power available to even the smallest independent hospitality enterprise. Computers can be used to simplify many routine cost control problems such as budgeting, inventory control, and recipe costing. The main difference between a computerized cost control system and a manual one is the speed with which computers perform the work.

Computers can arbitrarily be differentiated by size into three basic types: mainframe computers, minicomputers, and microcomputers (often referred to as "home" or "personal" computers). Although chain and large organizations might use mainframe or minicomputers, the microcomputer probably has the greatest impact on the independent hospitality enterprise. Today's microcomputers are so low in price and so independently versatile that it is often better (and cheaper) to buy an extra machine for a special type of job than to develop new software to run on an existing larger computer.

The hardware of a computer system is the physical equipment that follows a predetermined set of instructions in a self-directed fashion. Software is the set of instructions or program that causes the computer to do what is wanted. Software instructions are expressed in languages or codes that the computer can understand.

Hardware systems are made up of the central processing unit (CPU), the disk drives (which feed the software codes from disks into the CPU), the keyboard (which allows interaction between the computer and the operator), the monitor, screen, or cathode-ray tube (CRT), and the printer. The key to how well a computer will do what is wanted, however, is the software. Sometimes canned (already designed), software can be used. In other cases, for very special jobs, software has to be specially programmed. This can be expensive.

Software can be integrated; that is, one program can do a whole range of different jobs such as taking reservations, registering guests, assigning guests to rooms, creating guest accounts, handling charges from various sales outlets, providing housekeeping information, controlling accounts receivable, maintaining guest histories, and even controlling guest room security.

Application software is designed for one or only a few specific purposes and is much more simple than integrated software. Three common stand-alone or application-oriented software packages are word-processing packages, database managers, and spreadsheets. When these three common functions are designed into one software package, they are known as integrated work stations.

Another type of integrated package is an accounting one for handling general ledger, sales, accounts receivable, purchases, accounts payable, payroll, and inventory control.

Electronic cash registers (ECRs) have now evolved into point-of-sale (POS) systems, in which the registers or terminals at various sales outlets within an organization can be linked to a central processing unit (CPU) and to other hardware devices such as printers that can be situated in locations remote from the registers. These systems are basically sales-based, but they can provide information for the food and beverage cost control systems to use in compiling menu item sales mix records and inventory usage information.

Most food and beverage cost control systems are generally independent of the POS systems and are recipe- and ingredient-based. These systems provide purchase, storeroom, food production, and inventory control, as well as producing management reports that supply information for decision making.

DISCUSSION QUESTIONS

1. What is the main advantage of a computerized system over a manual one?
2. What is computer time-sharing? What are the problems associated with time-sharing?
3. Differentiate between a microprocessor and a microcomputer.
4. What is computer networking?
5. Differentiate between computer hardware and computer software.
6. What are the main hardware items that constitute a computer system?
7. What is a software language, and why is it necessary to use one in order to run a computer?
8. List the three ways in which one can obtain software.
9. Differentiate between an integrated software system and an application-oriented software system.
10. What is word-processing software? Describe a job in a hospitality enterprise that it could perform.
11. What is database manager software? Describe a job in a hospitality enterprise that it could perform.
12. What is spreadsheet software? Describe a job in a hospitality enterprise that it could perform.
13. What is an integrated work station?

14. Differentiate between an ECR and a POS.

15. Describe how a computerized recipe- or ingredient-based food cost control system works.

16. Describe how a computerized front-office guest room security system operates without using standard room door keys.

INDEX